PLAN FOR
PERMANENT PEACE

PLAN FOR PERMANENT PEACE

by

Hans Heymann, Ph.D.

Research Professor of Economics
Rutgers University

LONDON
George Allen & Unwin Ltd

Copyright in the U.S.A,
First published in Great Britain 1942

BOOK
PRODUCTION
WAR ECONOMY
STANDARD

Printed in Great Britain by
Bradford & Dickens
Drayton House, W.C.1

DEDICATED

to

my children and to the children of
my fellow Americans—in the hope
that theirs may be a happier future.

CONTENTS

MAPS AND CHARTS

(Prepared by Mrs. June Kilts Heald from sketches by the author.)

FOREWORD

By Richard T. Ely

*Honorary Associate in Economics, Columbia University; Research
Professor of Economics, Northwestern University; Honorary Professor
of Economics, University of Wisconsin.*

I HAVE read this work with interest, profit, and stimulation, and
I have no hesitation in commending it, because it is a constructive
contribution to peace. It points to a path which may lead away from
the chaos of hatred and selfishness toward a better world. It is a rare
combination of practicability and idealism. Some of Dr. Heymann's
ideas will probably long remain ideals, but we must have ideals as
a guide for present action. Isaiah's ideal for the future was peace—
"swords will be forged into plowshares." Long centuries have passed
since then, but this prophecy still has force. Most of Dr. Heymann's
ideals are of immediate practicability and in this hour of emergency
are worthy of serious study and consideration.

I was a student in Germany for several years and was well acquainted
with Germany as it was up to the first World War. In Heidelberg I
saw the beginnings of the evil forces which have at length triumphed
through Hitlerism. Knies and Bluntschli, my professors at Heidelberg,
were idealists who worked for international cooperation, mutual
understanding and good-will. I studied international law under
Bluntschli who drew up a code which was calculated to bring about
international peace. But Graf von Moltke answered him in an open
letter in which he stated, "What you want is only a dream, and at that,
not even a beautiful dream." Military force and the glorification of
war for which he stood have now triumphed for the time being.

Many of the things that Dr. Heymann says are in conformity with
my experiences in Germany. Dr. Heymann, during the days of the

xi

Weimar Republic, worked loyally for the prosperity of Germany and for other countries. In the first part of his book he recounts his experiences and shows how vital was a definite settlement of the international debts. To my mind no one has brought this out so clearly.

In the second part of the book Dr. Heymann presents a plan for a Bank of Nations. We already have, and in the near future can expect to see many more, plans for an international world hegemony. Dr. Heymann's approach differs from those we already have in that he treats of economics rather than politics and in that he presents his ideas, not in the form of a utopia or ideology, but draws upon his experiences to furnish a convincing technique, indispensable for the realization of the plan. We must never again neglect economics in making a future peace. In this section of the book he presents a functional economic mechanism to integrate our world economy.

There will be those who will scoff at the plan as an idealist's dream. In times of war—in times such as these—it is hard to think of peace. Yet if we do not plan for peace—whether it be Dr. Heymann's plan, or any other plan—we shall not have a good peace.

Many of us are confused today; the world scene does not make sense. In surveying events from a historical perspective, as best we can, perhaps we may better understand what is transpiring. As the human race has progressed, it has developed from the primitive family or tribal unit to the Greek City-State, and after a long lapse of time there has emerged the modern nation; and modern nations have developed into world empires. Perhaps what we are viewing today is the revolutionary throes of the growth of even larger spheres. If this is what is happening, we cannot glibly scoff at Dr. Heymann's ideals.

In any event, if a good peace is not to be had in the near future, if a large part of the world is to be dominated by totalitarian autarchies, we in the Western Hemisphere must be prepared to defend our way of life. To do this we must be prepared on many fronts. We must be as strong, and stronger, not only in guns, airplanes, and ships, but also in our economic weapons. In view of this Dr. Heymann's discussion of a Western Hemisphere Bank is enlightening. Whatever happens in Europe, and that is hidden in the mists of the future, the

FOREWORD

plan for the Hemisphere Bank deserves careful consideration as an immediate practical program.

Dr. Heymann had a distinguished career in Germany which he was ultimately forced to give up on leaving that country. He is now becoming an American citizen and is as loyal to our country as any native American. He is a democrat who brings us many valuable lessons from the Old World, to help us build a new world.

PREFACE

WE ARE fortunate to live in a country where objective research in economics can still be carried on. We are not required to make obeisance to any ideology improvised by dictatorial rulers for the exigencies of the occasion. We are free to seek after truth. Our democratic institutions and traditions permit and encourage this. The attainment of knowledge through the objective search for truth and the diffusion of that knowledge will make for an enlightened public opinion that will not easily fall prey to demagogic appeals. This, in my opinion, is a heritage to be guarded and a privilege to be cherished.

These words, spoken by Winthrop W. Aldrich, Chairman of the Chase National Bank, before the National Bureau of Economic Research in New York City, eloquently express my own feelings on being granted the opportunity, in this last haven of free thought, to study the economic elements which I consider vital for the attainment of a peace based on practical democracy.

The story of how this book came to be written abounds with coincidence. One evening, after a round table conference with my honor class at Rutgers University, a student, Theodore K. Robinson, asked me to give a series of talks to the Rutgers History and Foreign Relations Club about some of my experiences in Europe after the Great War. I am grateful for this request because it was the first incentive toward writing this book.

While looking through old letters and records for supporting material for these lectures, I came across certain documents which appeared worthy of publication. Two incidents in the course of my studies and public activities took on a special significance for future peace policies: (1) A memorandum drafted in 1922 for the Conference of Genoa, entitled "The Bank of Nations"—a document perhaps premature for that time, but assuredly more timely today. (2) Letters and documents

PREFACE

concerning the Franco-German understanding between 1930 and 1932, and the joint Franco-German opinion on the Definite Settlement of the International Debts.

In the light of these documents and experiences, there is no doubt in my mind that, primarily, neo-mercantilist errors, nationalist selfishness, and blindness to the first commandment of creative peace, namely solidarity of action, were the cause of the present war; in other words, misconception of economic theories, primarily, caused the war. Having learned this, what responsible statesman, what civilized nation or group, would again dare offend this peace commandment?

When we say that economic fallacies caused the war, it is by no means assumed that nothing but economics produced the war. We know only too well the influence of politicians, imperialists, dictators, and various private individuals on war, and we have certainly realized that economics is made by individual economists. But we have all too late discovered that the role generally attributed to economists or economics, as the underlying cause for war, has been constantly underestimated.

Thus, if we can prove with facts and figures that economic maladjustments and policies have been among the primary causes of war, we may be able to find first of all the economic path for the avoidance of war. The end of Adam Smith's "homo economicus" does not come about through denying that economics has an influence on our social or political order. The end of "economic man," the liberation of mankind from materialism, and the rebirth of "spiritual man" can only be attained by means of an international autonomous economic mechanism, coordinated with an international political authority.

First of all, a reconstruction of our economic world structure through some superordinated institution must be achieved in which all nations or groups of nations arising out of the present struggle may participate as equal partners. Collective security cannot function if it is based on only a small group of nations, and if it is not organized on economic fundamentals. Has not the new European war taught us the lesson that no nonaggression pact is able to guarantee a nation's security? The reason why, in the past, efforts at international peace and security have failed is mainly because such efforts have been based too exclusively upon political concepts rather than economic organization.

PREFACE

The peace problem is a functional, no less than a political, matter. The world needs, first of all, an all-embracing economic organization. In this genuine economic association, freedom and equality, the ideals of mankind since ancient Greece and Rome, may ultimately be attained. Through this universal mechanism of a sound economic organization, which has never been tried, humanity can be demechanized, released from the worries of its daily economic struggle.

Through the operation of such an international organization, man would be liberated and relieved of the burden of anxiety over the material world. His mind would be freed for devotion to the great ideals of democracy, freedom, justice, and peace. These ideals, in the long run, can be maintained and perpetuated only by the establishment of an equilibrium embodied in a vital and self-regulating international capital organization.

A design for this mechanism, which we have named "The Bank of Nations," is presented in this book. In spite of the fact that the term "bank" is now associated with a prosaic institution, we must learn to understand that the creative money and banking mechanism of the future will undoubtedly be so dynamic and socially enriching that the prejudice connected with its designation will prove unjustified.

"Money which represents the prose of life, and which is hardly spoken of in the parlours without an apology, is in its effect and laws as beautiful as roses," says Emerson. If this is true, the term "bank" needs no excuse. The ideal Bank of Nations is a money- and credit-creating institution. Three main tasks are entrusted to the Bank: (1) the issue of an international medium of exchange; (2) the extension of short-term credits to trade; (3) the creation of promissory notes for long-term investment purposes. These promissory notes are issued in series and amortized during the life of the capital objects, structures, and utilities of all kinds created by the Bank and its branches. National construction banks function as branch banks of the Bank of Nations and direct the flow of capital into the most productive channels.[1]

The international functional peace basis must, in turn, be supple-

---

[1] The nature, structure and functions of these national "construction banks," adapted to our domestic situation, will be presented in the author's next volume, now in preparation, "Alternative to Post-War Chaos," to be published by Harper & Brothers.

mented and strengthened by some future Federal World Authority and its various departments, forming the constitutional and executive bodies of an ideal United States of the World.

The power of credit, and the part that it can play in solving the enormous problems of production and distribution, is greatly underestimated. Credit is the electromotive force in the dynamics of economic activity. It establishes the contact between the energies emanating from the subjects and objects of our planet. From the creation of purchasing power to the exchange of just purchasing power parities between nations, there is nothing that credit cannot accomplish. At a time when the destruction of the world necessitates incalculable works of reconstruction and construction, credit is the only instrument capable of anticipating future earnings of long-life capital wealth and placing it at the disposal of the present generation.

The Bank of Nations, with its great staff, its army of auxiliary institutions, some of which I have tried to describe in this book, is the instrument which can fulfil the hopes and dreams of the classical social reformers of former centuries with the least possible disturbance. By pooling our gold in a common international fund or using it as a reserve or equalization fund, even this problematic question can be answered by the Bank.

In recent times, events have taken place which have influenced leading statesmen to dictate bloc or group formations on our globe. The individual is powerless against such developments, and individual nations cannot but answer such actions of force with similar actions in defense. But it is well within the reach of our power, and, in fact, it is a sacred duty of students in economics, to show the responsible guides of national policies that there must exist a higher functional order. We have the unavoidable obligation to prove to our best ability that this higher world order is no dream, no Utopia, but a relatively simple and logical aim. It is certainly necessary and enlightening to present ideological visions or ethical ideals to peoples in distress. But this is not enough. At the risk of being branded fantastic optimists, we must have the courage to invent realistic constructions, even if they are not perfect. Ideas without action are phantoms. We must make them work even if we must travel a long and weary path.

PREFACE

The following sketch of a plan for permanent peace might at least help to convince peacemakers that even groups or blocs or continental spheres in the organization of our society are and can only be transitory phenomena. Will these new groups fight each other with trade and production policies, with cartels and trusts, with armies, navies, and air forces; or will enlightened self-interest force these partial federations and empires to unite into a world economic organization?

The project of an ideal, creative, and constructive Bank of Nations, with all its interrelated departments, coordinated with a Federal World Authority and with a reformed International Labor Office embodying a new spirit of international planning, may guide our thoughts into channels leading to a new functional world order. If this ambitious program can contribute in some way toward the attainment of a just and lasting peace, these pages will not have been written in vain.

I am most grateful to Dr. Richard T. Ely, dean of American economists, who from the first day of my arrival in this country, has offered me his unselfish friendship and has given my work his wholehearted support. I would also like to express my gratitude to Professor S. S. Huebner of the Wharton School of Finance and Commerce, University of Pennsylvania, for recommending the draft of this book to Joseph H. Willits, Dean of the Wharton School, now Director, Social Science Division of the Rockefeller Foundation; further, to Dr. Willits, himself, and Miss Sydnor H. Walker, and Dr. Stacy May, of the Rockefeller Foundation, for their support of my work; to Dr. Stephen Duggan and Miss B. Drury of the Emergency Committee for the Aid to Displaced Foreign Scholars; to Dr. Edgar J. Fisher of the Institute of International Education, and Dr. Wilbur K. Thomas of the Oberlander Trust, Carl Schurz Memorial Foundation. I am greatly indebted to my friend Mr. Clarence L. Riegel of the General Electric Company, President of the New York Creditmen's Association, to Mr. Henry G. Parker, Sr., Chairman of the National Bank of New Jersey, New Brunswick, New Jersey, and to Mr. H. Griffith Parker, Jr., for their friendly assistance in introducing me to Rutgers University in 1939; further, to Dr. Robert C. Clothier, President, and to Dr. Walter T. Marvin, Dean of the College of Arts and Sciences, Rutgers University, for their kind interest in my work.

PREFACE

Further, I am indebted to the Carnegie Endowment for International Peace for its support of the book and especially to Dr. James T. Shotwell, its Director, to Mr. Thomas J. Watson and Mr. Willis H. Booth, former Presidents of the International Chamber of Commerce; and to Dean Leopold Arnaud and Dean Roswell C. McCrea, both of Columbia University, for introducing me to the Carnegie Endowment for International Peace; also to Mr. Marriner Eccles, Chairman, Board of Governors, Federal Reserve System, and the Hon. W. Warren Barbour, United States Senator from New Jersey, for their interest and encouragement in this work; to Dr. Herman Bruening, Professor of Government at Harvard University, Mr. Harold A. Lyon, and Mr. John B. Sparks for their constructive contributions.

On the chapters concerning the Hemisphere and Oriental Banks, Dr. A. A. Berle, Jr., Assistant Secretary of State, and Dr. E. A. Goldenweiser, Director of Research and Statistics, Board of Governors of the Federal Reserve System, have made constructive suggestions. I am indebted to Dr. Eugene E. Agger, head of the Department of Economics, and to Mr. Mark M. Heald, Professor of History, Rutgers University, for reading and revising the manuscript, and to Mrs. Jane Kilts Heald for her great patience and skill in preparing the maps and charts for the book; to my friend Mr. Maurice Emetaz for his loyal secretarial and research assistance, and to Mr. Louis Fiorini for his diligent stenographic work.

Lastly, it was my good fortune to secure the expert editorial assistance of Mr. Joseph A. S. Kenas, Associate of Dr. Ely at The Institute for Economic Research. His painstaking revision of the whole manuscript, and his many constructive suggestions were invaluable. I wish to thank all these persons and many others. I am solely responsible for the statements and conclusions in this book. More than I am able to express, I owe my gratitude to this country for offering me a new haven for independent thought and work.

New Brunswick, N. J.   H. H.
January 3, 1941.

PART I

ECONOMIC FALLACIES
CAUSED THE WAR

CHAPTER I

GROUNDWORK FOR WAR IN THE WEIMAR PERIOD UNTIL THE CRASH OF 1929

WHAT was the cause of the present catastrophe? Did Hitler commit an act of aggression? Did Chamberlain—by encouraging Poland to resist—cause the war? Did von Ribbentrop believe that Britain and France would not interfere? Is the Yellow Book, the Blue Book, or the White Book right? Was the real cause Imperialism, Fascism, Nazism, Socialism, Communism, Catholicism, or Judaism? How unimportant, how secondary, these questions are!

Certainly, Hitler has committed a clear act of aggression. Certainly, Chamberlain, by encouraging and sacrificing Czechoslovakia and Poland, has contributed to the disaster. Certainly, fascist, nazi, and communist dictators made war. And let us not forget that Britain and France were not such innocent virgins in war politics as they pretended to be.

But are these the real issues? Did they cause the war, or were there deeper reasons for the present catastrophe?

The present generation of students in history and economics will one day have to write the history of this period of human tragedy during and between two great wars. If such a history is to be written true to fact, and if we ever want to seek out the lessons to be learned from this period, we must carefully examine the beginnings of our present plight. We shall then understand that it was no one person or group of persons, but rather the abuse of a mechanism—the world economic system—that is at the root of our disorganization.

We have acted on the fallacious belief that one nation can gain only at the expense of other nations. This has made for fallacies in monetary policies, misconception of socio-economic problems, and lack of economic solidarity among nations. The rise of dictators and other power politicians was the logical and unavoidable consequence of the dusty old mercantilist, protectionist, and supernationalist errors. We deluded ourselves when we wrote the history of wars mainly from the political, imperialist, militarist, or strategical standpoint.

A financial strategem pursued by one important central bank, or by the government of one large nation, can destroy the equilibrium of all the nations and be the direct or indirect origin or cause of a world war, not to mention the effect of other shortsighted policies of currency, reparation, international war debt, armament, custom, trade; all of these policies are causally related to and have brought about the restrictionism and barter schemes of which the twentieth century has no reason to be proud.

The neo-mercantilist errors finally caused a fatal disequilibrium in world economics, disruption of trade and intercourse between nations, and culminated in the destruction of the capital and productive systems of the world. Our peace production was transformed into armament production with all its unproductive and wasteful consequences, at a time when tens of millions of human beings were starving or in need of the bare necessities of life.

We shall not accuse the Versailles Treaty of being at fault for everything. We shall leave this to the able demagogues who are forced to blame the Versailles Treaty in order to justify their own actions in the name of superpatriotism. We wish to state only that the unfortunate economic complications resulting from the creation of new nations with twelve thousand miles of new customs barriers and an increasing nationalist spirit, and from the evergrowing rearmament and war psychosis which followed Versailles, provided a fertile soil for the growth of ultranationalist and economically disastrous policies. Instead of division of labor and production among nations, neo-protectionism and hypernationalism were encouraged.

But let us now leave these generalities and retrace the interwar history as it presents itself to one who has been thoroughly identified with all the phases of these developments and who has sincerely endeavored to retain his independent position in spite of the distasteful and horrifying national and international political intrigues current during his activities as economic adviser to the German Foreign Office from 1921 to 1932—especially to Dr. Walter Rathenau and Walter de Haas.

The roots of the return of protectionism in Europe are to be found in Germany and the German classical economists Johann Gottlieb Fichte, Friedrich List, Adam Mueller and the Romantic School led by Heinrich von Thuenen. Thuenen's book, *Der Isolierte Staat,* has always been an object of adverse criticism and attack on the part of German students. When our teachers in Germany tried hard to paint for their students the merits of List's, Fichte's, and Thuenen's theories of protectionism and autarchy, we were always skeptical. We retained the impression after such debates that our teachers themselves felt rather uncertain of the merits of self-sufficiency. Friedrich List received his inspiration from Alexander Hamilton during his seven years stay in the United States, where he developed a profound admiration for Hamilton's protectionist teachings and was greatly influenced by them in his classic work, *The National System of Political Economy* (published in 1841). The statement of these facts and their influence on German and international economics does not by any means minimize the greatness of these thinkers and teachers. In List's case the opposite is true, for he advised the elimination of trade restrictions as a country became industrialized. Economists have learned that what is true for one time and place may not hold true at other times or places. Yet the history of ideas recounts how the great contributions of great minds are frequently perverted.

Protectionist theories have always existed. Plato, in his *Republic,* and the Hellenic philosophical school had supported the idea. Sparta was for self-sufficiency and Athens for free trade. No wonder that it was Athens which enjoyed a flourishing economy!

Even today in America, war contingencies aside, there are many isolationists and protectionists who like to reap the gains of international trade without contributing their share in the exchange. These are usually men who think of the present and not of the future— men whose philosophies find support among many industrialists and agrarians, or among statesmen who are badly in need of means to

3

produce some immediate relief in cases of serious unemployment, trade depressions, or other situations of distress. These are men who are ready to sacrifice genuine, definite, and lasting future advantages for immediate and visible results which may have fatal consequences.

The decisive moment in the history of protectionism, however—the moment which may be regarded as the origin of world disequilibria—was the overthrow of the German Minister Delbrueck by the great German Chancellor Bismarck. Bismarck was responsible for the re-introduction of iron and steel duties in the late seventies, which were designed to heal the wounds of the "Gruenderkrach" (crash of promotion schemes) of 1874. It was this German tariff policy which brought to an end an era of promising progressive free trade among nations.

Bismarck the feudalist, autocratic and independent in his actions, deliberately departed from the free trade policies advocated by British political economists and pursued by the British government. He supported cartels, state-socialized the railroads, and in a general atmosphere of prosperity pushed industrial expansion. After the successful wars with Austria and France, he received the support of trade unions and the Social Democratic Party by creating, between 1881 and 1891, insurance measures against sickness, accident, and old age—his so-called "paternalistic system."

Once industry had secured its protectionist privileges, it was only one logical step further that agriculture, supported by Adolf Wagner, should demand a just balance between industry and agriculture and itself cooperate with industry in protectionist policies.

In 1907, when I visited the United States for the first time, I observed the crisis and depression caused by overproduction and the withdrawal of gold from the London and New York Stock Exchanges by J. P. Morgan. In *Morgan the Magnificent*,[1] the Theodore Roosevelt-J. P. Morgan incident, in which Morgan played the role of saviour of the United States Treasury, is dramatically portrayed.

The repercussions of this depression were to be felt throughout the world and especially in Germany. At this time—if it was not then too late—Germany should have adopted free trade according to the

[1] T. K. Winkler, *Morgan the Magnificent* (New York: Vanguard Press).

theory of List. But she did not, and since then Germany has never fully recovered. The so-called "assisted capitalism" and protectionist policies, the neo-mercantilist policies (which had worked fairly well until 1907, but showed their fatal consequences between 1907 and 1912), were gradually driven to the point of absurdity and came to an end about 1912, because foreign countries were supersaturated with German goods and unable to absorb even the most cheapened of her dumped products. It was due to economic mistakes that the pace of international intrigue was accelerated in this period.

On the political horizon, the situation became equally threatening. Admiral Tirpitz' naval ambitions put England on her guard. In 1907, at the little Hotel Weimar, in Marienbad, England, France, and Russia laid the basis for their future alliance. At Agadir, where Kaiser Wilhelm had outraged the world by sending a battleship in an effort to influence a diplomatic conference concerning Morocco, the German Reichsbank leader Havenstein made it clear to the Kaiser that "wars cost money and there is no telling how much." The precarious economic situation in 1912, therefore, caused the Kaiser to give his significant order to the German banks for financial and economic armament about two years before the war actually broke out.

The situation in Germany from 1912 to 1914 was similar to that from 1937 to 1939, before the present war. Food storing and monetary policies prepared for war, and "capital was on strike" in the United States as well as all over the world.

It was above all an *economic explosion caused by protectionism and imperialism* which brought about the war in 1914. During the World War, the growth of protectionism in all kinds of war production was most natural; but it was only after the war that protectionism was carried to excess.

One important economic policy at the initial stage of the war in 1914 should be mentioned here. It was a question of great consequence, although not sufficiently recognized as such by historians.

Germany, while striding from victory to victory, was faced with the question of whether she should accept foreign financial help, which at that time was available from the United States.

In 1914, Germany was a creditor nation with thirty to forty billion goldmarks invested in foreign countries, especially in the United States. Because of the fact that exports exceeded imports, Germany was able to enter the war with a note circulation of one billion, eight hundred million goldmarks, and gold funds in the Reichsbank of about one billion, four hundred million goldmarks. Over and above that, gold coins to the amount of two billion were in circulation among the population.

There was no question that Germany could issue government bonds for war financing for some time to come.

A few farsighted economists, however, strongly recommended the acceptance of American war credits at least as "reassurance." But Helfferich and the majority of leaders in finance were so exuberant with optimism that they considered it beyond question, even "unpatriotic," to suggest the acceptance of outside war credits.

Some economists have disputed the consequences of this decision and believe that it facilitated American participation in the war and the complete collapse of the German credit and currency structure. (With regard to American participation, I am not of this belief. Today one can understand full well why it was unavoidable.)

A great achievement of the German war period was the creation of an agency for the organization of raw materials and resources created by Walter Rathenau, son of the founder and president of the Allgemeine Elektrizitäts Gesellschaft, and after his death chairman of the company. He was considered a genius of organization and selected by the government to head and organize the Raw Materials Department during the entire war period. When Rathenau, a patriotic and social-minded reformer and ethical philosopher, worked miracles and helped Germany so much to sustain a four-year war, he had not the slightest inkling that some twenty years later, long after his death, it would be accepted as the model for nazi four-year plans and war preparation.

To German patriots, the peace negotiations at Versailles caused sleepless nights. Shortly before the Treaty was to be signed, Rathenau, in a last vain effort to prevent the unavoidable, demanded in an outburst of protest, printed in the *Vossische Zeitung* in Berlin, that the German Commission refuse to sign the Treaty; but Professor M. J.

Bonn, a member of that Commission, has vividly painted the picture of why the German representatives had no choice but to do so.

A terrible depression weighed upon the nation after the fateful decision, when Julius Wolff, professor of economics, and I published articles in the *Berliner Tageblatt* and other newspapers, explaining why, from an economic viewpoint, there was not much to worry about for Germany; that if the Allies really insisted upon the payment of the astronomical reparation figures of a maximum of one hundred and thirty-two billion goldmarks or even the "small" initial amount of some thirty billions (five billion were to be paid by 1921) *the Allies would have to furnish Germany with a giant industry, production means, and income producing property values,* in order to enable the German economy to produce such gigantic amounts; and that the Allies would be forced to open their doors to German products and commodities if she were to transfer even a part of the amounts expected. A sincere will to fulfill reparations would therefore create a powerful resistance on the part of the Allies' industries and reverse the whole situation. Payments and transfers of substantial amounts in cash would definitely remain a great illusion. The idea that any such transfers were possible was undoubtedly one of the greatest and most fateful mercantilist errors of all time.

The psychological effect of these revelations was invaluable. Germany went to work.

We can omit here all those facts about the weakening of Germany through the war and the treaty, the loss in manpower, population, colonies, territory, resources, and the commercial fleet; how she was deprived of railroad equipment, livestock, benzol, coal, sulfate of ammonia, coal tar, etc.; and how she was "weakened to desperation" and delivered to political and social chaos.

On the side of the Allies, Sir Norman Angell, in his book, *The Economic Chaos and the Peace Treaty* (1920), and John Maynard Keynes, in his work, *The Economic Consequences of the Peace* (1922), were the first to have the courage of their convictions and predicted the chaotic consequences of reparations and exploitation of one nation to the alleged benefit of other nations.

Another psychological but practical task which I set myself was the

7

enlightenment of the German people on the subject of inflation. The German Reichsbank, under Havenstein and the government, showed a definite interest in maintaining the folklore conception that the inflation of the German mark was but a temporary measure. Counting on the belief of the man on the street that one mark equals one mark, even if it is greatly inflated, they appropriated the gold values of the country and in this way later rid themselves of their internal national debt. This was the time when every German thought himself a millionaire! Sixty million German inflation millionaires and multimillionaires looked down disdainfully upon the American "sixty family" aristocrats. In the last period of inflation, the value of the German mark was reduced to one-trillionth of its former value.

In 1921, I founded the "Association for Reform of Currency and Finance, e. V." in Berlin, which soon became extremely influential and included most leading German economists and government officials. Considerable courage was required, for at that time tinkering with currency and money management was considered as something almost akin to treason. As chairman and treasurer of the association, I had the delicate task of inviting more or less radical reformers—independent authorities with the necessary courage—to open people's eyes with regard to currency. Professors Geiler of Heidelberg and Mahlberg of Freiburg gave the first of those disillusioning talks. The most radical one was Sylvio Gesell, originator of the free land–free money theory, whose theories have recently been regarded, by John Maynard Keynes,[2] as superior to those of Karl Marx. These talks rang in the dawn of the era of currency reform and the people's awakening.

In order to bring about the much needed international understanding and an easing of the reparation question, my book, *The World Credit and Finance Reform* was published in 1921—a manifesto for solidarity among nations, dedicated to the pioneers of a true league of nations. The constitution of the League, although a hopeful attempt, did not appear to our group to be a true solution. The book, which was favorably received on the Continent and in England by Lloyd George, Sir Drummond Frazer, Keynes, and Barclay, culminated in a proposal

[2] John Maynard Keynes, *The General Theory of Employment, Interest, and Money,* page 355 (New York: Harcourt, Brace & Co., 1936).

for an international regulatory money- and credit-creating institution which I later named the "Bank of Nations."

Rathenau, then Minister of Reconstruction, tried hard, in international negotiations and speeches within the nation, to convince the Allies that reparations in commodities and products were the only possibility of at least partial fulfilment of the German reparation obligations, but his appeals remained unheeded. He read my book on his way back from Munich, where he had delivered his famous reparation speech, late in 1921. From Dresden, he sent a wire inviting me to Wilhelmstrasse for our first close discussion on international credit and currency questions.

The conference lasted almost four hours and resulted in my drawing up a memorandum on the "Bank of Nations" for the Conference of Genoa—where the economic fate of Germany was to be sealed. In this first conference with Rathenau, we agreed that the Conference at Genoa presented the first real opportunity for a complete change in the mentality of nations with regard to egotism, hypernationalism, and protectionism. In contrast to national egotism, "solidarism" among nations should be created—but only through a *superordinated*, powerful organization of the highest integrity—which by the excellence of its conception, construction, and functions would exercise a dynamic influence on the economy of nations.

We agreed completely on two points:

1. That Germany—as explained in my book—must bring about an economic cooperation with Russia. I have always believed that the two were economically the most naturally complementary countries, supplementing each other to their mutual benefit and to the benefit of the world. Even today, I am of the firm belief that, disregarding their political ideologies, Russo-German *economic* cooperation would be to the benefit of all nations and a definite prerequisite for a lasting peace. It would equilibrate one of the world's great economic maladjustments, and, reasonably recognized and organized, would eliminate and replace the German nationalistic aspirations with regard to their dream of a "Lebensraum" (living space). It would transform the sociopolitical schemes of national and state socialism into international solidarity, and at the same time permit the continuance of national

peculiarities and traditions. It would pave the way for a true Federation of Nations. Germany and Russia will never tie up their economies so closely that their relations to other nations would be affected or neglected. They are both too dependent upon the outer world.

2. That Germany was the obvious nation to offer to the world a definite economic and financial solution for the mess in which the whole world found itself. A real program not only would bring about help to Germany and to the former members of the Quadruple Alliance and Russia, but also would solve the problem of reconstruction in France and reparations in general; and, moreover, it would break the ground for the first foundation of international capital and credit-cooperation.

Rathenau first presented my memorandum on the Bank of Nations and discussed the plan at length with Lloyd George and Aristide Briand in the Credit Committee. Although it found strong support in Lloyd George, in Briand's opinion the time was not yet ripe for a plan of such vast proportions. Later, Rathenau recognized the Russian government and concluded the first trade treaty with Russia, thus bringing the whole conference to the brink of explosion.

Rathenau did not give up the idea of the Bank of Nations; he urged me to expand the treatise which was presented to the Genoa Conference, and as a result my book, *The Bank of Nations*,[3] was published in June 1922.

Having studied the book, Rathenau invited me to his home to discuss further action. He wished to have the proposition presented to the Sound Currency Association in London. But, two days before our meeting was to take place, he was assassinated by a group of misled, irresponsible young men who were hardly aware of the consequences of their crime. The death of Rathenau, one of Europe's *grands chevaliers d'esprit*, in June 1922, was a terrible blow to justice and solidarity among nations.

I have often been asked by friends outside Germany what was the

[3] This book dealt with the following main topics: (1) The currency and gold problem; (2) the establishment of the Bank of Nations; (3) the credit limitations of the Bank of Nations; (4) short term credits; (5) long term credits; (6) National Branch Banks; (7) the problem of reparation and the liquidation of war debts. A translation of this book is reprinted in the appendix of this volume.

real cause of the plot against Rathenau. The reason goes deep into the nature of the make-up of the German nation.

There have always existed two philosophies in German politics. One hailed exaggerated nationalism, autarchy, and some sort of exaggerated self-esteem: "Am deutschen Wesen soll die Welt genesen" (the world shall be healed by the German spirit). Racial and religious prejudices and general intolerance were partly characteristic of that group. The other, by no means less patriotic or nationalistic in the best sense, fought for understanding and cooperation among nations for solidarity and universalism as the noblest part of national tradition.

Rathenau was a philosopher of the latter type. He was called an "Erfüllungspolitiker" (fulfilment politician), that is, a statesman who believes in the fulfilment of obligations as far and fair as possible, with the conviction that such fulfilment would be recognized by the Allies and would render the whole reparations question absurd and promote a final accord. German ultranationalists lacked the instinct for conciliation and solidarity. They considered it a patriotic act to do away with men like Rathenau or Erzberger. But who ever succeeded these statesmen would have to take exactly the same attitude in foreign affairs. This Stresemann, Schacht, and Bruening did, with certain variations.

After Rathenau's death, I decided to continue this work. I called on Gustav Cassel at Stockholm University and on Vissering, the President of the Netherlands Central Bank, and in '23 visited England and the United States. In conference with Paul M. Warburg and Governor Benjamin Strong of the Federal Reserve Board and others, it became evident to me that the general opinion prevailed that no help could be expected from the United States unless Germany would give guarantees for abstaining from rearmament. But this, for political reasons, was impossible.

To go back to the internal condition of Germany: In November, 1923, when the German mark broke down, the ruthless industrialist and financier, Hugo Stinnes, who had succeeded in borrowing vast amounts from the banks and in repaying the credits with worthless marks, had appropriated and merged almost the whole of German industry and thus become the owner of the greater part of the national wealth. But after the stabilization the inorganic mixture of loosely connected industrial magnates could no longer exist. It was a disastrous situation without parallel. Germany's reentry to world economy depended entirely upon the success of the reconstruction of German industry.

By 1923, the groundwork for the stabilization of the currency had been well prepared by our Association for Reform of Currency and Finance. Germany, bared of any gold reserves, needed a fictive gold currency as an emergency measure for the period of transition into a definite sound currency situation. To meet this need, the Association conceived and promoted the idea of the "Rentenmark," a fictive gold currency, based on a first mortgage on German land and industrial values. Helfferich adopted the rentenmark form of stabilization. Schacht, at first opposed to it, later made it his own invention, creating the Gold Discount Bank and transforming the rentenmark into the Reichsmark.

Two other plans greatly contributed to the final stabilization: Dr. Luther's plan for a "Bodenmark," based on land; and the "Neumark," proposed and thoroughly prepared by Hilferding, providing for a new gold bank to be organized.

After the success of stabilization, the era of revaluation of German capital values and enterprises and a period of brutal deflation set in. Nobody who has not actually lived through the extreme inflation period can imagine the demoralizing influence of currency decay and the disappointment, heartbreak, and strain of currency reconstruction.

Schacht's rigid restriction of currency issues and the complete stopping of the note-printing press created confidence abroad and resulted in an international loan to Germany. In April, 1924, a committee of experts, representing the Allied Nations, recommended the grant of eight hundred million goldmarks, the so-called "Dawes Loan," to the Reich. This international loan gave German currency its final backing and security. The stabilization made one billion inflation paper marks equal to one goldmark.

After the stabilization in 1924-25, a cry for foreign credits emanated from Germany, where it was thought that England would be the fool's paradise for unlimited credits, and London was overwhelmed with applications. Again the idea of an international bank for money and credit creation was brought up.

MacKenna, President of Barclay's Bank in London, with whom the plan of a Bank of Nations had been discussed, was appreciative of the idea but saw no possibility of its realization. He was generous with good advice regarding the credit situation in Germany. "You must first clean up your financial house," he remarked. Credits were not even mentioned, and shortly afterwards England issued a credit embargo.

But the disentanglement of Germany's finance did not bring the ardently desired additional credits. England needed those credits for her own Empire purposes. And the American gold stream had not yet been released.

When I scored the foreign credit situation in the *Berliner Tageblatt*, the banker, Jacob Goldschmidt, President of one of the German "Big Five" and reconstructor of German industry, who had just created an international banking trust in Amsterdam, enthusiastically approved the article and wrote to me to that effect. We took advantage of his enthusiasm, proposing that he take the initiative in the formation of a Bank of Nations; as an individualist, however, Goldschmidt put all his faith in the efficiency of the big banks and was not in favor of an interstate banking organization.

But the general attitude toward the financial cooperation of European countries had at least improved. On January 18, 1926, a plan for a "Europa Bank" was issued in the *Berliner Tageblatt* for consideration by the world economic conference. It was translated into many languages and published in almost every country. The *New York Herald* went so far as to write about its impending formation, calling me the founder. This, of course, was premature. The plan never materialized and it was the privilege of Mr. J. P. Morgan to initiate the first international bank four years later. (The plan of Vanderlip named "The American Bank of Europe" was given much publicity, but Europe at that time did not feel favorably inclined toward a plan for a bank of Europe located in New York City.)

But let us return to the knotty reparations question. Until 1924 this problem was a source of great disappointment. As we had predicted and explained time and again, it was to cause the ruin of continental currencies, the complete collapse of the German mark, and partial exhaustion of the French and Belgian francs.

After the delay *ad infinitum* in the organization of the "Bank of Nations" in Genoa, which among many other proposals was advanced to assist in the reconstruction of the destroyed war areas in France and Belgium, these two countries continued to build up those areas at their own expense. They witnessed the partial breakdown of their currencies, which was precipitated by the fact that German reparation payments were very irregular and finally stopped altogether when the value of the mark dwindled to zero.

One of the worst experiences of that time was the occupation by French troops in 1923 of the Ruhr district, which represented three-fourths of Germany's coal, iron, and steel resources. This senseless action of Poincaré resulted in a complete failure for France. It did not pay at all and its only effect was to accelerate currency decay and to bring about revolutionary movements, with all their bitter consequences. In fact, it stimulated the Nazi movement more than almost anything else.

But—since there are always two sides to a picture—these hardships created a new spirit among nations. It became evident that economic problems should not be confused with political ambitions. In 1924, for the first time, "experts" were placed in the front rank. But political feelings of guilt and punishment were still deeply rooted in the hearts of chauvinists, and the experts were not allowed to make sound, objective, and radical reforms. Their independence was limited by the political considerations of the leading powers.

As Harry D. Gideonse in his study on *The International Bank* (published in the Rutgers University *Bulletin* of August, 1930) has rightly stated:

In the light of the experience up to 1924, nothing seemed more important when the Dawes experts met than the recognition of two principles: definite yearly payments within Germany's capacity to pay, and protection of the stability of the new German currency. The heart of the Dawes Plan, therefore, was its recognition of the so-called "transfer principle," that is to say, the Committee—following the idea already recognized by the Financial

Committee of the League of Nations in the plan for the financial reconstruction of Hungary—distinguished clearly between (1) the amount of revenue
that Germany could raise for reparation purposes, and (2) the amount that
could be transferred to foreign countries. The funds that could be transferred, the Committee pointed out, could not in the long run exceed the
sums which the balance of payments (which, of course, includes also the
so-called invisible items, such as shipping services, bank charges, travel, etc.)
made possible to send out of Germany without incurring the risk of monetary or budgetary instability.

Under the Dawes Plan the payment of the required amounts (of two
billion, five hundred thousand annually and prosperity index) by Germany
in marks to the account of the Agent General at the Reichsbank constituted
the definite and final act of the German Government, and if it did not prove
uncooperative in other respects—this payment represented a full discharge
of Germany's annual responsibility. At this point responsibility of the creditor
began, and this responsibility was left almost entirely in the hands of the
newly organized Transfer Committee. The Transfer Committee was to the
Dawes Plan what the Bank for International Settlements later became to
the Young Plan.

These negotiations under the Dawes Plan put a great trial of patience and nerves on the young German Republic. And it was
certainly nothing short of a miracle that the effects of the Versailles
Treaty were gradually overcome under the Dawes Plan. Germany
witnessed a rebirth under its Republican Government and a rising
spirit of democracy. Rathenau, Erzberger, Stresemann, and Bruening
all greatly contributed toward this renaissance, and their sincere fight
for improvement in international understanding met with a hopeful,
obliging spirit on the side of the Allies.

I can only mention here a few personal experiences during the
hopeful period of prosperity from 1925 to 1929. I shall never forget,
and still see before my eyes, the blue sky and warm sun smiling upon
the Lago Maggiore with Stresa, Isola Bella, and Locarno, where
Briand, Austin Chamberlain, Stresemann, and four other statesmen
met to prepare and sign the Locarno Treaty. It was an atmosphere of
"let bygones be bygones," of conciliation and peaceful collaboration,
which will always be remembered as the "spirit of Locarno."

PLAN FOR PERMANENT PEACE

The Treaty was an agreement between friendly gentlemen (rather than antagonistic statesmen) to settle differences by arbitration, to guarantee the frontiers between Germany, Belgium, and France, to end the war psychosis, and to form a basis for prosperous economic cooperation. Even the idea of a Pan-Europa Federation proposed by Count Coudenhove-Kalergi was discussed, and finally Stresemann could proudly state: "The long war between us is ended. Ended the long veil of mourning for the pains that will never be assuaged. Away with the rifles, the machine guns and cannons. Come here conciliation, arbitration, and peace." And there was indeed an economic peace after Locarno. German industry, banking, shipping, and commerce supported by foreign credits entered their flourishing period.

The world situation had become so promising that Delacroix, the Belgian Minister of Finance, and other international powers repeatedly urged the issue of additional amounts of the reparations bonds which had been delivered to the Allies merely *pro forma* at the first Hague Conference. One day I was visited by Baron Baudran, a French nobleman, whose position was never quite clear to me. He wanted me to produce an opinion in favor of the issuance of additional amounts of those bonds on the international market and offered me a large sum for preparing such an opinion. I immediately discussed the question with my chief, Dr. de Haas, of the German Foreign Office, who knew how strongly I was opposed to the idea of burdening the world market with still more bonds. "Excellent," he said, "write that opinion, but write it for us." I wrote the opinion, which, of course, contained just the opposite of what Baron Baudran desired; he received a carbon copy, Germany saved several billion goldmarks of debt, and the world was spared additional disappointments.

Later, I was again approached by Baron Baudran, and upon his request delivered an opinion for Caillaux on the stabilization of the French franc which must have inspired Caillaux, because his stabilization plan was similar to the one in this opinion. But he was not successful, for France needed a more forceful man to propose the stabilization; Poincaré deleted a few minor points from the program—and succeeded.

The growing confidence in Germany's political sincerity, as well as in her commercial and industrial capability, had also caused Governor Benjamin Strong to change his mind with regard to foreign credits. Not only in America, but also in England and on the Continent, Strong was recognized as

one of the greatest financiers of all times, who achieved wonders in world rehabilitation. For several years [this] one man was largely responsible for relatively stable prices throughout the world.

Marvin and Williams[4] are right in stating that

he understood the dangers of abnormal gold movements and the potential menace of a great boom followed by a collapse in prices. He managed the monetary system of the U.S. and indirectly of the world, with great adroitness. On the one hand, he kept a sufficiently firm grip on monetary conditions to check each threatened stock market boom within the country; on the other hand he maintained an easy money market in the U.S. enabling other countries to *borrow* freely.

The period which next followed was the most exciting and absurd epoch of the post-war capitalist system. Understanding this period means understanding the decisive causes for the present war.

Germany, we have seen, was overloaded with debts, but payment of interest and refund of principal *in natura* (that is, in products) was not sufficiently accepted. Furthermore, tariff walls were not lowered but raised higher and higher in the United States. The Tariff Act of 1922 with its flexible reform had changed the situation but little. The American tariff policy made any substantial foreign trade impossible.

We shall remember the influence of the United States monetary and economic policies of that time on the situation in Europe, especially in Germany; again the world was warned by us that, in these circumstances, Germany should not and could not take over great amounts in loans without adequate export facilities in commodities. Dr. Felix Pinner, editor of the *Berliner Tageblatt*, placed the editorial page in its commercial section at my disposal as a forum for warning. It was the time when Dr. Schacht was exercising his growing influence on

[4] Donald Mitchell Marvin & Gertrude Marvin Williams, *Design for Recovery* (New York: Harper & Brothers).

the nation's monetary administration, and when Parker Gilbert, the able American expert, had achieved an increasing influence on Schacht.

The real catastrophe and the decisive event of the interwar period was the death of Benjamin Strong. At his death came the turning point in American and international affairs. We, on the other side of the Atlantic, felt the impending catastrophe: Germany suffered indigestion through foreign loans too readily granted by the United States and accepted by Germany, and constipation because of the impossibility of transferring or of exporting products. America was to stop her foreign loans and thus knock out the prop sustaining the whole fiction. For what? To indulge in an inflationary spree of prosperity which in turn was to collapse.

One cannot condemn Benjamin Strong's monetary policy for allowing Germany to borrow about five billion goldmarks from the United States for productive industrial purposes. Germany was then seriously overburdened with loans, but a financial genius such as Strong would definitely have been able to master the international financial situation had he only lived a few years longer. One cannot even be so sure that he would have supported the Morgan and Parker Gilbert policies with regard to the Young Plan. But let us not break away from the logic of our account. As Marvin and Williams recount:

When, early in 1928, Governor Strong was called away from his desk by his final illness, he left memoranda which foretold the boom. These notes explained that while he had utilized an easy-money policy to speed the rehabilitation of a postwar world he was fully aware of the danger of a boom followed by collapse, from easy money getting out of control.

Unfortunately, with Governor Strong's illness and death, less powerful and less magnetic men took over control of financial policy. While they recognized the dangers of a boom, the measures they took to counteract speculation were neither bold, effective, nor timely.·

None of Governor Strong's successors recognized the danger of the continued inflow of gold to world finance. The governor's death and the loss of his guidance resulted in a most unfortunate sequence of events:

Gold continued to flow into the United States, weakening foreign financial structures. It became the base for an increasing, but not fully normal, volume of credit; our partial control of credit constituted tacit recognition of a need for: (a) control of the impending boom, (b) control of the gold standard. A boom developed through lack of firm measures to check speculation. The shortage of gold in other countries curtailed world buying power, reduced prices and ultimately constituted the determining factor which brought on the depression.

If we had permitted the unchecked inflow of gold to exert its normal influence upon prices in this country, and had allowed the automatic working of the gold standard to redistribute the gold, we should have been sure of a boom but it is improbable that it would have equalled that of '29. Certainly the inflow of imports incidental to the redistribution of that gold would have strengthened the industrial and financial position of foreign countries and, during our subsequent collapse, the strong financial position abroad would have acted as a cushion, preventing the widespread havoc which we experienced.

Governor Strong chose the more difficult course of attempting to manage world finance. He evidently hoped to prevent a major boom here, and certainly his policy was designed to increase rather than decrease the financial strength of foreign countries. It was a daring policy. It required deep understanding of international finance, skill in execution, and force and magnetism to secure the cooperation of other financial authorities who lacked such vision.

With lower tariffs and without the complications incidental to war debts, a man of Strong's ability might have made the policy effective long enough to create a new tradition in international finance. With lesser men in control, the dangers inherent in the policy materialized. The rate of gold inflow increased, *partial sterilization failed to prevent a boom* and, with the financial position of other nations weakened, the collapse of credit in the United States left no nation strong enough to fight world depression effectively.

A wide variety of factors in many countries *contributed* to the depression. Lack of balance between various forms of production and consumption, distorted relationships between volume of durable and consumers' goods and between farm products and manufactured goods were bound to be the aftermath of the war. Profits rose until they took an unduly large share of national income and the resulting speculation also had an adverse influence upon stability. These inequalities worked havoc upon normal monetary relationships, but they would not have become completely unmanageable *had wiser monetary control effected a continued slow readjustment.* From 1925 to 1929 financial observers unanimously admitted that the world was on a dollar standard and not on gold. Realizing this fact, they hoped for continued farseeing wisdom in the management of the dollar. With Strong's death, there was no financial statesman available to take over the control of money for the world.

All this is clear proof that even in 1928 and 1929 the Federal Reserve was not allowing the old gold standard free play. Prompt action at the proper moment and cooperation by the interests affected would have checked the inflation. The subsequent deflation of 1929 would have been less severe, or perhaps entirely avoided. By checking speculation before it gets out of hand a central bank can go far toward securing permanent stability.[5] (italics mine)

Marvin and Williams further complain about the unsuccessful control in 1930:

Undoubtedly a minor setback had been overdue at the end of 1929 but it need not have got out of hand. Stepping on the gas in July, 1930, might well have served to avert the catastrophe.

In Germany the pernicious influence of '29 and '31 developed into a situation of distress, internal disintegration, and rapidly growing political fanaticism. Lack of cooperation and the fatal monetary and tariff policies of nations created the atmosphere of desolation and despair which prepared the soil for the growth of dictatorial powers, and which finally brought about the war. On the part of the German Foreign Office everything possible was done to convince other nations that isolationist policies and lack of cooperation would have fatal consequences. But it was not possible to get sufficient support for German democracy from the Allied factions at the right time. When the economic and political negotiations were near the solution, it was too late. Extreme nationalist policies in Germany interfered. Volumes could be written about the failure of this task.

It may be considered lack of political intelligence in an economist for him to insist on blaming economic policies for political and social crises. But I trust that the reader will appreciate the spirit in which this criticism is given. My aim is to contribute positively toward the removal of those causes which lead to war.

The economic consequences of the Versailles Treaty were clearly foreseen by Sir Norman Angell and John Maynard Keynes. A general

[5] *Ibid.*

recognition, on the part of the Allies, of the deficiencies of the Treaty and mutual help in the removal of obstacles was under way in the twenties, and Europe—and especially Germany—was on the road to recovery under the Dawes Plan.

In the next chapter, however, we shall show that the growing understanding of the fatal and universal influence of certain economic policies surrounding the Young Plan and the Bank for International Settlements did not go far enough to produce a definite settlement. This, we believe, was at least the indirect cause of the new European disaster.

It is too late for regrets, but it is never too late for study and discovery of the means of avoiding excessive protectionist, mercantilist, and nationalist errors and to search for a road to universal socioeconomic solidarity in the spirit of "bear ye one anothers' burdens."

CHAPTER II

TO THE BRINK OF THE ABYSS AND THE ECONOMIC EXPLOSION

It is not easy to condense into one chapter the four-year period from the crash of 1929 until 1932, when the agreement under way between the German Republic and the Allied Nations was obstructed and wrecked. Eleanor Lansing Dulles has written a remarkable account of over six hundred pages, concerned solely with the Bank for International Settlements and the Young Plan, up to the year 1932.[1]

But my presentation will give at least those facts which I believe were decisive in leading up to the economic explosion of 1939 and some information not revealed until today, because only a few men, who dislike publicity, knew about them. If the best atmosphere for an economic peace movement is to be created, it is now time to lift the veil and present several significant documents which may guide us toward greater clarity regarding the influences of economics in modern history.

Let us reiterate: Immediately after Versailles, Germany—greatly weakened—was unable to export considerable amounts of goods or products. She had lost colonies, territory, manpower, her mercantile fleet, the iron ore of Lorraine, and had to deliver Ruhr coal, cattle and domestic animals, and other goods and services to France. During the war, Germany had used up a large part of her gold for war supplies from neutral countries, and the remainder had to be used for imports before credits were available. Seventy-five per cent of Germany's investments in foreign countries had been confiscated and sold. Then the reparation payments had to be made: at first irregularly; until in May,

[1] Eleanor Lansing Dulles, *The Bank for International Settlements at Work* (New York: Macmillan Co., 1932).

1921, three billion goldmarks, equaling seven hundred and fifty million old weight dollars, were demanded—to be paid annually.

After the World War, Germany was first obliged to import large quantities of foreign goods and there was a real need for German exports in products and commodities all over the world. In spite of Germany's reduced earning and production capacity, she was soon able and eager to export large quantities, but as we have seen in our first chapter many restrictions on the fulfilment of this task were imposed upon Germany.

This naturally caused a disequilibrium unequaled in the economic history of nations. With the gold funds vanishing, the German inflation machine was set in motion and the mark depreciated internally and in foreign countries. This was accompanied by internal rise in prices (expressed in marks), and that again was only an expression of progressing inflation. The Ruhr occupation was a great illusion and caused an accelerated economic and currency decay. In 1923 the German mark was stabilized. In 1924 the Dawes Plan brought great relief, but not a definite solution; it was an economic truce—not a peace. From 1924 until 1929 Germany's gigantic reparation obligations were met by means of borrowing, which was nothing more than "a shifting of debt."

With regard to the end of this hopeful period, Ernest M. Patterson, in his meritorious book, *The Economic Basis of Peace* (New York: Whittlesey House), has stated:

When prices sharply fell with their countless repercussions on business throughout the world the situation became an unbearable one. New foreign loans had stopped and the burden, already too heavy, was sharply increased. With prices lower, an enlarged volume of exports was necessary if obligations were to be met. Some increases were, of course, possible but other countries also were facing serious difficulties and trade barriers were raised. Many foreign claims were due on demand or on short notice and creditors, some of whom were under pressure, became insistent on payment.

With the crash of 1929, the fantastic idea of these payments became absurd, and the payments soon came to an end.

With five billion goldmarks borrowed on a long-term basis from the

PLAN FOR PERMANENT PEACE

United States, which in the war had changed from a debtor nation to a creditor nation, and about ten billions borrowed from other countries, mainly England, on a shorter term basis, Germany had again built up her industry, merchant marine, and one and one-half million houses and public buildings, recreation and sport centers. But two-thirds of the enormous amounts borrowed were again used as reparation payments up until 1929.[2]

The depression, the Hoover spirit of prohibitive tariff policies, preference systems, import quotas, the Hawley-Smoot Tariff (which, in the words of Secretary of Agriculture H. A. Wallace, caused "the insanity of the different nations of the world with respect to international trade" and engendered a general protest from thirty-three foreign nations), and the Ottawa System of the British Empire—all these thoroughly discouraged the German economy. Currencies were devalued in England, Japan, and the United States. Large gold funds were sterilized in France and the United States, and the gold standard was abandoned.

German exporters were definitely unable to compete under the high German price level. But, for Germany, currency devaluation, in itself a doubtful measure, was taboo after 1923. It was psychologically impossible. This situation paved the way for the rightist putsch and the Nazi revolution.

It is clear that the experiences of economic history were neglected after the World War—the lessons derived from post-revolution and war periods, that is, the economic experiences of the Napoleonic War of 1812 and the Franco-Prussian War of 1871. Today we, as Americans, may again be vitally interested in those lessons and experiences, because at the end of the present war the United States bankers may have to be the saviors of the world. The United States may find itself in a situation similar to that of England in 1815, when the father of the house

[2] The Information Department of the Royal Institute of International Affairs (Mr. C. R. C. Harris), estimates the total credits which Germany received, during the entire period from 1924 to 1931, as being about twenty-eight billion goldmarks and Germany's Reparation payments about ten billion goldmarks. In toto Germany received in credits about three times the amount she paid in reparations and during this period punctually lived up to her obligations and her debt service to foreign creditors. In 1932, Germany still owed about nineteen billion goldmarks to foreign creditors, of which about ten per cent, less than two billions, were repaid by the Third Reich under the dictatorial economic manipulations of Dr. Schacht. This is discussed more fully in Chapter III.

24

of Rothschild, whose picture has found a place of honor in the Royal Exchange of London, saved the fate of Europe. It was this little man, Rothschild, who financed England, gave the first reconstruction loan to France, and helped greatly in financing other European continental powers.

The experiences of the economic and financial history of nations following war developments were stupidly neglected after 1918. With the exception of President Wilson and his well-wishers, the world was blind to the true nature of peace.

Furthermore, the same United States that had taken part in the war had not actively cooperated in the peace, either politically in the League of Nations or in economic adjustments and the reconstruction of the world. The United States has observed, proposed, and generously lent money and engaged in great business transactions. But it neither constructively cooperated after Wilson's hopeful Fourteen Points were shamefully put aside, or offered definitely to compromise with its debtors. The Johnson Act was understandable, but it was protective rather than constructive. The consequence was that, after Poincaré's policy of hatred and revenge, the Allies in general developed the antiquated illusion of "reparation" as a postwar "must."

I believe that this rough digest of the 1929 situation is, today, commonly accepted as correct.

Now, let us see what was happening on the stage and behind the scenes of international politics, and look at the 1929 mentality.

When, about 1929, Morgan—through Parker Gilbert—actively stepped in to create the Young Plan and Bank for International Settlements, it was too late, and their propositions again became a protective compromise rather than a definite settlement. These new plans meant not much more than a modification of the reparations scheme. The Bank of International Settlements, in its narrow scope, was an impotent deformity of the Bank of Nations idea—an idea which may have had too wide a scope and therefore was premature in 1922, but could have been properly adapted to the situation in 1929.

As productive regulators, or better still as productive credit vehicles, to settle the distasteful reparation exaggerations, the Young Plan and the Bank of International Settlements in its original statutes were still-born infants. Schacht, however, was impressed, or was at least influenced, by Morgan's, Young's, and Gilbert's proposition.

What follows will show how those who tried hard to turn the wheels of history toward international cooperation and solidarity and to avoid the worst, namely, organized militarism, medieval barbarism, and war, did their duty to the utmost but were destined to fail because hypernationalistic interests reigned supreme.

The German business community did not like the Young Plan very much. So long as the Dawes Plan was in operation nothing drastic could happen to the German economy. It drew a borderline between creditor and debtor countries and discredited, in fact made impossible, encroachments on German economy. It avoided the worst. It created Germany's productivity and developed German exports artificially; but there was, as we have seen, a necessary limit to these exports, which conflicted with the economic interests of the creditor nations, and the transfer problem, as economists had predicted, became a burden to the Allies.

When the German banker Goldschmidt, who had always warned against any change of the Dawes Plan before it had found its natural end, discussed the transfer situation with leading English statesmen, the English could hardly stop laughing when he told them a parable. It really hit the point! Here it is:

A banker had accepted a large bill of exchange on a three-month term basis from his customer. Late one night, the customer tossed pebbles at the banker's bedroom window, arousing him from peaceful slumber. The bewildered banker opened the window and asked the customer, "What on earth do you mean by waking me up at this time of night?"

"I'm not going to pay my bill," came the answer.

"But your bill isn't due yet. You've still two month's time."

"Yes, I know," the customer replied, "but I haven't slept for the last four weeks, and from now on it's going to be *you* who'll not be able to sleep for the remaining two months!"

That just about sums up the situation. The creditor nations became at least as worried about the transfer problem under the Dawes Plan as the debtors. In short, Goldschmidt's former associate, Dr. Hjalmar

Horace Greeley Schacht now began to play his ambitious role on the international stage.

The chronological table of economic history shows the following dates:[3]

1929:

January 10—Reparation Commission appoints experts to discuss revision of Dawes Plan.

January 11—Reichsbank rate reduced from seven to six per cent.

January 19—Mr. J. P. Morgan and Mr. Owen D. Young accept invitation to conference.

February 11—First session of conference in Paris.

February 21—Rumor of International Clearing House.

February 22—Sir Josiah Stamp presents tentative plan.

February 24—Dr. Schacht presents plan for International Bank to Mr. Young.

February 25—Meeting of three committees presided over by Sir Josiah Stamp, Lord Revelstoke, and Mr. T. N. Perkins.

March 4—Mr. Owen D. Young presents plan for a new bank.

March 25—Complete report on proposed International Bank made to Young Committee.

April 12—Representatives of creditor powers present memorandum on annuities to Dr. Schacht.

April 13—Dr. Schacht rejects Allies' proposal.

April 25—Reichsbank rate increased from six and one-half per cent to seven and one-half per cent (capital flight from Germany).

May 16—Secretary Stimson issues statement that no officials of Federal Reserve or United States Government may take part in the new bank. (Mr. Benjamin Strong died early in 1928 and was therefore in no way responsible for this declaration.)

June 7—Young report signed in Paris.

What this chronological honor roll does not show may yet be of interest to us, namely:

Before the Young Plan was signed, Dr. Schacht flew to Mr. Krupp in Essen and presented the plan to economic leaders and industrialists, who were so strongly opposed to it that Schacht had to promise not to sign it. The leaders of German economy argued that the Young Plan

[3] Cf. historical data as listed in Lansing Dulles' aforementioned book.

implied gigantic obligations and would therefore arouse an overwhelming resentment within Germany. Schacht gave this promise, but the report was signed in Paris shortly afterwards. It really *was* signed with Schacht's approval; but at the decisive moment his conscience would not let him place his personal signature on the document. He had slipped away to the Bois de Boulogne, where he was found in a restaurant by one of his colleagues and actually was forced to put his personal signature on the treaty. This little episode would not have been mentioned were it not significant for understanding the developments which followed.

Let us continue the "honor roll." We read:

1929:

September 19—The New York Times stock average reaches high point of three-year rise. It was the boom of the boom.

October 2—Death of Stresemann—a great loss to the world.

October 3—Meeting in Baden Baden of Organization Committee of Bank for International Settlements. Basel is chosen as site. (This was quite contrary to the desires of German bank leaders; we proposed centers of banking activity, such as Amsterdam, London, or New York City as the location for the B.I.S.).

December 22—Hugenberg anti-Young Plan referendum rejected in Germany by six million votes. (The German people were suspicious of the publicity of the rightists.)

1930:

January 13—*At Hague Conference, Schacht refuses cooperation of the Reichsbank in the execution of the Young Plan and in the operation of the International Bank.* Reichsbank rate cut to six and one-half per cent.

Why did Dr. Schacht refuse? This incident, in our opinion, becomes a turning point in German politics. Was he opposed to the modifications, as he pretended to be, or did he in the end merely shirk the responsibility of helping to put them into effect?

Schacht, in his boundless ambition, had first promoted the Young Plan with all his vigor because he wanted to be considered the Saviour of Germany. Instead of permitting the Dawes Plan to reach its natural end, he wanted to alleviate the reparation situation by means of a new plan. But when he realized that through the Young Plan he had only perpetuated the debt calamity, without substantial change and without hope for ending the reparation monster in the near future, he used the first pretext to withdraw from the Young Plan, to quit the political stage, and conspire with the nazis behind the scene.

It was clear to the insiders. He wanted to shift the responsibility for the unpopular reparations question, including the Young Plan and the Bank for International Settlements, over to the government. He wanted to place the blame on the republican government; on German democracy, the co-founder and party member of which he had been, and which he had abandoned only in 1927. From that day forward, he about-faces and turns national socialist. Under normal circumstances this action would not have meant much. However, as it turned out, it was the beginning of the national catastrophe, because he had delivered the most dangerous material for propaganda to the German extremists. From this time on we see Schacht clearly preparing Hitler's course. The same Schacht, who had been selected by the social-democratic President Ebert for the presidency of the Reichsbank, and who was one of the founders of the democratic party, now in 1930 at one stroke becomes a satellite of the National Socialists. He becomes an active force in financing Hitler's rise with funds secured from Thyssen and other captains of German industry, in the hope of being able to rule the world by means of his own economic nazi dictatorship.[4]

1930:
January 14—Dr. Curtius promises German cooperation without Schacht and the Reichsbank.
March 7—Schacht resigns from Reichsbank.
March 11—Dr. Hans Luther appointed Head of Reichsbank.

At this point the Young Plan and the Bank for International Settlements became a reality. The Reichsbank acquiesced, the Reichsbank rate was cut to five per cent. The German Cabinet resigned, but Bruening formed a new one. The French Chamber of Deputies ratified the Young Plan, and at the first directors' meeting of the Bank for Inter-

[4] In his book, *The End of Reparations* (New York: Jonathan Cape & Harrison Smith), Schacht later endeavored to explain the motives for his action at the Hague Conference—not without success.

national Settlement Mr. McGarrah was elected President, Mr. Quesnay chosen as General Manager, and the German Dr. Huelse (my former schoolmate at the Royal Frederick's college of Koenigsberg (Koenigliches Friedrichs Collegium) was made Assistant General Manager.

All central banks, the Federal Reserve Bank, Bank of England, and Banque de France, reduced their bank rates; and the general public interpreted this as a sign of "central bank cooperation."

In October, 1929, after the signing of the Young Plan in Paris, in a stifling atmosphere poisoned with the pessimism of German entrepreneurs, I initiated the Franco-German understanding, finding in Dr. Mendès-France (at that time, Professeur des Hautes Etudes Sociales, later Under-Secretary of State under the Daladier government) a capable and cooperative comrade. Mendès-France was close to Daladier, who at that time was the guiding spirit of the Radical-Socialist Party (comparable to our American left-wing Democrats).

On November 9th, I spoke in Paris on the topic, "The reparations problem viewed by a German," and showed the deficiencies and advantages of the Young Plan. But this was not the essential task. Before, and while, experts discussed the statutes and bases of the Bank for International Settlements, and later, until 1932, I tried constantly in word and writing to influence world public opinion on the character of the international bank. I clearly recognized the inertia to which this *first international public banking institution* was condemned and the consequences and disappointments caused by its narrow scope.

Two contradictory conceptions prevailed both before and during its initiation: One faction wanted to restrict the activities of the bank to those of a clearing house for reparations—"to the more definitely monetary field"; the other wished to make it a creative and productive money and credit institution, to stimulate commerce at least, and if possible, to aid weak though promising economies of nations.

Some of those responsible for its implementation—Mr. Franqui, Sir Josiah Stamp, and Dr. Schacht—always insisted upon the extension of credit for commercial purposes, even if slight inflation was involved. But the committee had to delay these ideas and hoped for a miracle to happen in the distant future.

When Dr. Mendès-France published his standard work, *La Banque*

Internationale (Paris: Valois-Presse), which corresponded with my feelings on the inadequacy of the Bank for International Settlements, he invited me to write the introduction to the German edition (first published in *Les Chaiers Bleus*, Paris, October 4, 1930). I should like to restate here the closing words of this preface:

I have never ceased to be profoundly convinced that Walther Rathenau, by the power of his personality and the recognition which he enjoyed in Europe as well as on the other side of the Atlantic, would never have—had he survived—given up advancing the victory of the true Bank of Nations.

The reader of Dr. Mendès-France's work may himself judge how the death of a single individual has been disastrous for the fate of Europe.

Even though the problem had long been evaded, the International Bank had finally been established; *this was inevitable.*

But—because it had not been created in time, as a result of a *voluntary* movement—the world was now forced to accept it as dictated by the financiers with all its technical and political failings.

We greet in Mendès-France a young knight of European chivalry, one of those fanatic contenders for the cause of justice, destined to win or to die. May he, in the fight for the true Bank of Nations, be the champion in the tournament of world economic forces.

I extend my hand to my comrade in battle.

Soon there followed an invitation for me to speak at the Société des Savants in Paris on the subject, "The Future Tasks of the International Bank." Dr. Mendès-France was the commentator. It was my privilege to suggest, before these intellectual leaders of France, a broad outline of world economic organization. When the audience asked me to draw on the blackboard a sketch of how the plan would operate in the future with all related economic and social institutions and functions, I drew a sketch which is still the basis of my work on the Bank of Nations, as embodied in this book.

In 1930, Dr. de Haas, Director of the German Foreign Office and reponsible for the American and French Division, invited me to remain longer in Paris for the improvement of Franco-German understanding. And events again developed. The Dawes reparation bonds were burned and the Young bonds were issued on various markets, with European central banks participating in the subscription to the Bank of International Settlements' capital stock. The Reichsbank rate was cut to 4½ per cent and the United States and Germany made an agreement to settle their claims.

But all these actions came about *too late*. These two words, "too late," expressed the general European viewpoint. These words accompanied all subsequent actions until it really was too late.

After the dissolution of the Reichstag on July 18, National Socialists and Communists scored large gains in the election. German gold became flighty. Monsieur Moreau resigned as head of the Banque de France. Lee, Higginson gave the first 125 million dollar loan to the German Government. Oustric, in Paris, collapsed and stock scandals alternated with bank scandals. At the end of 1930, Kidder, Peabody in New York went into difficulties and the Bank of the United States failed.

On February 28, 1931, Chancellor Bruening declared that a moratorium would not solve the reparations problem. Both he and Dr. Luther urged a revision, while Schacht fought against the Young Plan in Stockholm. On May 11, the Austrian Creditanstalt went into difficulties and brought Austrian and general European conditions to their worst, and the American depression pressed from the other side with the full weight of its destructive consequences.

On June 15, Dr. Bruening and Dr. Curtius arrived in London to explain the difficult German situation. On June 20, the "Hoover debt holiday" was declared and, *on July 13, Germany's financial structure collapsed*. The German Bank, the Darmstaedter Bank, and the German Bourse closed, the Reichsbank rate was raised from 7 to 10 per cent, and in ten weeks 500 million dollars flowed out of the Reichsbank. There was a debt conference in London. The Reichsbank rate was raised from 10 to 15 per cent, and a credit of 250 million dollars was given to the Bank of England by the Banque de France and the Federal Reserve, but the pound fell sharply. The German banks reopened, the Reichsbank rate was lowered to 10 per cent. On September 19, the "Standstill Agreement" was signed by German bankers. (It has been maintained—with certain alterations—up to the present time.) On September 20, the Bank of England went off the gold standard. On October 6, Dr. Curtius resigned, but a new cabinet was again formed by Dr. Bruening. Premier Laval went to Washington and signed the

Hoover-Laval *communiqué*. In December, 1931, Dr. Melchior, partner of Max Warburg, Hamburg, presented a memorandum on Germany's financial situation, and on January 9, 1932, Chancellor Bruening declared Germany's inability to make any further payments. On January 19, Laval announced that France would not reduce reparation claims without having her own debt cut.

In Berlin, the big Dresdner and Darmstaedter banks were merged to ease the crisis and, on March 12, Ivar Kreuger, the Swedish match king, committed suicide—which caused one of the world's greatest industrial structures to collapse. On May 30, 1932, Dr. Bruening resigned as head of the German Government and on the following day Mr. von Papen was named German Chancellor. The English Prime Minister, Lord Grey, might well have said, "The lights went out all over Europe, never to be lit again."

May I now draw your attention to my own last semi-public activities, because they paralleled the efforts of Dr. Bruening and Dr. Curtius to bring about a final understanding between Germany and the Allies, a definite settlement of international debts, and the removal of economic obstacles.

I was fully aware of the great responsibility involved in these aims when Dr. de Haas invited me to participate in his endeavors toward a Franco-German understanding. Again in Dr. Mendès-France, who had meanwhile been elected to the Chamber of Deputies in Paris as its youngest member, I found an intelligent and competent collaborator, and, although my activities were to a large extent devoted to the Franco-German *industrial* understanding, we concentrated our efforts on a so-called Franco-German "Gemeinschafts-Gutachten" ("Joint Opinion") on the "Definite Settlement of the International Debts." We were completely convinced that, if France and Germany agreed on a mutual understanding on the debt question, it would be the key to a true world agreement.

During our collaboration, we had never entertained the idea that our two countries should propose a settlement without the agreement of England and the United States, because we knew all too well that only a solidarity of interests among all nations concerned would bring about lasting success. It was a daring undertaking and our combined efforts were those of cosmopolitan gentlemen trying to do the utmost to help their countries.

The drafting of the opinion, which finally comprised more than one hundred pages, was left largely to me; but Dr. Mendès-France helped to produce a French attitude favorable to an understanding.

There was a moment during one of our discussions when Dr. Mendès-France gave me the reaction of the leaders of his party, as well as that of the Banque de France and Bank of International Settlements. Could Germany, he asked, name an amount as a final reparation payment—a so-called "token" or "good will" payment—either to be paid at once or at any later date, or even on the basis of a loan from the Allies. If so, he hoped to be able to endorse the plan and to help to produce a favorable understanding.

I reported to Dr. de Haas, and to Valette, who was the specialist on the reparations question in the German Foreign Office, urging the necessity of mentioning a final "token" payment and asking for further directions as to formalities. Dr. de Haas was most cooperative, but his first serious symptoms of stomach cancer at this time hindered his activities considerably. Valette, whose political position was not always clear to me, was not so constructive in his attitude.

The main problem between Germany and France was this: While the German Government, in its dealing with France, always stressed the negative policy that Germany would not be able or willing to make any further payments at all, both Dr. Mendès-France and I knew only too well that for psychological reasons a "token" payment ought to be mentioned in order to bring about an understanding. How and when this payment was to be financed, credited, or paid was of relatively minor significance.

The German Foreign Office underestimated the French psychological viewpoint and its importance for a general international settlement. The German Government negotiated directly with England and with the United States, which at that time showed a growing spirit of conciliation and help. I continued with all my energy working for the satisfaction of the French desire, never leaving out of account the German-American and German-English policy of understanding; but

34

I was strongly convinced that in 1931 the way to international understanding led through France.

In answer to my report, Dr. de Haas wrote on July 10 from Berlin:

DEAR DR. HEYMANN:

In receipt of your kind letter of the 10th of July, I have carefully considered what action I should take in connection therewith. In view of the news that I received from Berlin I did not consider it wise to write to the Chancellor, who would not have been able to give the matter adequate attention. I therefore resolved to take the matter up with him personally upon my return. This was convenient, also, because my health was quite poor at the time and I had little inclination for work. I returned here at the end of last week and called the matter to Dr. Bruening's attention on Sunday; I should have had a conference with him yesterday, had he not left for Paris. I am happy about this trip, for he will most probably return with the conviction *that a complete cure can only be brought about through a reconciliation with France* [italics mine]. Thus, as soon as possible after Dr. Bruening's return I shall try to see him and discuss your letter with him.

On the other hand, I should not like to keep from you the fact that we should never enter a united front against America. Quite apart from our relations with the United States, the events which took place since the writing of your letter completely prohibit such action. Besides, the change of opinion with regard to the international debts is so unmistakable over there, that it becomes necessary to weigh carefully every word that is written, in order not to destroy the growing recognition of Americans that something must be done. When Dr. Bruening has returned from his trip the situation will appear much clearer than it does today and it will then be possible to discuss your plans with him.

In the hope soon to be able to give you more definite facts, I remain, with kindest regards,

Very sincerely yours,
WALTER DE HAAS

This letter of Dr. de Haas showed clearly that he agreed with Dr. Mendès-France and me that a "complete cure could only be brought about by a reconciliation with France" and that he hoped that Dr. Bruening would return from Paris with the same conviction.

De Haas, on the other hand, did not wish that we should enter a united front with France against the United States. This was never

Dr. Mendès-France's or my intention. We felt strongly, however, that the Franco-German understanding was the primary task and the *conditio sine qua non* for a "complete cure," as de Haas so effectively termed it.

Apart from political and psychological reasons, the whole financial construction of the international debt structure imperatively demanded the clearance via France. Germany was mostly indebted to France, France to England, and England to the United States. Perhaps the way via France was a more difficult one, but logically it would have eliminated the whole debt calamity for all time.

Perhaps France would not have made definite concessions to Germany without having its own debts to the Allies reduced. This position was officially taken on January 19, 1932, by Laval, ten days after Dr. Bruening's declaration that Germany was unable to make further payments. But was it not much more important to reconcile France and, via this reconciliation, arrive at a "complete cure," i.e., at the definite settlement of all the international debts, which have infected and poisoned the political atmosphere of Germany and all other nations up to the present day?

The letter from Dr. de Haas was followed by personal discussion in Berlin. Three months later, on October 30, during the course of the German negotiations with England, I wrote a letter to Valette from Paris.

Valette answered on November 10, 1931, from the German Foreign Office, as follows:

DEAR DR. HEYMANN:

Your letter of the 30th ultimate was only received by me upon my return yesterday, after an absence of several days. I should like to answer your letter with all due speed. . . . It is clear at present that we are not in a position to afford any conceivable sum of reparations for some time to come. No one knows when these economic difficulties which have made it absolutely impossible for us to pay will be lifted. Whether we shall be back on our feet in one or two years or in three or five years, and in what condition we shall be when the crisis has passed, it is impossible to foresee. I should consider it very dangerous if a declaration, concerning Germany's future ability to pay, were made. Before we can make such a statement we must know how we shall emerge from the crisis. Thus a fixed amount could be named only on the condition that we are in a relatively strong position when the crisis has passed.

There is certainly no objection to your mentioning the thought in your conversations with your French friends that possibly at a later time we might be able to pay *612 million marks*[5] *in addition to the service on the Dawes loan* [italics mine], after the crisis has been successfully passed. It would be an entirely different story if this were stated as a German opinion in writing, which, as you said, is to represent a German-French statement.

I beg you to remember that we are now in the middle of conferences which are to introduce a new settlement of the reparation question. At this time such a statement would be extremely inopportune. I should also like to emphasize the fact that what I have said is my own private opinion which must under no condition be utilized in any way.

For your work in Paris I wish you continued success. . . .

With my kindest regards, I remain,

As ever yours,
VALETTE

Dr. de Haas' health condition had weakened and I was recalled to Berlin to discuss the situation with him at his home, afterwards calling on Valette in the Foreign Office. Dr. de Haas was most appreciative and cooperative, and gave his advice to Valette over the telephone; Valette, however, showed for the first time the true nature of his attitude and his political position—an attitude which, in 1940, Dr. Bruening explained in a letter to me, to be quoted presently. Realizing that no help was available from the Foreign Office, I used Valette's tentative figure of 612 million marks in Paris, and continued with Mendès-France.

Unfortunately, Dr. de Haas died in December, 1931. The last letter that he wrote to me, on November 30, from his deathbed, has never left my pocket.

The progress and success of these negotiations was retarded because in 1932 French political opinion was divided into two camps. One party did not believe in the seriousness of the nazi movement; the other believed that the Nazis were already dominant and their triumph could not be prevented. Between these two opposite opinions, the action

[5] Later Valette maintained that this figure was suggested by von Buelow, Secretary of State in the Foreign Office.

for more active support of the German Republic, and for a definite amicable understanding between France and Germany via the definite settlement of the debt and reparations question, was greatly hampered. But it could not have failed had not the rightist putsch put an end to our endeavors.—

On January 8, 1940, I sent the two letters from Dr. de Haas and Valette to Dr. Bruening at Harvard, asking him kindly to furnish additional details concerning his own negotiations and endeavors to bring about an understanding and a definite settlement with the Allies; he obligingly responded on January eleventh:

MY DEAR DR. HEYMANN:

. . . I believe I have once before explained my ideas to you. Only once did I make the attempt to discuss with officials of the Foreign Office and the Ministry of Finance the question of what policy to pursue in regard to the Reparation problem. After two hours this discussion convinced me that proposals of these gentlemen would be quite useless. The copies of the two letters which you sent me reaffirm my conviction. Mr. Valette's letter, however, interested me considerably. If Mr. von Buelow had been aware of Valette's ideas and had reported them to me I should have caused him immediately to be transferred to another department. Several weeks before Mr. Valette wrote this letter I had informed Messrs. Laval and Briand that we should not be in a position to recommence the reparation payments in any form, not even in part. On the 19th of January, 1931, I expressed this opinion to the British Ambassador in a personal conference. While this information caused a hue and cry in France, it was accepted quite calmly in England. My conferences in Geneva in April 1932 were intended to cover the following conditions:

Germany can make a final payment only to the extent of an international loan which is to be granted to her. This loan must be concluded immediately, whereas the final payment cannot be made until ten years later. When I left Geneva the powers, with the exception of France, had reconciled themselves to the idea that henceforth no more than a "token" payment was to be made, in the form determined between the war debtors and the United States as a result of one of my conferences. It was Mr. von Papen who was later prepared to make larger payments. He even exceeded the sum which had been suggested to me by the British Government by way of the Bank of England and which I had refused.

This fact will enable you to interpret correctly the contents of Dr. de Haas' letter. I should merely like to add a few remarks. An understanding with France always was the aim of my policy. On the other hand, it was perfectly clear to me that such an agreement would only succeed if I were able to secure the backing of England and the United States. This policy had advanced much further than the gentlemen in the Foreign Office realized. ... I was not overthrown because of failure in the reparation and disarmament problems. My overthrow was caused by the opinion of the clique surrounding the President, that these questions were practically solved and I was no longer needed. It was made clear to the President (of which he in turn quite frankly informed me) that, if I should be permitted to remain in office for three more months, my successes would be so widely recognized by the public, that he would not dare to dismiss me and to prepare a coup d'état of the rightists.

As for the Bank for International Settlements, all my endeavors during 1930 and '31 to find some support for the financial stability of Europe in this respect were in vain. This does not mean that the Bank of International Settlements may not play an important part in future.

I hope that you do not entertain the idea that I intentionally carried on a neo-mercantilistic policy. It was forced on us by the provisions of the Young Plan. In the conferences of Geneva in 1932, I set down orally such basic proposals as would have enabled a return to a freer trade policy within a year. The fate that awaited these plans is, more than anything else, responsible for the situation in which the world finds itself today.

Wishing you best success in your work, I remain,

Very truly yours,
H. BRUENING

I can only repeat what I have explained before. I have always believed that Dr. Bruening, the most distinguished spirit in German politics, who stood far above all political intrigue, a pious and upright man, a pillar in the turmoil of events, did his utmost to carry the understanding to success. I have always known that his success was envied and begrudged by the rightists. I still believe, moreover, that the agreement with France would have made his success complete and lasting. With a relatively small token payment of, say, six hundred and twelve million marks or less, on the basis of an international loan with deferred payments and all necessary concessions in amortization, interest, and so on, *the question of international debts could have been definitely settled in 1931.* Why was that of such overwhelming importance? It is my personal opinion that it would not only have brought about the salvation of the German Republic at the right time, but it would have cleaned up the international atmosphere once and for all.

Neither the United States nor any other nation has considered it imperative to their well-being to see that the obligations are fulfilled, but the absence of a definite settlement will weigh heavily upon the world, and at the peace table the shadow of the debt monster will appear as an evil spirit to the peacemakers.

With regard to the neo-mercantilistic errors and such mistakes, represented by the reparations "must," the Young Plan, and the B. I. S., I fully agree with Dr. Bruening's viewpoint; they were "responsible for the situation in which the world finds itself today." Capitalism missed its greatest opportunity when it set up a passive and sterile tool for reparations clearance in lieu of a creative and productive instrument for the consummation of our society's potential. Ten years of agony and futility, climaxed by the economic explosion of the present war, were the ignominious results of this egregious blunder.

In the same letter of January 11, Dr. Bruening states that the time is not yet ripe to give any part of his memoirs out for publication. "Only he who has drafted and performed the plan is in a position to give a presentation, suitable to serve as a basis for historical research." He states further that, during the critical period of his chancellorship, many interesting and valuable propositions were not brought to his attention, because they were not in step with the actual developments. We are therefore looking forward to the publication of his memoirs, which will disclose his negotiations with Laval in Paris, and from which the world will undoubtedly realize why he allowed himself to be overthrown by President Hindenburg, then an old man and a helpless instrument of a clique, instead of himself overthrowing Hindenburg and the rightists.

More than that, we know that leading democrats of that time, such as Minister Albert Grzesinski, often urged Bruening to make an end of Hitler and his partisan activities. Why did he not follow this advice and act accordingly? Only he, who executed the political plan, can give us the true story. It is therefore to be hoped that his work will soon be brought before the public.

When Dr. Bruening abdicated, Germany was close to a settlement with the Allies—which would have brought about the success of the German Republic. But, as Dr. Bruening has stated, the extreme rightists, including President Hindenburg, Papen & Company, thought that the understanding had practically been reached and they could not afford the success of Bruening and the Republican government. A putsch was planned and the dazzled rightists did not realize that their narrow-minded attitude meant the beginning of the end. They overthrew the Republicans and paved the way for Hitler.

Papen, who replaced Bruening, was a Hussar officer with few, and not favorable, diplomatic experiences here in the United States. He and the militarists could perhaps also have saved the situation. But here again the Social Democrats begrudged Papen such a success. They could not endure the idea that Papen and the conservatives should succeed. The *tertius gaudens*, the man who laughed to himself, was Hitler, who reaped the fruits of Versailles, the Ruhr occupation, the reparations monster (ruthlessly employed in propaganda), and the distress caused by the crash of 1929 and the economic depression after 1931.

With Hitler's arrival upon the scene, the war of 1939 was practically declared in 1933. Of what value is it if nazi leaders constantly emphasize: We *do* not want the war, or we *did* not want the war. They have systematically and cold-bloodedly prepared and organized this war since the beginning of their existence. Nor does it alter the situation if one threatens the whole world with the greatest army and air force ever produced and begins to occupy and conquer country after country without bloodshed or declaration of war. Such peaceful acquisition of neighboring countries ends with the moment of resistance. What a ridiculous justification to say: We did not want the war, but you encircled us—*you* resisted, therefore *you* made the war.

On the other hand, let us be frank and just. Is it surprising that lack of solidarity and love for one's neighbor, absence of any definite settlement of the stupid monstrosities or of any reasonable economic system or order, and lack of a spirit of cooperation and fair play among the nations of the world breed nationalistic upheavals, fascist dictators, and wars? Is it not natural that any country in the midst of such a situation will produce its Hitlers, its Goebbels, and its Streichers?

Once this nazi regime became established, the snowball started the avalanche, which rolled downward with overwhelming force, swallowing peaceful peoples in its path.

After Dr. de Haas passed away, Dr. Bruening was overthrown, and the Weimar Republic came to an end, I gave up all public activities. In the summer of 1932, upon my last visit to the Bank for International Settlements in Basle, Dr. Huelse, the German director, told me that Schacht, before leaving for Berlin, had just informed him, "The Nazi wave must come. It is unavoidable."

The wave has come. It has swollen into a flood of blood. But floods are controllable and shores can be protected; and behind hospitable shores a great and peaceful nation must prepare itself for the task of re-organizing the institutions of society. A mighty and wealthy nation must take it upon itself to mould the economic basis for the reconstruction of our world when it has spent its fury. What nation but the United States of America is in a better position to show how economics, which has made war, is also capable of making peace?

CHAPTER III

NAZI ECONOMY VIEWED AT A DISTANCE

As HAS been pointed out, many facts contributed to the rise of national socialism in Germany. Let us, briefly, review the most important of these:

The German Republic was denied by the Allies the support indispensable to its success. The Versailles and Locarno settlements and the recovery that followed did not represent an economic peace, but were more in the nature of a truce. Germany and Europe in general recovered; but the entire set-up of the Dawes Plan, the Young Plan, and the Bank for International Settlements, with its prolongation of the debt insanity, was doomed to failure. The men who might have saved the fate of the world either had been killed or had passed away.[1]

One more fact, frequently neglected, must be mentioned here: During world recovery in the period from 1925 to 1929, a gigantic overcapitalization of production, accompanied by a unique rationalization of industry in all capitalistic countries, especially Germany and the United States, carried the situation to the boiling point and created an unprecedented unemployment problem when the crash brought an end to prosperity.

The effects of this overcapitalization have been strongly felt until the present time. One of the leading German bankers, Otto Jeidels,

[1] I shall mention only three: (1) Walther Rathenau, who might have brought about solidarity of world economy culminating in a Bank of Nations as an organizing mechanism for solving gradually most of the vital international economic problems; (2) Benjamin Strong, who might have created an ingenious new world monetary policy which would have counteracted the crash of 1929 and the depression that followed; (3) Walter de Haas, who might have insisted on carrying out the Franco-German understanding, the definite settlement of the international debts via France, and, as a logical consequence, international disarmament. His sickness greatly weakened his influence, and his death practically brought the Franco-German reconciliation and "the complete cure" (that is, the fundamental elimination of the obstacles to world reconciliation) to an end.

(after Fuerstenberg's retirement the leading spirit of the Berliner Handelsgesellschaft, now partner of Lazard Brothers in New York City) went so far as to believe that this supersaturation of the market with production means and real capital completely halted recovery during the New Deal period of 1933-39.

Two movements could have changed the situation after Dr. Bruening was overthrown and before Hitler came into power: Von Papen and Schleicher might have saved the nation, but they lacked the energy and decision, and failed to start a timely military revolution to be followed by an economic reconstruction. On the other hand, if the Social Democrats had joined with the Communists in a united labor front, carried out the revolution, and instituted economic reform, nazism would have been avoided. But they, in turn, lacked group unity and the spirit of organization.

Hitler, with the help of his adherents, succeeded in convincing the German industrialists of the bolshevik peril and in this way obtained their financial support. He and his party members had already well prepared the revolution and fascist organization for many years, using the most ruthless and aggressive tactics.

Whoever started the revolution in Germany would have had to create a national movement to unite the national forces in one powerful organization and to create public works and employment. The nazi government concentrated exclusively on war preparation in the broadest sense and on a vast scale, and therefore from the beginning was more or less excluded from economic reconstruction on a world-wide scale. It exploited and created its economic forces independently of and in opposition to the outer world. This is the cardinal point and the great weakness of the nazi constitution.

I do not underestimate the effects of their ruthless squandering of the nation's resources and the functioning of their dictatorial organization created by militaristic tyranny, cruelty, and fear. I will not pass judgment on their nationalistic and bureaucratic achievements. But economic isolationism, in a highly industrialized country like Germany, which is largely dependent upon the importation of foreign raw materials, can be maintained only for a limited time. Concentration on war industry and complete militarization must lead to internal disequilibrium and fatal maladjustment or to external explosion, to war, which is never profitable.

Neither the rightists nor the leftists would ever have ignored the simplest laws of economic dependence on international economic forces so completely as this was done by the Nazis. National socialism is in itself a contradiction. Socialism is an international movement and cannot survive national limitation. I am convinced that men like Dr. Schacht recognized this fact and may have done their best to change the situation, but I know only too well how ignorant of economics are most fanatical nationalistic politicians.

It would be superfluous to explain the details and technicalities of a totalitarian economy in this book, because so many excellent books have already been published on the subject.[2]

Our aim is not national autarchy and restrictionism, but an international system of economic solidarity, of just division and distribution of economic forces among collaborating nations.

The author lived in Germany until the summer of 1936 and saw that the immense, the almost complete, employment of the country's labor and productive forces resulted in no miracle of progress.

The rigidly controlled "Wehrwirtschaft" was patterned after the Rathenau system of the World War, after the Kriegs-Rohstoff organization, and also after Bernard Baruch's War Industries Board in the United States. These wonders of coordination and organization of war economy were copied and adjusted to the nazi scheme of things.[3]

[2] Williams D. Bayles, *Caesars in Goose-Step* (Harpers).

Rudolf Brinkmann, *Wirschaftspolitik aus nationalistischen Kraftquell* (Gustav Fischer, Jena: Publ., 1939).

Peter F. Drucker, *The End of Economic Man* (New York: The John Day Co.).

F. W. Foerster, *Europe and the German Question* (London: Allen & Unwin).

C. W. Guillebaud, *The Economic Recovery of Germany* (New York: Macmillan Co., 1933-38).

Douglas Miller, *You Can't Do Business with Hitler* (Boston: Little Brown & Co.).

Gunther Reimann, *Germany* (London: Secker & Warburg).

Gunther Reimann, *The Vampire Economy* (New York: Vanguard Press).

J. T. Shotwell, *What Germany Forgot* (New York: Macmillan Co.).

Henry William Stiege, "Wehrwirtschaft: Economics of Military State," *American Economic Review*, Dec. 1940, Vol. 30, No. 4.

Gustav Stolper, *German Economy, 1870–1940* (London: Allen & Unwin).

Otto D. Tolischus, *They Wanted War* (Reynal and Hitchcock).

Frieda Wunderlich, "Germany's Defense Economy and the Decay of Capitalism," *Quarterly Journal of Economics*, LII, May, 1938.

[3] The origins of other measures are to be found in partly misunderstood adaptations from

The financing of party needs by underconsumption is copied from Lenin's N.E.P. (New Economic Policy). Russia applied this method even more thoroughly. Nearly 97 per cent of earnings in the Russian people's economy were assessed for the Soviet Communist Party, and not much was left for housing, clothing, and food. If we were to apply such rigid methods to employ the idle population of the United States we should soon have a revolution on our hands, because the "führer" complex, the spirit of militarism, and servile subordination fortunately are foreign to us. We should be thoroughly aroused if such pressure were imposed on the American people.

Mussolini and the fascist pattern of Italy were godparents to most of the other movements. But the statement of these facts is not intended to minimize nazi achievements in organization, economic planning, co- and sub-ordination. Prussia has always been considered supreme in its unique power and skill for organization, and much is to be learned from its achievements in this respect.

The man who was responsible for the financing of the gigantic rearmament of Germany and for the financial management of the nazi regime was Dr. Hjalmar Horace Greeley Schacht. His ingenuity in organizing financial management and restrictionism cannot be over-emphasized. Credit for the existence and relatively long preservation of nazi national economy is due to him and to the fact that it was financed by underconsumption for the major part and by inflation for the lesser part. When Dr. Walter Funk took over Schacht's office he was unable to stop the printing press and inflation machine, already doomed to run out of control. The only thing keeping the system together is the power to control prices, wages and profits by guns that are always pointed. (There has been talk of a nazi financial revolution, whereby inflation can be controlled for an indefinite period. This is discussed later in the chapter.)

The astonishing results obtained during Schacht's era were, of course, only possible through drastic price-fixing measures and through

---

other nations and literatures. The financing of the internal economy through long-term antic-ipated public credits and the attitude toward the interest problem have been analyzed in my book, *The World Credit and Finance Reform* (Berlin: Ernst Rowohlt, 1921). Most of the re-maining measures are equally unoriginal.

expropriation and assessment of the middle and upper classes for the benefit of the lower classes; but the lower classes also had to sacrifice about 20 per cent of their already reduced earnings. Further, a severe export, import, and currency control and restriction enabled the nazi regime and its reign of terror to continue. The confiscation of Jewish and Catholic property did not contribute much economically; it was part of the nazi propaganda machine to excite the masses.

It is the merit of Norbert Muhlen and his commentator, Johannes Steel, to have described and preserved for posterity the surprising actions and typical characteristics of Schacht, who was not a "magician" but actually the absolute financial dictator of the Reich, and who has earned for himself the name of Hitler's Machiavelli.[4]

As Steel states, it has always been Schacht's dream to become "the economic Napoleon of the twentieth century." History alone will some day be able to judge whether Schacht's dream has come true. Certainly, he has turned out to be a high priest of armament finance and a Fra Diavalo in national and international credit and property. By financing the *furor teutonicus* with confiscated foreign credits, foreign and domestic property, and underconsumption, he enabled Hitler to carry out his Napoleonic ambitions.

It would be flattery to compare Schacht in his political activities and his political convictions—if he had any—with Machiavelli. But with Napoleon? . . .

When Schacht was considered for the presidency of the Reichsbank, a leading German banker, upon being asked by the president of the Chamber of Commerce whether the rumors of Schacht's evil character were true to fact, answered with a blunt, "No! That is grossly exaggerated. Schacht has no character at all!" It is hardly understandable why, in spite of this, Schacht was appointed Reichsbank President by the social democrat, President Ebert, in 1924.

Schacht has a vivid and sparkling personality—dangerously ambitious and wily—with a reputation for always doing the unexpected. Muhlen explains his unlimited personal ambition and will-to-power as

---

[4] His mysterious ambitions and his influence on world events during the inter-war period are ably criticized in Muhlen's book, *Schacht, Hitler's Magician* (New York: Longmans, Green & Co.).

being the result of a certain inferiority complex derived from his experiences and environment in early youth. He is insatiably and mercilessly ambitious and most probably will never cease striving to become the "economic Napoleon" of world affairs.

The unscrupulous and confusing tactics and methods which he applied gradually to rid Germany of her private and public foreign debts and interest payments—in order to keep the Third Reich solvent and independent, to save the mark, to avoid or postpone inflation; to put "capital in a concentration camp," to make other countries involuntary creditors of the Reich, and, as traveling salesman, to force the dumping of cheapened exports onto foreign markets—are nevertheless achievements of great resourcefulness. Viewed from a historical perspective, and disregarding his aims and methods, these ruthless and original actions must in themselves be considered as ingenious.

Once committed to nazism and entrusted with nazi alchemy, he developed into a model Machiavelli, Cagliostro, and Savonarola all rolled into one. As Muhlen's book so lucidly explains, he could on the one hand solemnly declare before the New York Bond Club on October 9, 1934: "Germany will pay all the debts which she has contracted after the war; no one who has invested any money in Germany after the war on long term or short term, whether he has invested it in industrial credits, commercial credits, or in credits to the public authorities, will be disappointed, because Germany will pay those debts, and I include the Young Plan. . . . We Germans want to maintain our honesty as orderly business people. . . ." But within a few years he had ignored "every single one of these promises."

He denounced the Dawes and Young Plans, to cheering nazi crowds, as "political treaties without moral validity" and stated in the same year: "Germany will not pay these coupons of the Dawes and Young Plans." A few years later, he decided once and for all: "Not a pfennig to the creditors."

There is a grandiose swing to his unscrupulousness which may be explained in history by his fanaticism for the national socialist idea and cause—which was in fact his own cause—and his detestation of Germany's foreign debt burden. Muhlen characterizes it as his boundless ambition "to rule through the Nazis, who cannot rule alone"—as Schacht is said to have told Dorothy Thompson in 1931.

These are only a few highlights on his conduct as financial dictator at the peak of his career. The more he has fooled the world, the more he has been idolized and may go down in history, if not as a Napoleon, at least as the Tyll Eulenspiegel of our time; because "mundus vult decipi" ("the world wants to be deceived").

The main result of Schacht's crafty scheme of tactics was Germany's ability to finance the most stupendous armament program of all time, to a great extent at the expense of her creditors.

Do we really learn by experience? I am not so sure. Experience seems to indicate that mankind's whims of imaginative fancy are only too easily tricked into worshipful admiration of the diabolic, mysterious, and cunning statesman, and are prone to admire such a man as Schacht as an economic demigod.

What was the reason why other nations remained relatively calm toward the Nazi movement and did not concentrate equally on rearmament? Was it not a strange attitude on the part of the British and French to tolerate the fanatic elevation of a nation so well known for its military efficiency, and not to step in when the Rhineland was occupied or later when the German war machinery grew to menacing proportions? Why did Britain discourage France from interfering in the occupation of the Rhineland, and why did she not fear Germany's increasing military power?

One of the main reasons why nazi Germany was able to exercise her provocative rearmament policy in 1934 and 1935 was apprehension on the part of Britain and France that an overthrow of the nazi regime might bring about communism and open the door to bolshevism in Germany. This fear is in fact an explanation for the import credits which Germany received from England and other countries in spite of the fact that she had defaulted on her foreign debts early in 1934.[5]

[5] Paul Einzig, in *World Finance Since 1914* (New York: Macmillan, 1936), page 39, writes: "In the case of the British Government, the Nazis succeeded in obtaining credit at first through the operation of an exchange agreement, by which German imports of British goods were . . . to discharge their liabilities by the payment of Reichsmarks into the Reichsbank. Subsequently, when this arrangement broke down, a payment agreement was conducted and the Bank of

It is this fear of bolshevism in Germany and its spread over Europe, that may again have played a great part in Mussolini's appeal to President Roosevelt and Sumner Welles's mission to Europe early in 1940.

Was there any other reason for the attitude of the Western powers against nazi Germany? Did they believe in Hitler's assurances in *Mein Kampf* that war against Soviet Russia and the "liberation" of the Ukraine were, in fact, the aim of nazi foreign policy?

To a great extent they did. When I visited English leaders as late as in the spring of 1936, I still heard the belief expressed on all sides that the *furor teutonicus* would be directed toward the East and that so long as it could be diverted in that direction, England would not fear, nor interfere with, nazi policies.

Here again Dr. Schacht played a significant role in world affairs. It was at the time when Schacht negotiated with English bankers for a thirty-million-pound-sterling loan to Germany. The loan was supposed to be a model loan, to be enlarged later, with French participation provided for. Lloyds of London underwriter groups were asked to participate in the negotiations and to examine the credit insurance of the loan. The political demands which England made conditional to the granting of the loan, with regard to the cessation of racial and religious persecution and armament limitation, did not meet with Hitler's approval, and although Schacht did his best to bring home the loan he did not succeed. But during the entire nazi period, Schacht always publicly declared, even as late as 1937 in Paris, that the Third Reich sought no foreign loans.

Muhlen gives us a very interesting comment on these negotiations. In 1936, when Schacht again tried to get foreign loans to cover his gigantic armament expenditures,

---

England granted a loan of £750,000 with the declared object of assisting those British exporters whose credits were defaulted upon by Germany. The real result of this transaction was, however, that those exporters, having received their money back from the Bank of England were promptly prepared to grant new credits to Germany, so that in reality the transactions amounted to granting a credit to Germany."

Gunther Reimann in his book, *Germany, World Empire or World Revolution* (Secker & Warburg, London, 1938), reports that Sir Montagu Norman is quoted as having said in the City of London: "We shall have to give a loan of £50 million to Germany later, if we refuse to give her credits now. The money may never be paid back, but it will entail smaller losses than a collapse of the nazi regime."

he thought to find lenders in the City of London. A representative of City financiers came to Berlin to negotiate with him.

"Now," objected the London financier at the very outset of the negotiations, "it is customary for a banker to see the accounts of a firm, before he gives it credit. The Third Reich," he continued, is "the only firm in the world which asks for credit without presenting a single figure of its accounts."

Schacht turned and twisted. He had sent his assistants for fat files of papers in which statistics had been compiled of Germany's huge economic progress. But the man from London shook his head. He asked for the fundamental figures, the figures of the unpublished German budget, the profit and loss account of the Third Reich. In the end Dr. Schacht, hoping for a new stream of credit, weakened and did actually bring forward the official figures. The figures of Germany's expenditure for armaments until the end of 1935 were:

Budget Year	Total Expenditure[6] on Armaments (in million marks)
1912	645
1926	518
1927	539
1928	553
1929	490
1930	515
1932 (budget estimate)	674
1932 (actual expenditure)	630
1933 (budget estimate)	671
1933 (actual expenditure)	3,000
1934	5,500
1935	10,000

The man from London glanced at them, said he would like to study them quietly at home, and flew back to London, with his purse in one pocket and in the other a sheet containing the secret budget of the Third Reich.

Thus it is that we know the official figures of the expenditure of the Third Reich on rearmament. The British negotiator soon sent to Dr. Schacht a letter coldly regretting that at the moment he was unable to continue the credit negotiations.

In February 1937 "The Banker" published Schacht's budget confidences. The figures said little for the credit worthiness of Mssrs. Third Reich Ltd.,

---

[6] In 1936, these expenditures amounted to 12.6 billion marks. In 1940, these expenditures are estimated at 13 billion dollars. Hitler boasted in one of his speeches that up to the beginning of the war the nazis had spent 90 billion marks on armament.

but much for the ability of that firm's managing director, Hjalmar Schacht. They spoke plainly as only figures can.

At the beginning of these credit discussions, Dr. Schacht informed his friend Montagu Norman, Governor of the Bank of England, of Hitler's intention to march against Russia, although historically it has been proved that Hitler at that time no longer believed in a war against the Soviet Union. It is true, and has lately been confirmed in the official White Book published by the Polish Government-in-Exile, that Germany attempted over a period of many years to lead Poland into a joint war against Russia.[7]

After Field Marshal Hermann Goering's visit to Poland in 1935 however, where he ultimately proposed that Germany and Poland should conduct a joint war against Russia and divide the spoils of war in the Ukraine, the dream of a joint German-Polish war against Russia definitely came to an end. The Poles refused or "side-stepped" the idea of cooperation with Germany in a war against Russia, because they believed "the offers were intended merely as the first step toward German domination of Europe," as the White Book states. In 1935, Rosenberg and others, who may have tried to influence Hitler on the subject of war against Russia, lost ground and other cool-headed leaders—especially the brain trust surrounding Goering—gained in influence on German policy. Montagu Norman, however, gave credence to Schacht's fairy tale of 1936 and told it to the City of London, thus relieving the English people of a nightmare, and all was "quiet on the Western front."

In August, 1936, when I visited an English friend, a partner in one of the large Lloyds underwriter groups in Leadenhall Street, he repeated what he had told me during the loan negotiations of Schacht

---

[7] The part played by Germany in the complot of the eight Russian generals to overthrow the Russian Government and to form a military power in Russia is not quite clear. The White Book reports that Hitler himself declared in a talk with Joseph Lipski, last Polish Ambassador to Germany, in 1935, that General Kurt Schleicher, who was killed in the Nazi blood purge of June 30, 1934, aided in the formation of a military power in Soviet Russia, and that "that alone sufficiently justified General Schleicher's end."

It is not the task of this book to bring to light this sad and mysterious affair, which brought to an end one of Germany's most able, hopeful, and intelligent strategists and political geniuses; but it is the aim of this book to detect the economo-political reasons, which led to the present war.

with London bankers in Berlin early in 1936: "Schacht has set the City at ease. The *furor teutonicus* will be diverted toward the East; so we have been informed by his friend Montagu Norman." The City of London remained at ease until it was too late.

There in Berlin and London, through Hjalmar Horace Greeley Schacht's assurances to his friend Montagu Norman, Governor of the Bank of England, the fate of Austria and Czechoslovakia was sealed, and not in Munich. I happen to know that Schacht told nazi leaders in Germany, to the accompaniment of uproarious laughter, how he had fooled the City of London. But posterity will probably maintain that he has always acted in the best interests of peace and the capitalistic world. This action was the only plausible explanation of why England was comparatively unprepared for the war of 1939. But all these experiences which England suffered will by no means hinder Schacht's influence as monetary "wizard" of international affairs.

Knowing the British and American attitude toward Schacht, I am convinced that he will again be considered as a "jolly good fellow" when economic rulers sit down with him at the peace table. And there is a plausible explanation for this peculiar play of logic. In currency and credit questions, inventive spirit, skill, and expert knowledge are evidently considered as more important than character. It is an old story that politics spoils the character. National political acts can always be explained in terms of patriotism. Moreover, there is still a deep mysticism attributed to money, currency, and gold problems; and Schacht is considered as *the* German "expert" in monetary management, certainly the one man who has had practical experience and showed resourcefulness under excruciating circumstances.

It was through a muddle of intrigue that Schacht first succeeded in overthrowing his rivals, Dr. Alfred Hugenberg, Gottfried Feder, and Dr. Kurt Schmidt, the more liberal and capitalistic-minded nazi members. But, when Schacht had "no more rabbits left in his hat," he was in turn overthrown by Hermann Goering and his brain trust. Dr. Walter Funk, Schacht's successor, does not enjoy the confidence and friendship of foreign statesmen and the "trust Schacht school." It was Schacht's ingenious deception in arousing the protection of foreign creditor interests and the seemingly "moderate" course which he promised, and which the world attributed to him, that succeeded in appeasing Chamberlain and those responsible for English foreign policy.

But has the world ever realized how much Schacht was driven by his selfish interest and thirst for power, and how little by his aim for appeasement, when he hunted out and always found "friends" all over the world who supported him and will probably continue to do so as long as he lives? Schacht was always successful in finding his backers abroad, such as J. P. Morgan, the late Parker Gilbert, Benjamin Strong and his successors, Montagu Norman, and most of the international captains of currency and finance.

On July 16, 1926, Lord d'Abernon, then British Ambassador in Berlin, wrote in his memoirs:

Norman, the Governor of the Bank of England, and Benjamin Strong, the head of the Federal Reserve Bank, are both here on a visit to Dr. Schacht, the President of the Reichsbank.

Norman tells me that the purpose of the visit is, partly, to establish a basis for future cooperation, but still more to give Schacht a lift and increase his prestige.

How familiar does this melody sound and how harmoniously was it sung again when, before the outbreak of the new World War, we heard about Schacht's honeymoon trip to India. The public talked seriously of his advices to the Bank of India on behalf of the British government. Or in 1940, when Sumner Welles lunched with him in Berlin. Or when Schacht was searched for at Gibraltar, on board the "Conte di Savoia" which brought Mr. Welles home. It leaves much to the imagination as to just what the British customs hunters might have done had they really found him.

Schacht's last action in favor of "appeasement" is worth mentioning. When Goering had gained supremacy in Nazi economy and the "four year plan," and Schacht was politically a dead man,

the immediate reason [as Steel reports] for Schacht's dismissal was a conference between him and George Rublee, Director of the British Governmental Committee for Refugees.

The final session of conference between Dr. Schacht and Mr. Rublee took place twenty-four hours before Schacht's dismissal.

In the course of the conference Schacht agreed to try to work out a settlement of the refugee question without forcing the payment of ransom upon an outraged world.

Schacht previously had suggested through the good offices of Mr. Montagu Norman, Governor of the Bank of England, that an orderly dispersal of the emigrants should be financed by a loan of two and one-half billion dollars raised by Jews outside Germany and covered by additional German exports admitted by other countries under special export licenses. Schacht promised Montagu Norman that Germany would suspend anti-semitic measures for a time, if this scheme would be accepted.

Dr. Schacht's acceptance of Mr. Rublee's proposal was all the excuse necessary for Dr. Walter Funk, who had long been anxious to succeed the President of the Reichsbank.

Dr. Funk succeeded in convincing Hitler that Germany absolutely needed the money to be obtained for Germany from the Jewish refugee ransom plan, and that he, Funk, could obtain it, if Schacht couldn't.

Dr. Funk, after Schacht's dismissal, saw to it that the negotiations with Mr. Rublee continued . . . Dr. Funk's first act in office as President of the Reichsbank was to order a survey of the resources and real estate properties of the Catholic Church in Germany.

Dr. Funk is no magician, no sorcerer, no genius. He had to produce and print the means necessary for the party's and the people's gigantic needs. Schacht did not envy him, nor do we. Without Schacht's unpurchasable international "prestige," and within the "splendid isolation" of the Third Reich, nothing can stop the inflation avalanche.

What was the result? Internal disintegration? Breakdown of German economy? No! Ersatz, and *war*! The sad fate of beautiful Germany and her afflicted population. Having lived in Germany during the World War, I know what it means to old and young—born to die, for whom? for what?

We repeat: In 1935 the idea of war against Russia was abandoned. In 1936 and 1937 this policy was gradually replaced by a plan for Russo-German cooperation. The anti-comintern movement led by Germany was a political propaganda measure to make the Western powers believe that the anti-Russian war idea was still alive. The agitation against Russian communism, and especially the Italo-German intervention in Spain, were above all directed toward the breaking of the Franco-Russian pact. Today we know that this policy was successful. From 1937 on, Dr. Schacht openly favored Russo-German cooperation and followed, by doing so, the Bismarckian and Rathenau traditions. For insiders it was not at all surprising that the new war found Russia on the German side. In spite of Hitler's opportunism, which later led him to turn upon her, eventually Russia and Germany must find each other in permanent *economic* collaboration.

In general, the peculiar economic situation of Germany, a highly industrialized and overpopulated country with great dependence upon foreign raw material resources, is understood in England and France as well as in the United States. The hardships resulting from the Versailles Treaty and the error of demanding monstrous reparations are well appreciated on both sides of the Atlantic. More and more, recognition is breaking through that foolish mercantilist blunders have been made by nations on all sides.

So long as the hymn of peace was being sung by Hitler and other nazi leaders, there was even a certain sympathy evident on the part of the Western powers. Outside of totalitarian countries, even the drastic nationalist measures of organization and national security, of re-employment and labor provisions, were appreciated and even envied. It became evident that the German people, and even economists such as Rudolph Brinkmann and many others, earnestly trusted in Hitler's peace appeals. In the spirit of Albrecht Schaeffle's philosophy, in the period at the turn of the twentieth century, that "a nation which strives to secure its peace development must be and remain well prepared for war" (a philosophy derived from Vegetius' slogan, "si vis pacem para bellum"), they may have seriously believed that nazi leaders did not want the war and that war among civilized nations is unnecessary or even impossible.

The fact that Hitler was unable to carry on his power policy with diplomatic and political threats, and that war finally broke out, has changed the situation completely—not so much outside of Germany, where the peace sermons of Hitler have never been taken seriously, but evidently within Germany.

The German people have long since realized that the so-called "moral armament" of the nation was nothing but a brutal militaristic preparation for war, and even if Hitler further succeeds in conquering all Europe he will only leave, behind his armies, destruction, hunger, wounds, and despair.

The consequence may be an overwhelming desire, a most passionate longing, for international understanding from within Germany. But so long as no other chance, no other economic solution, is in sight, the Germans will deceive themselves with the delusion that nazism is their true ideal. We know the German soul too well. The German spirit of humanism, liberty, individuality, and brotherhood is still alive, and in fact has never vanished, even in a state of all-embracing militaristic array and enforced subordination of the entire nation under the thumb of the Gestapo. The spirit of individual freedom can be oppressed, gagged, threatened, and misguided, but it cannot be killed. Books and papers can be burned as products of heresy, but the spirit of freedom and the search for truth cannot be extirpated.

High German spiritual ideals are stronger than all tyranny. In times of distress and war, the German people can be kept obedient and patient for an extended length of time, but in the long run they will not tolerate a tyrant. The spirit of Wilhelm Tell and Schiller's spirit of liberty as expressed in *Die Raeuber*, Goethe's spirit of humanity and humaneness, Heine's lyrical spirit, Lessing's spirit of wisdom and justice, are alive. Germany, especially academic and intellectual Germany, hates serfdom and regimentation and longs for liberty no less than do France, Britain, and America.

He who knows German history can tell from what direction the overthrow of tyrannical powers will probably come some day. It will come from the sphere of those spirits who once shook off the yoke of Napoleon; from those spirits who inspired the Prussian youth; from the spirit of Koerner and Lützow, York and Hardenberg; from the spirit of liberty that animated the revolutionaries of 1848; from the ranks of those true patriots who once stood up as one man, when the World War broke out, and died in action at Ypres, Verdun, and Soissons, with a song in their throats; who died for their Fatherland because they thought that theirs was the just and righteous cause.

In the national socialist movement this spirit of sacrifice, this conviction to die for a just cause, is not true and genuine. In the nazi movement, which is a product of misery and distress, the good spirits of the people have been diverted toward an evil cause, the low instincts of the people have been incited and driven to medieval witch trials and church incendiarism. Corruption and lies have become established principles. The German people were threatened with vicious demons: first the Communists; and when this did not convince the masses, the Jews, the Catholics, the Protestants, the Bolsheviki, the Czechoslovaks, the Poles, and last but not least the British and the American plutocrats.

In order to excite the masses over and over again for further sacrifices to the Party, devils were found and put to the pillory. This medieval procedure must go on until the eyes of the people are opened; until the masses understand that they have been driven up a blind alley, that Hitler's martial victories are not victories of the German people and the German soul. Nobody can forecast the exact hour of mental liberation, but the moment must come and will come—at the latest, when the war is over and peace assured. We must only show the German people a way out of their situation. Unless they see and find a way out of their dilemma, they will hang desperately onto their misleaders and their false idols.

As soon as the German people realize that there is a way out, they will find out their false gods and demigods and with them their heresies, superstitions, and fallacious doctrines. They will throw overboard their erroneous ideologies. This step must be prepared from the outside. It must be prepared and offered by those nations which may have contributed to the state of mentality of Germany and are therefore not free from guilt and now share the responsibility for the catastrophe. In spite of the military success of Germany, the people are open to a *mental* revolution. It is now up to us in the lands of freedom to show the ways and means to liberation, to show the ideals which have their roots in the old classical thoughts of freedom and equality and are inspired by the high ideals of universal justice and solidarity.

We must show the skeptical and despairing peoples of the East that we are not as egotistical and selfish as they may believe; that we also can find the way to practical Christianity. We must make them believe we have thoroughly understood and learned that protectionism can be as godless as restrictionism, and autarchy as stupid as supernationalism; that there is only one way to overcome false idols and ideals, only one way that leads toward the spiritual and economic satisfaction of our society, and that is through international socio-economic liberty and justice, while appreciating and sanctioning all national traditions and peculiarities.

I am thoroughly convinced that a socially minded and socially conscious new order, the socio-capitalistic world organization of the twentieth century, is strong enough to replace and overcome national totalitarianism. Germany's sense of universal imagination will fully understand and appreciate these social philosophies of practical international solidarity.

We must arouse the good spirits of the world; they are not dead, they are merely sleeping.

CONCLUSIONS ON THE "NAZI REVOLUTION"

Economic fallacies caused the war: Was this not sufficiently proved in the first part of this book? I hope that by presenting established facts and chatting about some of my most impressive experiences I may contribute in some way toward arousing the economic conscience of our contemporaries. Historians may be animated to study the inter-war period more and more from the angle of mercantilist errors committed by statesmen and nations everywhere. Economists may more easily be able to read between the lines of economic history where economic details and technicalities have by necessity been omitted, as in this book. For the public at large, however, it might be useful and helpful for an understanding of the economic peace requirements to draw some conclusions before we actually visualize the constitution of reconstruction.

There can hardly be any doubt about the fact that both world wars were first of all economic explosions. The war of 1914 was a result of hyperprotectionism, overproduction, and unsound competitive rivalry (dumping). The war of 1939 was the fruit of the same nonsensical economics which led to the first war. It was the fruit of unprecedented economic maladjustments caused by the World War and the Versailles Treaty. It was, further, the result of mercantilist errors which led to

the unnatural boom of 1929 and the crash and depression. This in turn
caused deplorable conditions and despair. The lower and middle classes
were merged into one. As a result of the first World War, currency
breakdown, economic disequilibria, and mercantilistic errors between
the wars, social revolutions were started with ease and success. State
socialism or state capitalism, fascism and nazism were born out of the
dissatisfaction and despair of the masses. All these totalitarian dictator
ships were forced to create public works and giant armies, navies, and
air forces, and in this way shunted their economy from its natural
purpose. These creations transformed our advanced international ex
change economy into a regressive nationalist armament, self-sufficiency
and restrictionist economy. Economic laws were neglected and replaced
by noneconomic rules. Totalitarian restrictionism and armament caused
depression and counterarmament in nontotalitarian countries.

It was clear from the outset that the abolition of economic golden
rules and of the laws of solidarity and interdependence of nations and
the transgression into unproductive war investments would lead to
still greater economic disequilibria and monstrosities. In 1937 and 1938
it became evident that this insanity could not go on for any length of
time. Nontotalitarian governments were forced to compete in the arma
ment race, and after the "Anschluss" of Austria capital openly prepared
for war. Since 1937 capital has been "on strike," and the capital and
gold flight has set in. Democratic governments have had to spend gigan
tic amounts for re-employment and grossly unproductive armament
expenditures, and the world's capital formation system has run amuck
The reparations and debt jugglery runs like a red thread through the
whole inter-war period. Today we rack our brains as to how this
unprecedented, this complicated and confused, puzzle was possible
and wonder at how much brain power and effort was wasted on this
mercantilist phantom. When we realize the absurdity of this provoca
tive scheme, we can only be ashamed of our lack of good judgment.

In order to make feeble, blood-drained Germany pay reparations, it
was fattened like a goose. The golden eggs were dispersed all over the
world in the form of coal deliveries, port construction, railroad mate
rials, chemical products, etc., and presented as gifts to other countries
In technical terms these were "payments on reparations account" with-

out any returns from the receiver countries. Thus the natural exchange
of goods and services was interrupted and trade diverted into undesirable channels. About ten billion gold marks were "paid" in this way
until the Bank for International Settlements went to work.

The amounts lent to Germany for fattening purposes, the "debt
burden imposed upon Germany," as well as the "reparation payments"
became unequaled propaganda material for German extremists and
were successfully exploited for political reasons. So much so that, with
Hitler's and Schacht's arrival, counterpressure and reaction on the part
of nazi Germany found an excellent echo in public opinion in both
camps. Too late the capitalist world began to understand the drama
which was being played and to realize that the tables had been turned.
Schacht turned the trick. He refused to "pay another pfennig" and
with all kinds of stratagems and insolvency arguments retained and
confiscated foreign credits, including interest, to the amount of nineteen
billion goldmarks which represented a definite loss to the creditors. In
fact the loss was much greater because of Schacht's currency and stock
exchange manipulations and the indirect or consequential losses.

Hitler and Schacht used this appropriation for three main purposes:
(1) For financing the enormous armaments of the Reich, which, in
    turn, forced similar armament expenditures in other countries.
(2) For dumping exports, which created confusion and unsound
    emergency practices in world trade, shrinkage in productive in-
    dustry and employment with consequent reduction of consump-
    tion and purchasing power all over the world.
(3) For world propaganda which prepared the path for war success
    in small countries and dangerously infected the mentality of the
    peoples of all countries.

In retrospect it appears to have been the destiny of human short-
sightedness to generate and reproduce evil and vice in increasing proportions. ("Es ist der Fluch der bösen Tat, dass sie fortzeugend immer
Böses muss gebären.")

The use of the foreign credits, in conjunction with the employment
of all available national economic resources, enabled the Third Reich
to spend about ninety billion marks (through 1939) on armaments—
in the broadest sense—until the war broke out. How many more bil-

lions are being spent during this war nobody will ever be able to count accurately!

And the other nations? Latest statistics indicate that the annual investments in armaments in the whole world amounted to about 12,500,000,000 gold dollars at the outbreak of the new war compared with about 2,500,000,000 at the outbreak of the World War in 1914, or about five times the pre-war armament investment of the world.

But these again are only the direct consequences. Imagine the indirect economic and social consequences of these misdeeds! Imagine the influence on the socio-economic structures of all countries!

Inside Germany, the whole economy was regimented for political purposes in accordance with the four-year plans and their countless departments and substitute enterprises. Although unemployment has vanished, a characteristic of an economy of autarchic totalitarianism, the standard of living has sunk. Wages were stabilized only nominally; the value of these wages was doomed to decrease. Labor and its product were invested in war and power policies. It was exploited for the purpose of conquering weaker neighboring countries and absorbing their economy in the realm of the Reich, imposing the same rule of terror and regimentation upon these "coordinated economies." There is no difference between Hitler's dictatorial militarism and Schacht's imperialistic finance and trade policies. Both wanted to be the Napoleons of Europe and possibly of the world. The Napoleonic psychosis of nazi leaders is the second very weakening and vulnerable issue of nazi Germany. It creates more and more points of attack and a rising spirit of hatred and rebellion.

Totalitarian economy resembles an insatiable octopus, holding in its choking embrace the entire personal and material wealth of the nation (and now of the conquered nations) and draining as much of its life-blood as possible without sucking it entirely dry. Theoretically, private capital and ownership are still in existence; but they form only the weak skeleton of the socio-economic body of the nation. With the prolongation of the war—even after the inclusion of the entire European continent in the German economy—strength and substance are inevitably vanishing.

There is scarcely any initiative, independence, or individuality left to private enterprise. Everything is regulated, commandeered, assessed, or confiscated for war and power purposes. If a manufacturer needs raw material, besides undergoing an endless process of red tape, he must employ a middleman, a briber and corrupter with "influence" upon party members and leaders. And, even if the manufacturer happens to be successful in his production, he cannot freely dispose of or invest the fruits of his labor. What is left over, after deductions, taxes, and party contributions, is likely to be forced into export subsidies or into enforced war loans, etc. Industrialists must invest part of their earnings in substitute enterprises although they realize all too well that these war and self-sufficiency undertakings are doomed to destruction and elimination when the war is over. They must make these and innumerable other sacrifices to the glorious ambitions of the nazi octopus.

Similar symptoms can be observed in Italy and Japan with varying degrees of severity.

Among the Western powers preparation and preparedness for war, and active war, is gradually transforming the entire national economy into an emergency and war economy with all the useless waste it implies. In Great Britain, "for the sake of victory," Sir John Simon, Chancellor of the Exchequer, estimated in 1940 England's rate of spending at £1,500,000,000 a year, rising during the fiscal year 1940-41 to £2,000,000,000 and increasing from year to year. According to a recent statement of Sir Kingsley Wood, Chancellor of the Exchequer, this estimate has proved to be too low. The rate for 1940-41 will amount to £3,967,000,000 (or about $15,900,000,000) and if the war lasts through 1942 over £5,000,000,000 (or at least $20,000,000,000). The daily military and civil expenditures in Great Britain are believed to amount to about $50,000,000.

Taxes in England are reaching a maximum in history. The standard income tax is 50 per cent and may rise further. Excess of income over £2,000 pays surtax on a sliding scale running from 10 per cent to 47½ per cent. A gross income of £66,000 is reduced to £5,000 by taxation.

Although the leading economists of the empire, such as John Maynard Keynes, are considering and introducing methods and measures to avoid inflation, Great Britain has issued its first war loan, a

3-per cent, 15-year bond issue, totaling $1,179,000,000, representing the first long term war loan since 1918. The Chancellor of the Exchequer has frankly admitted that this is only the forerunner of much larger sums.

Germany and France followed suit with gigantic bond issues. Before the collapse of France the French budget was close to the annual average for 1914-18. Conquered France is now paying astronomical figures to the nazis. Germany estimates her yearly war expenditures at about $13,000,000,000.

Annual war expenditures of $33,000,000,000 dollars or a daily total of about ninety millions were estimated by the belligerents. These vast amounts cannot be covered by taxes alone nor could such devices as the savings plan of Keynes in England or Paul Reynaud's "closed-credit circuit" in France or the impenetrable totalitarian nazi octopus economy be a remedy.

When the nazis built their express highways, their public administration and defense structures, and their war and "ersatz" industries, they pointed out that two-thirds of their cost would be returned in the form of taxes on producers and contractors or covered by productive employment relief. Only one-third of the total expense was to be considered as actual investment.

Almost from the very day that the nazis began constructing their vast non-productive military machine, the collapse of the entire system has been predicted. This collapse has not materialized, and economists and writers, in increasing numbers, are searching for an explanation. A recent article in *Harpers* strikes the note that the reason is that there has been a "German Financial Revolution."[8]

Briefly, according to this article, the system the nazis have developed is this: The nazis came upon a scene in which idle men and idle money were going to waste, and simultaneously people went hungry and unclad. To finance their war machine the nazis exchanged the idle bank money for government interest bearing securities. Thereupon with cash in its bank account it started the productive facilities of industry and labor going. When the banks became loaded with the securities, and the deposits became so large that there was the threat of an over-supply of liquid funds, the nazis saw to it that private sources absorbed

[8] Dal Hitchcock, "The German Financial Rtvolution," *Harpers*, Feb. 1941.

the securities. Thus savings which "forced" the government into debt finally were transferred into interest bearing government securities which landed, after the regular series of capitalist transactions, in the hands of the former savers themselves. In this way the government created a form of investment for surplus savings. The savings were thus given the opportunity to move the economic machinery. The reason necessitating this procedure is that "capitalism requires the continuous growth of business enterprise." This growth manifests itself in savings which must be invested, the process taking place at a somewhat geometric progression.

Since business could not—or would not—absorb the surplus, the government securities did, and put it to work. By permitting a reasonable profit and interest on the securities the stimulus came from the profit motive. Thus there was established a system for continuous and full production.

This, in brief, is the instrument of the nazis' financial revolution as presented by Mr. Hitchcock. Now, can we accept it as a true *revolution* and what lessons are there in it for us in the U. S.? There are two elements which we must be careful to observe. One is that we are discussing an economic instrument and policy potentially applicable, in adapted form, in the U. S. and elsewhere, and the other is the use of the instrument as it has been applied by the nazis.

It is beyond the scope of this volume to go very deeply into the former problem, since it more properly belongs to the next volume which the author has under preparation. The nazi "financial revolution" which grew out of desperation and emergency, is nothing more than a perverted and opportunistic version of the Keynes plan carried out without regard for its safeguards and limitations. The Keynes plan in itself is a useful economic policy, and here in the U. S. we have already made limited and useful application of it. In all probability even greater use would have been desirable. But in itself it is not a total solution for we are faced with a situation in which factors other than unemotional economics must be considered. Unlimited extension of it infringes on the realm of what is generally, as yet, conceded to be the sphere of private business.

Used in the public sphere it creates debt. *This debt in itself is not a bad thing if it represents productive results.* (And in this case what we ought to do is enter the productive result in our budget as an asset.) But this means a certain amount of government control—control larger than many of us are as yet willing to tolerate, but certainly nothing of the kind exercised by authoritarian governments. The question boils down to this: Are we willing to pre-empt the sphere which is still acknowledged to be private? If we are not, the alternative is *to increase and safeguard instruments for productive borrowing in the private field.* In this manner we may balance the one by the other, each complementing the other.

The nazi "financial revolution" has been nothing but a shrewd fraud. The government "securities" are but scraps of paper representing nothing productive, which are purchased at the *"suggestion"* of the Gestapo. The whole instrument functions for only two reasons: prices, wages, production, currency and banking are controlled by threat of dire punishment; and secondly, once having invested in the securities the investor, hoping to maintain the value of the securities, becomes, willingly or unwillingly, a fellow conspirator—collapse of authority means loss of property.

Subjugated countries like Denmark, Norway, Holland, France, etc. which had every reason to be proud of their financial and monetary policies are being equally subjected to a system of disguised robbery. Paper currency is generously paid for goods that are scarce in Germany. By accepting German paper money under pressure of the emergency situation, with the Gestapo always in the background, these countries too become involuntary captives of the nazi finance scheme, and as investors in German paper money become interested in the fate of the currency and securities of the Reich.

But even the expansion of their scheme over the greater part of the continent of Europe can not save the nazi financial situation. The nazi scheme can control inflation only to a limited extent. As it produces for war purposes, this production appears to be productive as long as war is successfully waged. If, however, the war is carried to a stalemate or exhaustion, with the blockade unbroken, the effects of the war production will prove to be unproductive and the whole scheme will arrive at the point of absurdity. Paper money, treasury bonds, government loans (voluntary and enforced), will lose their substance and value, and what appeared to be productive borrowing will develop into a situation of unproductive inflation with its concomitant disastrous and demoralizing results.

It is very easy to accept the theory that the nazis have found the stone of wisdom and that they can apply the scheme with equal success to a peace economy—and that we in America can and should apply it to war and peace. But if we think out the scheme to its logical end, we must arrive at the conclusion that the nazi emergency scheme may save them from internal collapse as long as the war does not come to a deadlock; but that we, here, in this country of abundance, not yet at war and valuing certain economic and political freedoms, must face our situation quite differently.

Nowadays those nations are most efficient in armament production which are best able to control wages and the general standard of living.[9] By financing armaments and war through underconsumption, assessments, compulsory contributions, and forced investment of savings in

[9] Bruce Bliven, Editor of *The New Republic*, has presented a revolutionary interpretation of German statistics of national income and its distribution (*The New Republic*, November 11, 1940, p. 649). He has claimed that we were deluded into believing that the German standard of living had fallen. He says that she financed her armament preparations, and in addition has not only maintained her standard of living as of 1932 but has even raised it, for the nation as a whole, by raising the national income.

This startling interpretation, coming from one who is unquestionably opposed to nazism, will undoubtedly be questioned in the light of the preponderance of evidence presented to America for many years. Unquestionably as a result of the full use of labor reserve and productive facilities the national income rose. The uncertainty, however, has been about how large a proportion of it went into productive uses. We must remember that, when there is a lack of food and clothing, not only is armament unproductive, but even public works, which are usually a necessary part of the standard of living, are uneconomic.

Using 1932, when the national income was 45 billion marks, as a base year, Mr. Bliven's statistics show that through 1938 the increments of each year over 1932 added up to 104 billion marks. Subtract from this the 90 billion marks which Hitler claimed was spent for armament and the surplus was about 14 billion marks; spread over seven years the addition to the national income was about 2 billion marks a year over 1932. This hardly warrants Mr. Bliven's assertion that there was created "a handsome surplus for other purposes" than military when we remember the state of Germany in 1932, particularly since we do not know what part of this 2 billion is in stored reserves. Moreover, we must remember that these figures are from nazi sources and must be appraised with the greatest reserve. In spite of my doubts, however, the whole problem is worthy of concentrated study since there are probably some lessons we can learn to our advantage.

From my own experience, living in Germany until August, 1936, I question Mr. Bliven's conclusions on the standard of living. My own opinion is that it has been at a minimum tolerable level, and that the "efficiency" of their system is the efficiency of force and control.

government loans and similar appropriations, and last but not least by drastic price fixing measures, government and war policies can be expanded and prolonged considerably and inflation partly controlled. The nazi "miracle" of economic perseverance, self-financing, and self-sufficiency is no miracle at all. It is merely the forced and curtailed utilization and consumption of all economic resources in whatever direction and to whatever end those in control dictate. Further, it is the anticipation and consumption of future income for generations to come.

But this method of war financing finds its limit in the final unproductiveness of a war economy and the dissatisfaction and resistance of the working populations in conquered countries and within the nation. This situation is aggravated by the blockade and dependence on foreign raw materials, by lack of gold and foreign currency. But even if the blockade were lifted and Germany had access to foreign goods and credits, in the long run inflation could hardly be avoided until the war is definitely liquidated.

And in the United States? Without any extravagance our budget will still have to be increased because of our rising armament appropriations. Armament expenditures of some ten to twenty billion dollars may soon appear to be normal figures; and the eventual additional taxation, not only upon war profits but upon those income groups now relatively undertaxed, and a radical tax reform which may soon appear unavoidable, may make all previous attempts at increased taxation look like mere bagatelles. We must not fool ourselves: The American defense program will require some 50 to 60 billion dollars annually, or a total of $200 to $300 billions. In Western countries state regulation of economics may be increased by the necessity for war measures.

In this connection we cannot too greatly stress the fact that in preparing for all emergencies to ward off totalitarian governments we do not create an inflation rising out of defense or a deflation after that phase has passed and thus let the enemy in by the back door. Inflation will take place only when there are not enough consumers goods to go around. To avoid that we must not only have total defense, but also total production. We must supplement our defense production with investment in truly productive enterprises and income producing properties. This total production will also help us avoid post defense deflation.

A second measure to forestall inflation is to make government securities attractive enough to private and institutional investors so that they do not pile up in the banks and become the basis for an over abundance of idle deposits. This was one of the recommendations of the Federal Reserve Board in its special report on the first day of the year 1941.

When sooner or later the war is ended, it is hard to visualize the difficulties and revolutionary changes necessáry to transform the war economies into normal peace economies. We may be forced to maintain at least for some time many of those political, social, and economic pre-war and war creations, because removing them would cause a complete collapse of the socio-economic structure in the countries involved in the present struggle. Will we ever be able to bring order into this chaos?

One thing is certain. Future history will admit that the economic monstrosities of the inter-war and war periods have led the capitalistic system ad absurdum, awakened the world and forced nations to do what they should have done at least in 1922, when Walther Rathenau proposed to responsible statesmen a world solution based on economic solidarity.

This war and economic revolution will destroy hypernationalist and hypercapitalist narrow-minded selfishness. Nations will be forced to become friendly neighbors and to support each other in their mutual interests. It is unavoidable! All nations must join in the hard work for the functional organization of the world which is in fact the only hope of mankind!

Some 150 years ago an industrial revolution shook England and the whole world. Machine production displaced human labor with the well-known tumultuous effects. Weavers arose in impotent desperation and mutinied against the domination of machinery. But, when these waves of violence had calmed down, an era of unprecedented industrial expansion developed.

In our time another industrial transmogrification will take place, produced by entirely different causes and events: the rationalization of production through a geographic division of labor and technology on a quasi production-for-use basis. For lack of a better term, we may call this a technologeographical revolution. Again it will originate in Europe, but this time on the continent.

In the inter-war period the European continent presented a pitiful picture. Dozens of nations of all sizes and constitutions, proud of their newly acquired or re-established national status and independence, but hopelessly nationalistic and even chauvinistic, created their own more or less independent industries and accepted some form of protectionism, autarchy, and large-scale armament production. Instead of creating an intelligent division of labor and production on the entire European continent, they surrounded themselves with an impenetrable wall of customs and tariffs, isolating themselves like manorial villages of the Middle Ages. A mad race of nationalistic policies and self-sufficient production was begun.

The modern "blitzkrieg" has destroyed the walls. Not with trumpets, swords, or cannon, but with dive bombers, tanks, and "fifth columns." And unwittingly nazism has played the part of Providence in this act of nature or this logic of the law of economics.

We might safely state that Europe will never go back to the miserable times of the castles of hypernationalistic enchantment and protectionist isolation. Whether Germany wins or meets a Waterloo, whether it comes to terms with the other nations in a negotiated peace or ends in sheer chaos with the entire continent, there will be organized a customs union in Europe that in a not too distant future eventually must spread over our entire planet.

This is a sound basis for a functional peace, which need not discourage those who hope for a re-establishment of national boundaries, traditions, ideals, and heritages, because a sound modicum of nationalism is well compatible with the idea of a customs union. On the other hand the creation of a customs union will revolutionize the national economies and the national industrial policies of the continental countries and in one form or another create a new European system of political economy. It is unavoidable that a new organization of industry and finance take place, an organization based on division of labor and production, of raw materials and products, of money, credit, and investment.

As Thuenen's "isolated state" or List's "national system of political economy" inspired the forties of the last century in Germany, so the Schachtian, Funkian, or Goering-brain trust philosophies will influence the forties of the twentieth century in Europe. The nazi conquerors have thus been forced to devise plans on a continental scale to maintain their victories.

In the early twenties of our century, when Hugo Stinnes, the captain of German finance and industry, combined almost the entire German industrial wealth into one huge vertico-horizontal trust, he combined entirely disharmonious units into a completely inorganic structure. This complex was doomed not only by reason of currency decay, but primarily for lack of division of its functions; it was not a living organism.

This time—during and after the war—the problem of industrial reorganization will be dictated by the desperate and vital necessity for the unification of weakened nations which may not be able to preserve their economic independence when the war ends. The unification of Europe, however, can only last and prosper if it is created by the free will of the European peoples.

It is not satisfactory to state fixed commonplaces like the following: "Economics does not make men, but men make economics." Modern philosophy recognizes that there is a relationship between the energies emanating from matter and the energies emanating from man. The center of gravity may be nearer to matter or nearer to man. That depends upon the relative dynamics of the sources of energy. Goethe went so far as to say that men are merely the instruments of action inspired by the dynamics of nature. "We believe we push—but we are pushed." Modern economics respects the *relative* theory of value. History, however, records visible facts and usually ignores invisible influences.

We note that today another industrialist of brute force has arisen in Germany. But this time he is financier, industrialist, politician, and militarist all in one. He evidently considers himself as the instrument to carry out the reconstruction and reorganization of European industry and economy. He represents a very original type of national socialist entrepreneur. Not only has he acquired large packages of shares in armament and "ersatz" industries as well as direct or indirect ownership of stock majorities, estates, and other financial and art treasures; but he has surrounded himself with a brain trust of executives, with a board of directors of the modern politico-capitalist type of national socialist. Wilhelm Goering has become the visible representative of a plan for European political and industrial reorganization which goes far beyond the Schachtian program,[10] and Walter Funk is now Goering's financial adviser and treasurer.

While Schacht, the currency and credit specialist, has placed more emphasis on European economic union and reorganization in general, the Goering-Funk plan is based on the idea that control over European industry is the best political guarantee for a German-dominated Europe —a diabolically clever conception. While Schacht organized the German foreign trade monopoly, the Goering plan provides for a European trade, currency, and credit monopoly controlled by Germany. Control over all natural resources, raw materials, and means of production, a complete division of production, labor, and productive processes is the goal. This plan provides for a redistribution of factories, machinery, and workmen in unprecedented dimensions on a continental scale, and an abandonment of unprofitable or politically undesirable enterprises for the enhancement of Germany's political and economic supremacy.

The militaristic elements of the nazi regime visualize a form of reorganization that is based less on economic essentials than on national security and defense requirements. They wish to subdivide nations into "autonomous minorities," vassal states with their own nationalistic ambitions, so as to prevent unity of purpose and action and avoid too much concentration of power in a huge government-controlled European trust. The controversies raging between the "Mitteleuropaeische Wirtschaftsraum" or "Grossraumwirtschafts" plan of the Goering-Funk faction and the plans of Schacht, and between the militarist ambitions of the generals and the more radical and communist ideas of the Goebbels-Ley-Himmler trio, who support measures of a more permanently revolutionary character, may one day produce political and power clashes within Germany.[11] Further, there still is England, which

[10] The Schachtian plan is further explained in Chapter V.

[11] For a further description of these nazi plans see Peter F. Drucker, "Germany's Plans for Europe," *Harper's Magazine*, November, 1940.

will not easily give up all influence on the continent; there still is Soviet Russia, which will have to take part in the fate of Europe; and, last but not least, there is the United States, which will not permit a world peace unless based on solidarity of all nations or groups of nations.

But, when the great day comes when America can take the initiative or cooperate in the formation of a just and lasting peace, she will also be involved in the problems of customs unions, trade relations and repercussions, and the great and unavoidable industrial and socio-economic changes in the broadest sense.

England will probably undergo a social and industrial revolution of no lesser degree than will the continental powers. She may have to transplant entire industries to Canada or to other colonies. And America, in order to solve the surplus commodities problem and to maintain her relative competitive position, may have to combine the basic minerals, raw materials, industries, and labor of our entire hemisphere into a mammoth industrial and financial organization.

Customs unions of a number of highly industrialized nations in other parts of the world may force us to an expansion of our United States customs union over the entire Western Hemisphere. We must admit that another industrial revolution is on the way and nothing can stop it.

The success of these revolutionary economic changes in the world depend to a large degree upon a sound and elastic, a safe and stable, currency, credit, and investment system, and that in turn depends upon a new universal socio-political order of solidarity in the spirit of live and let live.

Twenty years ago it was the aim of the statesmen conducting the peace negotiations to bring about a better world. How miserably they failed we all know, and the reasons why they were bound to fail have just been recounted. In the future if we are to attain a lasting peace we must know better how to make use of economics.

In the remainder of this book a program will be presented which takes into account all those financial and economic mechanisms necessary for a smooth-functioning exchange of the world's goods, services, and treasures, and the continuous creation of new wealth through the utilization of the world's limitless resources, thereby making it unnecessary to wage continuous warfare for the control of the world's wealth.

There remains a well-founded hope that the European continent which has produced its Spinozas, Kants, and Rousseaux will return to reason, to moral and natural law. In the long run the world will not neglect Kant's philosophy of admiration and awe for "the starry heavens above and the moral law within," and Spinoza's eternal wisdom of reason: "Quatenus homines ex ductu rationis vivunt, eatenus tantum natura semper conveniunt."[12] One day reason will again become supreme law for the people of our earth.

[12] Spinoza, *Ethica*, Pars. IV, Prop. XXXV.

Part II

SOCIAL CAPITALISM
CAN MAKE PEACE

CHAPTER IV

THE BANK OF NATIONS

WHEN the great social reformer Charles Fourier worked as a clerk in Marseilles, he was ordered by his employer to bring about the sinking of a rice-laden ship in order to keep the price of rice high. At that time, in 1799, the world was not yet as civilized as it is now, when wheat, coffee, and cotton are burned, milk poured into gutters, and hogs and cattle destroyed. Fourier was, however, greatly impressed by the command of his chief and this started for him a train of thought regarding the state of society and the organization of harmony in our economic system.

Today, one and one-half centuries later, after the changes brought about by the industrial revolution and expansion, and by the era of capital accumulation, the problem of organizing harmony and equilibrium in our society is still with us, and our experience has made us no wiser. We are once again shocked and disillusioned by a world war and are perhaps more powerfully impressed by the state of disharmony in our society than ever before. In view of the obvious futility of our present struggle, we cannot be surprised that a strong desire for the best attainable organization of our social body is being felt all over the world. At least, I am sure, we want a society in which there will be no more war! But it has become an urgent question whether this organization shall be enforced, regimented, and dictatorial, or whether we shall be able to establish such an order *with a minimum sacrifice of our democratic heritage.*

Today, however, the problem is not so simple as Fourier visualized it some one hundred and fifty years ago. Nations, feeling insecure, have prepared for war and have learned the bitter truth that the means for war can only be obtained by drastic reduction in consumption. The disturbance in the free flow of capital and exchange of goods and the disruption of international relations have induced nations to "save their national economy first," a true world organization being in the nature of a dream. Nations have created international disharmony in the vain belief that harmony in our society can be achieved on a national basis. They have brought pressure to bear on national society, instead of trying to solve the problem without compulsion internationally. This narrow-minded attitude has left us one strong hope, namely, that this fallacious concept may hold only during a transitional period, after which it will eventually clarify itself. After the debacle an international organization will be imperative for the well-being of society as a whole.

When the violent doctrines and delusions of autarchy and lust for power have been driven to starvation and have finally arrived at the point of exhaustion and bankruptcy as the result of war, the people will become painfully aware of their desperate situation.

It is still beyond comprehension how disappointed and utterly miserable those people will feel when, at the end of this debacle, they take stock of their state of poverty, their unbearable loads of debt, and their depressed standards of living. It may take years before the whirlwind has been completely spent. The reaction will take the form of an unprecedented breakdown.

Perhaps there is a deeper reason for this frightful punishment of our society; for have we not sinned by wasting and destroying the riches of our earth and at the same time preventing others from obtaining them, by compelling and regimenting human effort toward destruction, and by exploiting and persecuting helpless minorities?

When the inhabitants of our earth have destroyed all that is noble in the world and are brought face to face with the results of their crime, then their better nature may be awakened. Then they may once again wish to help one another and to cooperate with each other to their mutual interest. Then finally they may begin to understand that the world is one large treasure house of valuables, and its inhabitants perfectly able to live an abundant and full life, to create progressive works, and to multiply. We would need no neo-Malthusian restrictions, no provocative and dead-end customs walls, no concentration camps for labor, money, and raw materials, no Gestapos and Ogpus, no popu-

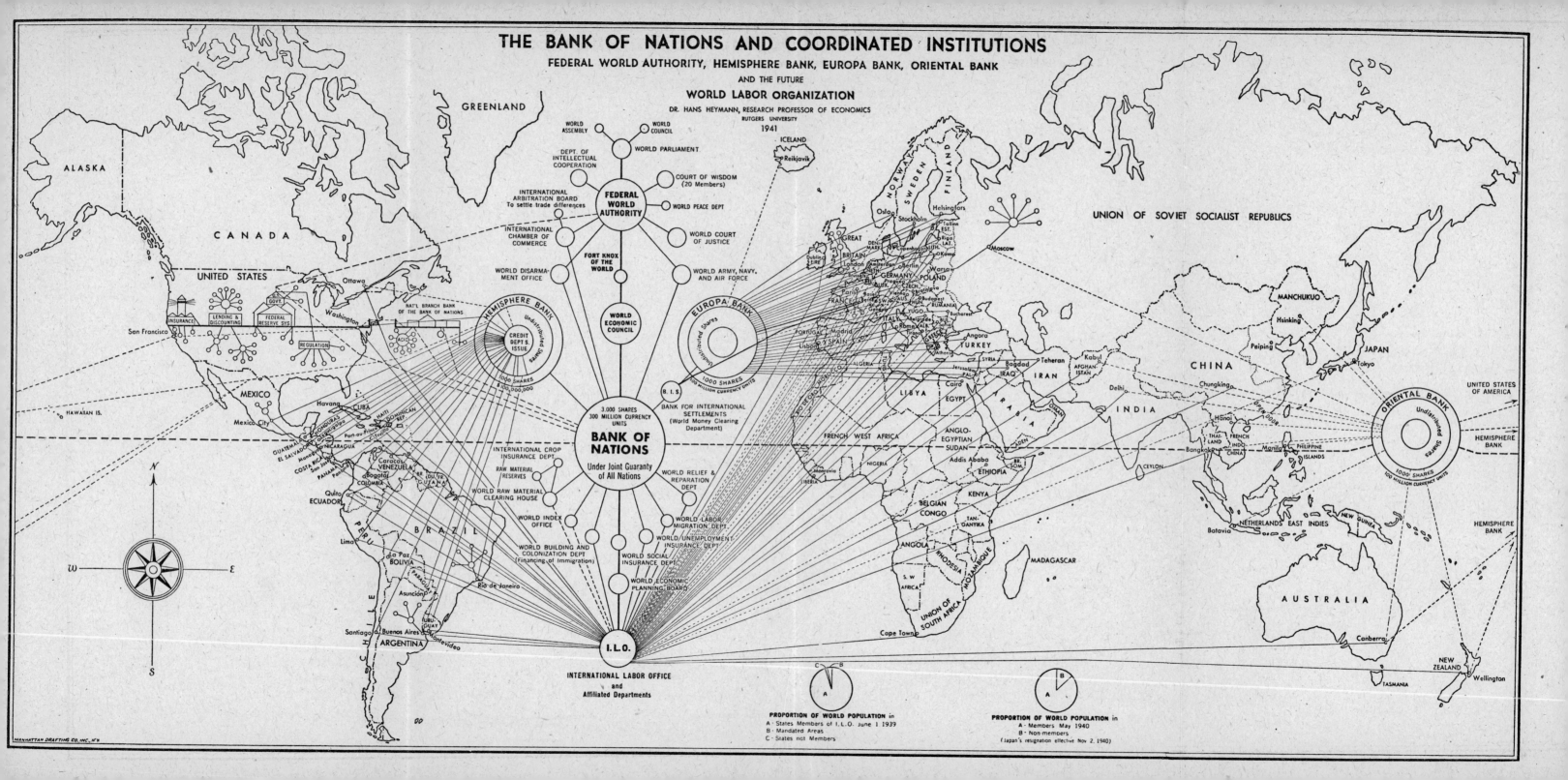

THE BANK OF NATIONS AND COORDINATED INSTITUTIONS

FEDERAL WORLD AUTHORITY, HEMISPHERE BANK, EUROPA BANK, ORIENTAL BANK

AND THE FUTURE

WORLD LABOR ORGANIZATION

DR. HANS HEYMANN, RESEARCH PROFESSOR OF ECONOMICS

RUTGERS UNIVERSITY

1941

PROPORTION OF WORLD POPULATION in
A · States Members of I.L.O. June 1 1939
B · Mandated Areas
C · States not Members

PROPORTION OF WORLD POPULATION in
A · Members May 1940
B · Non-members
(Japan's resignation effective Nov 2, 1940)

lations in arms, no bombers, dreadnoughts, or poison gases—if we would apply to these problems just a little common-sense, organization, and humanitarianism.

But of one thing we may be sure: The world we have known will be no more—and I mean this literally. It will be no easier to bring it back than to unscramble a scrambled egg. It cannot be done! The fires of the war have reshaped and congealed old institutions into new forms. The sooner we recognize this fact the larger will be our part in shaping the world of tomorrow to our own desires. We, in the United States, have the means—the power and the wealth; we need but a clearer understanding and the will. We must become a united nation and we must be willing to make certain sacrifices. We must not fool ourselves. Unless we make sacrifices voluntarily we will lose all we have. This is no abstract social reform cry—look at Europe.

Any system of economics is constructed on sociologic fundamentals. It is no hard and fast science; it is rather a tool, a way of thinking. Plato built his society on slave labor—and in his day it was quite natural. Up until the 1860's English economists of the classical school believed there was just so much wealth which labor could share in, and no more. Of what avail, therefore, were labor unions? The larger the share of one group, the smaller the share for others. If all labor were organized it would give them no greater wealth. We could go on and on recounting similar economic fallacies. They would all point to one fact: throughout all economic history we have always thought in terms of a closed, instead of a dynamic, economic system. The concept of economic man—man motivated solely by self-interest—held sway. Permit man to follow his own self-interest and we shall have the best of all possible economic worlds. Of course there has been an expanding area of restrictions, but, by and large, this has been the psychology and philosophy of economists. We have permitted the individual to take as large a share as he could grab, even when his economic behavior has had the effect of freezing the status quo. Instead of foregoing a certain share of economic activity so that at a later date all would have more as the result of a dynamic expansion we have practiced no moral restraint. Society has seen fit to segregate those of us who commit criminal offenses. We must recognize that certain economic activities

79

are equally destructive—economic crimes. If we don't, we stand to lose everything. This is not to say that there is no longer to be an economic sphere for individuals to conquer, or that self-interest must be submerged, but we must recognize that the line between individual self-interest and social welfare must be redrawn. As I have stated elsewhere:

Today, at the threshold of a new economic era, we have come to the realization that capital, the source of the well-being of us all, is a matter of national concern; that we may not allow capital produced by the diligence and industry of an entire nation to be exploited, wasted, or allowed to decay according to the arbitrary will of individuals, since, in the final analysis, its returns are for the benefit of all citizens.

In this book, I carry this concept further so that it encompasses world economy—world capital and world citizens.

The fundamental importance of economics in the appeasement of conflicting social philosophies cannot be overestimated. At the risk of being branded materialists, we economists and social philosophers must emphatically stress again and again the vital importance of an equitable economic structure for the welfare and satisfaction of our earthbound community.

Although we may have sinned and erred, the sun still shines upon our land; there are yet enough resources, fertile soil, grain treasures, and rich unexploited countries for all of us and for ten times our present population. But what is missing is the mechanism, the instrument, the system, the vehicle of organization and coordination, which would bring those riches to the needy classes and peoples. To provide the poorer classes with adequate means of subsistence, to let them share in the great abundance and wealth of our earth, to give them adequate work, and to avoid the "grapes of wrath" is the great problem of our twentieth century. It is so vital and imperative, that the survival of our capitalist system completely depends upon its solution.

In many parts of Europe this problem has already led to the complete demolition of our present system, to one of the most disturbing revolutions of all times—namely, to national totalitarianism, which I hope and believe represents the last violent flaring up of excessive nationalism.

Through the most Draconian and cruel methods of autocratic dictatorship and national restrictionism, totalitarianism has tried to solve this problem on a national basis by financing its internal economy through underconsumption and inflation. The results have been that *poverty has been organized*, and that, instead of bringing the riches of our world to the needy classes, it has brought to them much too much work and all too little wealth.

This problem can never be solved on a national scale alone—not even by the most perfect national, private, or public organizations and not even by the most intelligent and hopeful national subsidy measures, such as the New Deal, the N.E.P. (New Economic Policy), or the Four-, Five-, and Ten-Year Plans. To bring the possible riches to needy classes and peoples, an international organization of this wealth and of men must be constructed. Social capitalism of the twentieth century must replace national totalitarianism.

When the rage of this war and revolution has spent itself, and national political ambitions have reached a deadlock, we must view the state of society from a distance and join in the preparation and establishment of an international organization of a higher rank and authority than any we have today. In connection with the present war, many voices have been heard calling for an international political body with authority over the individual states. The English labor leader Atlee has proposed that an international authority superior to member states be created. This is but one of a host of such proposals.

The antagonistic economic systems of the East and the West must find an instrument which endeavors to achieve a compromise between them, and to attain an equitable distribution of the resources and man power of this world, a division of labor and production, and an approach to many other social ideals. The absence of a mechanism of authority in international politics has been recognized as the reason for the failure of the League of Nations. The absence of a vigilant and creative international economic body to arouse the economic conscience of the world has been the reason for the failure of an economic understanding among nations, and the underlying cause of the present war. We are aware of the fact that economic projects do not enjoy equal popularity with political proposals, although they are the prerequisites for idealistic attainments. But if they are inspired by sufficiently powerful ideals they may meet with consideration and eventual acceptance among our contemporaries.

Let it be stated, once and for all, that there is no system of economics in the world by which one nation may profit for any extended period of time from the distress of other nations. There is no system by which one nation can achieve enduring advantage to the detriment of any other nation. In our modern economy, the interdependence of nations has become so evident that any act committed by one nation or a group of nations against the equality and solidarity of all nations will react sooner or later on the nations at fault. It is therefore in the interest of the United States, as well as in the interest of all other nations, to strive for the establishment of an organization for concerted economic action for the benefit of all member nations which are willing to cooperate. It is plain utopianism to imagine that, after this war, America—for any length of time—can remain an isolated isle of prosperity in a world of distress.

The United States is faced today with a completely revolutionized outer world, transformed into a few economic spheres of interest, under totalitarian or state-socialized regimes, with forced, sweated, or even slave labor, with dumping prices and industrial government monopolies. Exports and imports are restricted, regulated, and used as a weapon against countries which cannot dispose of their raw materials as usual, because large parts of the world are under restrictions and blockade, and suffering from depressed purchasing power. Their gigantic war expenditures do not allow them to satisfy the most urgent needs of their peoples.

Against a system of such opportunism and of such aggressively and militantly monopolistic state power policies, how could our system of custom walls, protection, hostile or unharmonious labor unions, unproductive unemployment relief, and disorganized competitive individualism pass through such dangerous times unchanged or isolated? We cannot stubbornly carry on an ostrichlike policy and keep such a system going.

It becomes clear that we must abandon this "great illusion," and the sooner we do so the better. It is a fallacious notion to believe that we can establish any peaceful international order by retaining even the most "splendid" isolation. Without sacrifices, without tearing down, stone by stone, our tariff walls and actively helping to build up the new credit structure of the world, this ideal becomes illusory. The hopeful policies of Cordell Hull, with regard to reciprocal trade agreements, are only a beginning—a means for transition toward an internationally organized trade policy.

It is entirely up to the present and coming generation to understand that the welfare of our nation depends upon the relative welfare of others. It is for our contemporaries and their offspring to decide whether all the nations shall live in wealth or in poverty. If it is to be in wealth, we must find the great mechanism of solidarity, collectivity, and mutuality. We visualize a new form of organization for our society, in which restrictionism and protectionism is outlawed; in which free trade and economic world organization is not a contradiction, but a permanent condition; in which nations and states are economic and political provinces of the world realm; in which national traditions will be conserved as precious jewels, but in which international loyalty will be the supreme ideal. We are looking straight forward—toward the dawn of a new era of peace and a golden age.

We have already made a beginning. President Roosevelt has pursued a course of action which aims to encourage American participation in the economic post-war reconstruction. In an attempt to save the world from the financial debacle which is to be expected at the end of the war, with liquidation of war industries and universal price collapse, and the attendant world unemployment and revolutionary disturbance, the administration should make plans so that we may cooperate in the world-wide economic reconstruction which is bound to come. The President should have, prepared and on hand, long-range national and international plans which would, when needed, be available. In this way we may be able to help to cushion the otherwise unavoidably destructive chaos which will undoubtedly affect us.

These many preparations must inevitably culminate in a huge new international banking mechanism, which may first be put to the test through the proposed Inter-American Bank in the Western Hemisphere. The experiences and the new technique of international money and banking, derived from this experiment, can then be applied to a world banking institution.

I do not doubt that, at the end of this war, the eyes of the world will look to this country of liberty and justice as the one into whose hands that responsibility might well be placed. We shall have the privilege, if we are willing to accept it, of reconstructing the financial and credit structure of the world, with the cooperation of all nations as equal partners. For those among us who believe in a harmonious family of nations, this is faith and hope.

Between thirteen and fourteen million men were killed in the World War. How many tortured, oppressed, killed, and disinherited will there be as the result of the present war and revolution? If a harmonious and efficient supernational economic structure cannot be achieved after the war, in twenty years another war may completely destroy our civilization.

But economists cannot succeed unless teachers, priests, and statesmen cooperate and offer their helping hands, and unless schools, universities, churches, parliaments, and governments recognize national and international economic ideals and make them part of their political, moral, and ethical ideals.

Before we can reap the benefits of the manifold ideas of socio-economic reform and utopianism for our capitalist system, we must build upon a foundation of moral, ethical, and religious ideals. The ideas of brotherhood and brotherly love, of justice and righteousness, of altruism rather than egotism, have all contributed to the recognition of certain economic ideals which consciously or unconsciously all of us have in mind when we visualize a humane and lasting peace for the brotherhood of nations.

It was Masaryk, founder and first president of Czecho-Slovakia, who wrote these immortal words into the book of history: "No state or policy can prosper unless the groundwork is moral." Economics is capable of making a lasting peace, but only if it is based on the highest moral and ethical principles of our society. What are those economic ideals? At the risk of being considered an idealist, may I be permitted to set forth

Fourteen Ideals for a Living Peace

1. The fundamental idea of economic solidarity among nations, based on the relationship and interdependence of national economics. Economic internationalism or universalism is greater than nationalism.

2. The idea that protectionism must be abolished, mercantilistic errors discredited, and tariff walls torn down, stone by stone. Restrictionism must not only be given up, but also outlawed.

3. The belief that free trade, though on an organized basis, should be made the goal, with free access to resources and organized distribution of raw materials.

4. Division of labor and production among nations. Nations should specialize more and more in those products and commodities which they are best able to produce with the greatest economy.

5. International control of production in proportion to needs (production for use), to avoid over- and under-production. The systematic setting aside of reserves in raw materials during fat years, in order to have them on hand in lean years; an international insurance reserve system *in natura* ("in goods").

6. The assurance of a minimum of subsistence for every human being.

7. National and international social security. Bellamy visualized work years as encompassing the ages of twenty-one to forty-five, with work hours greatly reduced. By full utilization of our technological achievements in accordance with national and international human needs this could probably be attained. Opportunity, however, should be given to those over forty-five who desire to continue their work. In other words, the opportunity for suitable work and income should be assured during the working life of the individual, and adequate protection for the health and welfare of labor in the matter of wages, hours, and the conditions of employment should be provided for.

8. Organized international social and unemployment insurance.

9. Labor migration, emigration, and colonization of immigrants under the auspices of all nations.

10. Trade through exchange of just spending power values, facilitated by an internationally guaranteed and unified medium of exchange.

11. A free road for the capable, and equality of opportunity through credits for the able and competent who have not had the privilege of inheriting capital.

12. Participation of labor in profits from the products of its labor.

13. The creation of productive national and international credits, with the greatest possible moderation in the rate of interest, based on permanently repaired, replaced, and *reproduced* property values according to the life expectancy of those physical properties; in other words, organized reproduction and perpetuation of capital.

14. The adjustment and equalization of conflicting socio-economic systems between the East and the West, between individualism and socialism, between liberalism and collectivism; a system of government in which we attain the "four essential freedoms" expressed by President Roosevelt: freedom of speech, freedom of worship, freedom from want; freedom from fear.

How can these ideals be approached or gradually achieved? The statesmen of the East believe in state socialist and nationalist power policies, and those of the West in capitalist practices. Both apply militarism and war as the ultimate arbiter. The East practices bolshevism and propounds an economic world revolution, or even permanent revolution. And the West?

If we are to have a living peace we must recognize that all nations must be included from the beginning. The exclusion, even temporarily, of Russia, Germany, Italy, or Japan would be, in the economic sense, an inexcusable imbecility, incompatible with the organization of peace. However, before any reasonable political solution can be thought of, a socially conscious economic structure must be created when the fury of this war has subsided.

Such an order cannot be achieved by prospectuses or ideas, with which the world will presently be surfeited. It can only be brought about by an instrument, a practical mechanism, which is so simple, exact, and convincing that the gigantic difficulties the world faces can be overcome. It is the thesis of this book that such a mechanism is to be found in the Bank of Nations described below.

But before we present the technique of such a mechanism, let us first, briefly, make certain that we understand the problems and processes of international economic relations as they function today.[1]

The great problem in world trade is this: How can the exchange of unjust and unequal labor values or spending power parities—today represented in cheapening and dumping—be avoided?

In contrast to the ideals and techniques of international trade, what have we today? We have abandoned and paradoxically perverted our highly advanced trade relations by reverting to barter.

Barter in our time is the fruit of the fatal obstacles in the intercourse of nations caused by egotistical and narrow-minded politics and lack of solidarity. When the distress of the German people, caused to a great extent by the nonacceptances of a cooperative superordinated banking and credit apparatus by all nations (as proposed by Rathenau in 1922 to the Genoa Conference and later replaced by the Bank for International Settlements, in Basel, with its narrow scope), came to its climax, the nazi government led the entire economic postwar system to the point of absurdity.

As has been pointed out above, the German government used all the savings of the people, and the anticipated savings of generations to come, for entirely unproductive purposes—for roads which are empty and serve chiefly strategical uses; for its gigantic mechanized army, navy, and air force; for rebuilding and projecting entire city sections, triumphal avenues, pompous administration buildings, and so forth. But in order to import necessary missing raw materials, Germany was obliged to export at any cost. Products had to be cheapened and dumped on the market, with a resultant loss in labor values, in purchasing power,

---

[1] For further discussion on the problems of international trade see: Herbert Feis, *The Changing Pattern of International Economic Affairs* (New York: Harper & Brothers, 1940); and J. B. Condliffe, *The Reconstruction of World Trade* (London: Allen & Unwin).

and, last but not least, in business reputation in general. Italy had similar problems, although on a smaller scale.

Similarly, in the process of barter trade, Russia, in order to build her giant industrial machinery, her army, navy, and railroads, has sometimes not even taken account of her own raw materials and has given consideration only to labor and transportation costs. She dumped chiefly her raw materials when using barter, and thus lost in purchasing power. As for the recipient countries, the customers of dumping nations, such as South America and Mexico, they in turn had to dump their raw materials (coffee, sugar, wheat, cotton, oil, and so forth) and had to accept doubtful products in exchange.

Even our own country has now been forced in an ever increasing degree—sometimes even when such a course becomes a burden—to resort to barter in commerce with Latin American and other countries because these weaker nations (weaker in gold and foreign currency) need assistance. This must be done for political as well as economic reasons. It is considered gool policy and merits the unanimous support of the entire nation at this time.

The new European war has greatly increased, for the time being, the necessity for barter among the democracies and the nations of our Western Hemisphere. In spite of our meat packers and producers of wheat, corn, oil, cotton, and artificial silk we shall increase our purchases of meat and coffee from Brazil as well as of sugar from Cuba, and we shall build, with our United States dollar assets now resting idly in Mexico and South America, artificial silk factories, dams, power and steel plants, and so on, throughout the southern continent, instead of concentrating our efforts in this respect solely in the United States. The alternative of having these countries fall out of our sphere of influence would be even more costly. England has exercised similar policies in her dominions.

The Export-Import Bank of Washington is the first institution to support these policies. The second project is an inter-American bank with a proposed share capital of one hundred million dollars sponsored by the Inter-American Economic and Advisory Committee in Washington, in which South American nations are invited to participate with share capital. This so-called "hemisphere bank," a purely public enterprise, is to be authorized by a special act of Congress.

But we must not nourish the illusion that all the countries involved are enthusiastic about barter or will make it a permanent establishment. Under the nazi government, even Dr. Schacht, when Minister of National Economy, frankly stated: "It is incredibly barbarous to exchange machinery against grain or radio sets against tobacco, as if we were savages bartering ivory against shells or rubber against cotton goods. Is such a system worthy of a cultured human society?"

Maybe the Phoenicians were content to exchange shells for amber or women for cows; but in our days, five thousand years later, it is unnecessarily inefficient and no more than a makeshift. However, trade must go on; and, when war is over, it will, we hope, not be nazi Germany, the great barter juggler, who will rebuild the economic structure of the world.

We must plan for a Bank of Nations which will bring about just spending power parities between nations, so that trade may once again be a net gain to all—a mutually profitable and agreeable exchange, as it was in the times of classical free trade. Not elimination of free competition; but planned, joint, and cooperative action among equal partners. That is our goal.

With this before us we can go on to design the functions, purposes, and structure of the Bank of Nations.

Twelve Basic Functions of the Bank of Nations

Here I wish to offer my Twelve Basic Functions of the Bank of Nations, as presented by Walther Rathenau to the Genoa Conference.[2]

1. First step in reconstruction must be the introduction of an international auxiliary medium of exchange.
2. Introduction of such a medium of exchange would necessitate

[2] This plan was discussed in detail at the Conference of Genoa and in the Credit Committee, as explained in the first part of the book. Lloyd George supported the plan, but Aristide Briand believed that the time was not yet ripe for this instrument of economic solidarity among nations in its all-embracing scope. This condensed summary of the original documents, adapted to the present conditions, can still be considered as up to date and even so timely and comprehensive that I have tried in vain to discover important inadequacies with regard to its character and scope. See footnote 3 below for the proposals of J. E. Meade.

establishment of a superordinated bank with power to issue bank notes technically in accordance with the highest money creating principles.

3. Principal task of the Bank of Nations to be the granting of short- and long-term credits on a basis of sound collateral.

4. Establishment of branch banks in every member nation, consisting of issuing and credit departments.

5. Establishment of subordinate national trust banks to finance new productive enterprises—factories, soil reclamation, public utilities, etc.—and to maintain and enlarge existing business and trade. Because of their productive character, these banks would be called Construction Banks.

6. Bank of Nations to grant long-term bank note credits to Construction Banks. These credits would be amortized by a new method, according to the depreciation of objects on which credits are granted.

7. Aside from soliciting capital, the aim of the Construction Banks would be to extract capital gradually from the market through bond issues. Payment of interest on bonds would be dispensed with until the bonds were issued. Free-of-interest period might last three to ten years—this for the benefit of weak debtors.

8. When issued, bonds to yield customary rate of interest as first-class securities and to be provided with a flexible share in the profits derived from the objects it has financed.

9. Until the end of the free-of-interest period, bonds to be held by the Bank of Nations or branches as securities. At the end of the free period they should be issued in series in accordance with the ability of the market to absorb them. Payment by subscribers to be made in Bank of Nations bank notes, which are to be destroyed when returned to Bank of Nations.

10. Aside from amortization of their capital, the debtors to pay the following additions: (1) fee to cover operating expenses of the Construction Banks from the end of the free-of-interest period; (2) interest on bonds; (3) share in the profits derived from the productive enterprises created by the loan. Loans to be guaranteed jointly by all debtors and superguaranteed by the Construction Banks, whose obligations thus become gilt-edged securities.

11. In order to assure their value, objects serving as collateral for loans to be insured by maintenance insurance, which would cover premature decay of property and provide funds for upkeep and vital repairs. This would assure maintenance of value during the useful life of the objects.

12. Amortization of loans by debtors to proceed steadily until the debt of the Construction Bank is completely repaid. Amortization to be carried out according to statutory regulations in Bank of Nations Construction-Bank notes which are to be destroyed when returned to Bank of Nations. Thus Bank of Nations would be completely covered (even during the time when the bonds yielded no interest). The joint guarantee of debtors could also serve as security for *short-term trade credits*. These credits would be examined individually and approved by the central bank in series.[3]

[3] Mr. J. E. Meade, in his *Economic Basis of a Durable Peace* (London: Allen & Unwin), proposes (cf. Condliffe, *op. cit.*, pp. 389, 390) that the following powers be given to an International Central Bank:

1. Power to regulate the issue of international currency so as to combat the onset of economic depression and "the ultimate power of controlling the total supply of money within the Member-States."

2. The sole power to vary exchange rates.

3. Power to engage in open-market operations.

4. Power to forbid the use of national exchange equalization funds.

5. Power to appoint representatives to the national boards of control over the foreign trade of the Member-States with planned economies. These representatives would have final power of decision over the actions of such national bodies.

6. Powers of supervision of the operations of "various bodies which already control prices, production, sales or exports of various primary commodities. . . ."

7. Powers to prevent any Member-State from putting an embargo on the issue of foreign loans, the purchase of foreign securities or other forms of foreign property, and other powers over international capital movements.

8. Power to forbid the type of trading system which uses exchange control and clearing agreements.

9. Power to supervise exchange controls directed against speculative transfers of capital and of import and export controls.

10. Power to enforce the principle of the Open Door which might be assured by handing over the colonial territories to the International Authority for actual administration by a competent international body.

11. Power to supervise international cartels.

12. Power to insist gradually on the relaxation of restriction schemes as a permanent method of maintaining the incomes of the producers of raw materials.

13. Power to insure freedom of migration. The International Authority might have an army, police and taxation powers.

14. Power to establish some effective means of ensuring collective security.

The layman may well ask why we place so much stress on su financial and materialistic ideas, and how such great benefits may gained from applying them. The answer lies in the fact that heretofo the instrumentalities of credit and banking have been exploited in tl interest of personal commercial advantage, and we have thereby tran ferred to these instrumentalities our mental associations with regard the institutions. In the process we have overlooked potentially powerf mechanisms for the social welfare of the body politic.

In his standard work, *The Life and Structure of the Social Body* the German philosopher Albrecht Schaeffle has stressed the analog of the socio-economic organism of a nation to the organism of tl human body. Banking furnishes the life structure and the vital eco nomic functions of the national organism, its skeleton; credit its veir and arteries; and currency the blood corpuscles, streaming throug the nation's economic body. In the same manner we might say that a international banking, credit, and currency apparatus would create th organic life and structure of the international socio-economic body Only on the basis of a living organism with sound health, good diges tion, and well coordinated muscles and limbs can we establish a soun and permanent economic order and a living and functional peace.

The Bank of Nations apparatus was first designed to help the badl weakened and anaemic European nations after the World War. Th new international currency was designed to give them a blood trans fusion in order to avoid pernicious anaemia in 1922; along with currency, long-term promissory notes on the basis of a new systen of securities, with especially safeguarded and amortized collaterals were designed to reconstruct those countries and especially the destroyed areas of France and Belgium. Today the plan of the Bank of Nation is even more appropriate. It must function not only to stabilize and reconstruct currencies, but it must also give blood transfusions to anaemic national economies, help trade with short-term credits, and reconstruct, transform, and create productive enterprises all over the world.

Through this world banking institution a sound basis would be laid for the revival and complete utilization of productive forces in our world economy. For the discovery, acquisition, and exploitation of new

aw material resources, in the interests of human progress, a center of
financial activity would be created. Moreover, the financial institutions
of the Bank of Nations could function as distributors of labor forces
into the most fruitful channels and into those productive areas of the
earth which are most capable of development. With the power of its
capital it could indirectly encourage and support new ventures by
means of credits to existing industrial and commercial organizations,
or directly finance new productive institutions in cooperation with its
constructive national branch banks. In other words, the Bank of Nations—with its great capital resources—could· support those institutions which made it their task to create productive undertakings in
the best interests of the people at large. The volume of its capital
would finally depend upon the funds deposited in the bank by creditors
and creditor nations. Only if the Bank of Nations were able to cope
with these difficult tasks in the interests of all nations would it enjoy
the confidence of the world, indispensable for its efficient functioning
and lasting success. Only by fostering and encouraging projects of a
distinctly practical value, could it expect, and would it find, support
and confidence on all sides.

I state at the outset and in no uncertain terms that this mechanism
need not interfere with existing private or public institutions. On the
contrary, if there can be an instrument effective in supplementing and
supporting existing industrial, commercial, or financial institutions, it
is the Bank of Nations with its constructive and flexible limbs. The
more we study the problem, the more do we feel certain that most of
the economic ideals we have mentioned before can gradually be
approached and realized by means of the Bank of Nations. In this
mechanism of economic solidarity one dream after another, one ideal
or utopia after another, finds its most natural fulfilment. This neocapitalist instrument, with its refined technique of banking and insurance, appears to bring the wishes of the majority of mankind to a
common denominator and satisfy needs which, until now, could not
be realized in economic life. This will give it favorable chances for
realization.

We may consider five main possibilities for a regulative world institution:

1. The *Western Hemisphere Bank*, which might be expanded into a more actively operating world bank for money clearing and creation. It may first be empowered and authorized to sell and lend United States gold funds to central banks of foreign countries and in this way gradually redistribute our large idle gold hoardings into international channels. The second step may be the creation of an inter-American medium of exchange. The inter-American currency could later be expanded into an international currency and the bank gradually be entrusted with broader powers of short- and long-term credit creation.

2. The *Bank for International Settlements* in Basel, Switzerland, which might be transformed from a mere clearing house for reparation payments into a more productive and constructive Europa Bank for money clearing and for money and credit creation. For this purpose the bank, logically, should first of all be located in a center of banking activity such as Amsterdam, Zurich, London, or Paris. Our attempts to locate the bank in one of these key points during the Baden-Baden discussions were in vain. We may be sure that, to consolidate his conquests, Hitler, through Schacht, will take steps to organize such a bank in Berlin.

3. An *Oriental Bank*. The situation is such that a similar institution might be set up in the Orient for the economic settlement of East-Asiatic problems, with international financial support.

4. Or, an independent *Central Bank of Central Banks*, as suggested by numerous economists since 1920 and by Marvin and Williams in their aforementioned book, might be organized. This bank might serve as a board bank for the central banks of nations (for instance, Federal Reserve Board, Bank of England, Banque de France, Reichsbank, and so forth), to avoid gold shipments and to maintain a financial balance between countries. Such a bank, of course, should have powers similar to those formerly held by the Bank of England or by J. P. Morgan & Co. during the classical gold standard times.

5. A *Bank of Nations*, a creative bank—located, for instance, in Washington, D. C., or New York City; in Toronto, Ottawa, or Montreal, Canada; in Zurich, Switzerland; or in Stockholm,

Sweden—to issue short-term credits, in terms of an international medium of exchange placed under the joint guarantee of all member nations, and in this way regulate and facilitate international credit and trade. The bank should also issue long-term promissory notes in a new form and on a new basis. Branch banks, so-called "construction banks," in all member nations should be organized in order to provide the indispensable safeguarding long-term investment apparatus. This all-embracing super-organization of banks would be the highest economic world authority, the Federal World Board for the entire world economy. It would be superordinated to the Hemisphere Bank, the Europa Bank, and all Central Banks. It would be the ultimate vigilant authority, custodian, and regulator of economic world affairs.

At the outset we must recognize that the Bank of Nations must be kept free from particularistic interests of nations or capital powers. It was a deplorable experience to observe how at the last Hague Conference the various nations brought their selfish interests to the foreground. Only an equalization of interests on the basis of solidarity can give us the guarantee for the permanent prosperity of this institution—an equalization of political interests and the interests of capital and labor, and of the existing conflict between world economic spheres of interest. The autonomy of its banking technique imperatively demands a certain economic independence. Only under these conditions can it endeavor to fulfill its high tasks of influencing the fluctuations of world markets and of promoting capital formation and maintenance.

It cannot be denied that the new European war has temporarily disrupted the already disordered international capital cooperation; but projects of such universal and embracing character as a world bank must in any case be prepared long before their introduction, and can greatly help to reconcile the alienated parties.

The basis for the program of the Bank of Nations in its modern form is substantially the same as it was twenty years ago. The economic disequilibria, predicted for the future of international economic relations at the Conference of Genoa, if national egotism and lack of solidarity among nations were to make impossible the introduction of

a higher economic order through world organization, have surpasse
all expectations and have finally led toward a new world war.

The first task of the Bank of Nations would in all probability be th
promotion of a gradually expanding international trade with rates o
exchange as stable as possible. In so far as the international exchang
of goods is performed through bills of exchange, by and large, goods o
equal labor value are normally exchanged without profit or loss. Th
use value of these goods in the consumer countries may be as variabl
as ever. In normal times and in a just international exchange, which i
not based on monopoly or power conditions, each product is paid fo
with a corresponding quantity of other merchandise of approximatel
equal labor value. Price, which mediates the exchange, merely repre
sents the value of the labor hours expended by both parties in th
manufacture of the products, and is expressed in money units as :
standard of measurement.

If we consider the entire exchange of goods from the viewpoint o
exchange equivalents, the task of our Bank is clearly indicated. Th
first task of a bank which is founded to promote the exchange of goods
in the best possible way is to facilitate the exchange of commodities by
keeping in readiness the necessary media of exchange and by improving
such exchange by means of credits.

Over a period of several centuries, up until the first world war, our
Western civilization evolved a system centered around the use of gold
to serve this exchange function. There have been strong arguments
both pro and con as to its effectiveness, which we need not go into
here, but it is an established fact that since the first world war the gold
standard has been either in a state of disuse or performing its functions
badly. It has long been contended by many economists that gold has
ceased to function as a currency basis for use within a country. Since
the onset of the depression their opinion has seemingly been justified.

It has also been contended that relief from foreign exchange difficulties is to be found in an international currency. The question of whether
a gold coverage is provided for the newly created international paper
money (as was provided in the statutes of the Bank for International
Settlements), and the question of how far the Bank ought to assist and
partake in the stabilization of currencies and the protection of fluctuat-

ng gold coverages in those countries, will depend upon the statutes
nd upon the powers with which it is endowed.

Recently, Dr. E. A. Goldenweiser, Research Director of the Fed-
ral Reserve Board, has correctly admitted that gold, which is not
ised directly for currency, and only part of which is necessary as a
nonetary reserve, "is an asset which is of little value now, and whose
alue in the future is unpredictable."

Secretary Morgenthau goes a step further. He made a statement
egarding the future of gold, on May 3, 1940, as reported by the
New York Times, which was regarded as

he greatest concession he has ever made to gold pessimists and was his first
oublic admission that the future value of gold is at issue in the struggle
broad.

"To be sure," says Mr. Morgenthau, "if the political picture of the world
hould undergo a drastic change in the future, so that instead of fifty or sixty
ndependent nations there should exist only one or two groups dominated by
uthless powers, then international trade and finance may assume the char-
cter of domestic trade.

"There would cease to be independent monetary systems, as there would
cease to be independent foreign policies. Balances between countries would
be settled as balances between our States are now settled—that is, by transfers
of deposits.

"Under such circumstances it might well be that gold would no longer be
needed. But under those circumstances life would be so different that the
possible loss in the value of gold would, I am sure, be the least of our
troubles."

Some financiers and economists [the Times continues] recognizing the
bearing of the European war's outcome in the value of gold, have made
various proposals for utilizing the gold stock.

Prominent among these proposals are the return to gold coinage, which
would renew the interest of individuals in gold as money and more directly
relate gold to our currency, and the redistribution of some of the gold stock
among other American Republics to enhance their ability to purchase our
products and thus cement economic ties in the American Hemisphere, which,
in the event of a Nazi victory, would be the primary sphere of the United
States interest by sheer force of circumstance.

PLAN FOR PERMANENT PEACE

The Bank of Nations attempts a solution similar to the vision of Morgenthau, but without totalitarian "troubles." By pooling the world's gold in a common reservoir held by the Bank, even this precious metal could be preserved for some time to come, until it would be replaced by international agreements and gradually dispensed with.

The return to the gold standard or gold coinage and private ownership of gold, as advanced by Walter E. Spahr and his adherents, can by no means be recommended in this book. Neither "coinage of gold" nor "restoration of its private ownership" can contribute to a sound solution of the currency and gold problem. In times of uncertainty and inflationary tendencies, such as these, allowance for private ownership of gold may lead to hoarding and other undesirable conditions. It would be absolutely unproductive and lead private funds into dry channels.

To those who believe in the preservation of gold for currency purposes, the large idle gold funds owned by the United States or entrusted to us and stored in Kentucky should not cause too much embarrassment. Gold does not disintegrate. So long as the world wants our goods, so long will the world need our dollars to get them; so long as gold can buy dollars, gold will be internationally valuable. So long as gold is valuable, we shall have the power inherent in that value—power to command something in exchange.

The idea of gradually distributing our idle gold hoardings into international channels is commendable and may well appeal to other countries. But this policy should not be accompanied by reactionary steps which we may eventually regret. It cannot be stated too often that for the definite settlement of the gold question we need more peaceful minds and times. This is first of all an international problem and we must keep our hands free for its future final international regulation. As a hopeful sign for the gold adherents, I may mention the fact that Great Britain is still the largest gold-producing nation of the world, and Russia is next. The time may come when United States gold will again play its important part in world affairs.

The loss that the United States has suffered through buying gold at $35 per ounce instead of for some $20, which would have been closer to its production cost, may be considered as balanced by political advan-

98

tages for our nation during the present war. By purchasing gold at $35 from England, our Government is indirectly financing the Allies with a gift of approximately one billion dollars yearly in spite of the Johnson Act, which forbids direct credits to those countries which have failed to repay their debts.

If there is a suitable instrument for reintroducing our idle gold funds into international channels, it is a Bank of Nations with the power of international money and credit *creation*. Ever so many suggestions have been made, of late, for the use and employment of the idle gold hoards of the United States and other nations (that is, England and Russia). It has even been recommended that the gold be used for buying up all the armaments of the world and sinking them in mid-ocean. But it is my suggestion that, if gold is to be conserved for the perpetuation of the confidence which mankind has bestowed on this precious metal since dim past ages, it could be pooled by all nations in the Bank of Nations as a "Nibelungen treasure," a memorial to mankind's fanciful imagination.

If this suggestion seems too remote, we may be sure that the practical experience of the Bank of Nations, with a world medium of exchange under joint guarantee of the member nations, will show whether some day our gold coverage can gradually be replaced by a better and more elastic yardstick. Maybe, in the not too distant future, the world will recognize that the true purchasing power of a medium of exchange, regulated in accordance with the turnover of goods, is not dependent upon the extent of gold coverage. Such purchasing power in a medium of exchange is dependent upon the costs of production, which are to be calculated according to the average work cost of production, wages, and other cost factors.

An international agreement as to the complete elimination (demonetization) of gold, however, could only be considered after the introduction of a unified regulated world medium of exchange, which at its inception might perhaps be adjusted to the purchasing power of a specific quantity of gold. But the conversion of such world money into national currency units would, as before, be carried out on the basis of the rates of exchange, which are dependent upon the purchasing power parities of the individual countries.

PLAN FOR PERMANENT PEACE

If a Bank of Nations, the establishment of which we are proposing as an instrument of the aforesuggested international agreement, should itself issue any short- or long-term promissory notes which would in turn be placed under the joint guarantee of all civilized nations, then the general realization might spread that for such notes no gold coverage at all would be necessary or useful. If it becomes evident that this new system will accomplish great savings in our economy at home and abroad, America will be quick to accept it.

Again, if the Bank were granted the right to issue bank notes as a method of creating or initiating credit without interest, gold as an international medium of exchange would then be replaced by a conventionally fixed value unit, which would then be theoretically equivalent to a fixed quantity of gold. But this quantity of gold itself—as Marx has rightfully stated—represents a certain precise quantity of socially necessary labor-time in the countries producing precious metals (in so far as the exchange value and not the use value is to be considered).

One of the most important requisites of the Bank of Nations is the power to regulate note circulation according to the exchange value of the quantity of merchandise that takes part in the international intercourse of goods, whereby the extent of money demand certainly depends upon the velocity of circulation and the frequency of the acts of payment. The permanent preservation of the gold currency for those countries participating in the Bank of Nations is of relatively minor consideration.

My position on the interest-free note credits of the Bank is this: So long as interest is the governing factor in the capital market, we should not overemphasize the importance of this question. But there is certainly a fair chance that the Bank of Nations may limit its profits or dividends and thereby reduce the interest rates on its credits as far as possible.[4]

It would, furthermore, be the task of the progressive and experienced leaders of the bank to decide upon the volume of augmentation and

[4] In Parts 7 to 9 of the "Basic Functions of the Bank of Nations" (see page 90), a free-of-interest period from 3 to 10 years on the bonds of the constructive banks is proposed for the benefit of weak debtor nations.

THE BANK OF NATIONS

creation of money possible without endangering the liquidity of the bank. This would be best decided upon from time to time as changing situations present themselves.

In our plan for the Bank of Nations in 1922, another task was suggested which today may be regarded as still premature, but which is perhaps the most important, namely, the issuance of a new type of long-term promissory notes based on productive capital objects and constructive enterprises, safeguarded by the joint guarantee of specially qualified, preserved, and reproduced objects, to build up the missing means of production, public utilities, housing and transportation facilities, and so on, in countries of capital need and promising possibilities. After the war, the idle American private and public capital funds will be acutely needed for national purposes and international reconstruction. However large these funds may be, they will certainly not suffice to satisfy even the most urgent and immediate capital needs. An entirely new creative long-term credit system must therefore be invented to master the situation. This long-term credit system can be sketched only roughly in this chapter. If, after this war, the world finds itself in a situation where sufficient savings and idle funds are not immediately available, we must anticipate the future, that is, the future earnings of those productive enterprises which are most urgently needed and which must be constructed long before the world has again accumulated the savings necessary for this purpose.

But to anticipate future earnings requires a new sense of responsibility; it imposes new obligations on mankind and requires a well-supervised and controlled system of security. If we must undertake to anticipate the future and the earnings of properties of future generations which can only be undertaken and allowed for *productive* long-term purposes, we must insert a mechanism into the economy of the world which systematically assures the proper maintenance, replacement, and renewal of those productive capital objects which are to be constructed by means of this new system of long-term credit creation.

The long-term promissory notes, which the Bank of Nations is to issue over a series of years, must be issued, amortized, and safeguarded on the basis of the life expectancy of the credited capital objects, production means, plants, utilities, and so forth, in a new mechanized form of insurance protection. It is imperative to make use of entirely new and rather elaborate and very accurate credit and insurance systems in order to solve this very constructive undertaking, which can only be touched upon at this writing.

These long-term credits would be matched by recipient organizations located in member nations, which institutions are to function as branch banks of the superbank. Besides, trust banks, so-called "construction banks," are needed for reconstruction and long-term financing. An example of territories with promising possibilities for the activities of our long-term credit and investment system would be our southern states with their vast unexploited resources. Other American examples would be Canada and Latin America, but there will be other districts of the earth in great need of creative credits after this war, such as China, Spain, Poland, Finland, and others.

SHARE CAPITAL

For the Bank of Nations, as proposed at the Conference of Genoa, a share capital of 100 million currency units—for instance, 100 million world dollars—was suggested in 1922 as perhaps sufficient to get the Bank of Nations started. Today a share capital of 300 million currency units seems more appropriate, and this amount could be increased in accordance with the mounting volume of world production and trade.[5] Before the outbreak of the new war in 1939 the total amount of international trade alone was approximately thirty billion dollars per year; the total world indebtedness between sixty and sixty-five billion; and the interest on that debt, at 3 per cent, about two billion, or at 4 per cent, about two and a half billion.

For the participation of member nations, a proper key must be found. In the setup of the Hemisphere Bank each participating nation is invited to subscribe to the share capital a minimum amount in accordance with the respective annual trade volume of the individual nation. If, for instance, the annual export and import volume amounts to 25 million dollars, 5 shares (each of one hundred thousand dollars in value) is the designated minimum participation; if the volume of trade amounts to over 25 million and up to 50 million dollars, 10 shares

[5] For all further details regarding this 1922 Bank of Nations see Chapter III and Appendix.

valued at 1 million; and so on. Argentine, Brazil, and the United States are to participate with at least 50 shares, equal to 5 million dollars share capital, because their annual trade volume exceeds 500 million dollars.

Another method of finding and adjusting a proper key to participation would be an annual assessment upon each nation or group in per mille of the average national income of individual nations or groups during a certain period of years. (This method would assure the United States and the British Empire adequate influence in the bank.) Voting powers are to be granted in proportion to the amount of share participation. For withdrawal from participation in share capital, notice may be given on a five- or ten-year term.

For the first three or five years, no dividends should be distributed. After this waiting period all earnings over and above 3 per cent dividends are to be accumulated until surplus equal to the share capital and reserves, large enough to counteract depressions, is accumulated.

ADMINISTRATION AND PERSONNEL

The Board of Directors should be composed of a government representative from every nation, the governor of every central bank or leading bank or his representative, and representatives of industry, trade, agriculture, banking, and labor. A similar board would be required for the national branch banks, which in turn must be represented in the Bank of Nations.

For the study of all special questions a permanent advisory committee should be appointed, to be composed of specialists or experts from all fields of economic activity.

A world-index office, a statistical department, and a research department would be integral parts of the administration.

The management of the bank must retain a certain independence in its actions; i.e., it must not be checked in its initiative by too stringent and unwieldy regulations. The knowledge of monetary management and private commercial credit banking must be a prerequisite to the governing position of the Bank of Nations. The leaders must be well qualified by their world experience and territorially unlimited background. The officers must be equally competent in banking and commerce, and in world-wide organization.

Credits to trade and investments in needy or other economies with good prospects must be carefully examined. If they are prequalified and appraised as to their economic justification, their safety, chances of profit, reproduction possibilities, and life duration, they are to be approved by a majority of the board members of the Bank of Nations in conjunction with the board of the branch bank of the nation or group for which the credit is needed.

． ． ． ． ． ．

In brief, we have first of all required the issue of an international medium of exchange to influence fluctuations in world markets through a sound monetary policy of contraction and expansion, and to stimulate trade and capital movements.

We have pointed to the necessity of international loans for financial as well as economic reconstruction of those countries which are most in need of such support. We have sketched the technique of a mechanism for the purpose and explained the primary requirements for its success, namely a readjustment of the balances of international payments of the member countries of the Bank of Nations, the assurance of a reduction and, finally, removal of international restrictions and trade barriers.

After the war the Bank of Nations may first have to reconstruct and support national currencies. The various nations or groups would conserve their own national currencies to be pegged at certain values in terms of the unified regulated medium of exchange of the Bank of Nations. The great advantage, especially for weaker nations, to participate in the Bank rests in the fact that instead of credits of the kind extended in the interwar period they can command purchasing power over raw materials in the open market by drawing on the international currency funds of the Bank five to ten times or more, at one time, their share capital participation. In this way the motor of international trade is set in motion.

We have explained the role that gold might play in this process. The international bank notes might perhaps first be adjusted to the purchasing power of a specific quantity of gold; but the conversion of such world money into national currency units would, as before, be carried out on the basis of the rates of exchange.

Further, a new system of international long term credits has been devised, a system of long term investments which anticipate the future earnings from those investments. The promissory notes, issued in series for these purposes, must be amortized during the life of the objects and through products to be created. In this manner the objects created become sound and safeguarded collateral. This represents a procedure of revolving credits for production and reproduction, for permanent generation and rejuvenation. The issue of these promissory notes requires a well functioning international peace economy, but we can anticipate that day by the initiation of national construction banks.

An international exchange equalization fund might counteract speculative short term credit transactions and take all measures to support and stabilize international trade. The foreign exchange control to prevent short term capital disequilibria might be maintained by the member nations. Totalitarian and nations with planned economies would not readily be able to abandon the control of their foreign trade. Non-totalitarian nations would therefore have to adjust their foreign trade to these conditions through the organization of export-import bodies; but the Bank of Nations will have to regulate these various export-import boards, and establish certain standards, rules, and modes of operation. A certain control over international cartels, trusts, syndicates, conventions and restrictions seems to be equally indispensable.

When this basic new order has been established, the flow of international long term capital movements can gradually be opened under the informed and vigilant direction of the Bank of Nations, and all the other movements of labor migrations, immigration, colonization, etc. can be initiated.

We have endeavored to sketch the basic functions of an ideal Bank of Nations. The unavoidable shortcomings of this design for universal credit reform and economic recovery can be smoothed out and perfected only if the student of world social and economic problems does not refrain from constructive criticism. So long as our human race exists, mistakes and errors can never be avoided; but we can control the exercise of selfish nationalist greed and power policies and excessive acts of nature by means of a socio-capitalist credit and insurance system, which our present generation has brought to unprecedented efficiency and perfection.

We cannot yet fully appreciate how a creative Bank of Nations, even if it did not include all suggested powers at the outset, would be able to eliminate most of the frictions and obstacles to peace. Most of those powerful economic disequilibria and incentives for war would disappear and the system of accumulative and national capitalism would be transformed into an enlightened system of organized international social capitalism. Without eliminating the efficient and rational parts of our old system, the new world-wide banking mechanism would give new life to our traditional democracy.

Why do capitalist countries become enshrouded in passive pessimism? Why do they not visualize and endeavor to apply a solution for the world on a reformed capitalist basis which encompasses the advantages of national socialist ideas and practices without indulging in their reactionary and illiberal schemes? Neither old capitalistic methods of the Western democracies or empires nor the illiberal methods of economic strangulation in the dictator nations or areas can reconstruct our economic system. The all-comprehensive and collective mechanism of an international social and capitalist order will be found to be of real help and will be superior to excessive national or group capitalism and restrictionism. When presidents, kings, or dictators call their families of nations, or subject nations, to a conference to form new integrated economic groupings, they must hereafter decide whether they can afford to ignore the forces making necessary an all-inclusive and truly creative Bank of Nations.

THE BANK OF NATIONS: ITS FUNCTIONAL SUBSIDIARIES

In MY opinion there is no doubt but that the establishment of this international instrument for the creation of money and credit would be the first decisive step in the unification and voluntary organization of our world economy. We realize that we have still a long way to go before we can succeed in organizing a completely unified and systematic world economic policy. But if we ever wish to achieve this ideal organization of society, without disastrous revolutions, we must construct this mechanism on the basis of an improved capitalistic system with an entirely different sense of social behavior, as outlined in my Fourteen Ideals for a Living Peace (see page 85).

There can be no doubt that, within and outside of the capitalistic sphere of influence, transformations are in the making which will lead toward a more systematic utilization of all human and material productive powers in our world economy. The problem of a functional, socio-economic world organization is so complex and momentous that within the range of this chapter we can only sketch a few important projects which could be correlated into an organism with the Bank of Nations as its core.

I should like to suggest, first, an approach to one of our most urgent world problems, namely, the utilization and protection of idle labor, especially in the leading industrial nations. This is by no means a purely national economic problem, but one, more or less chronic in the capitalist system, which cannot be overcome by national measures alone.

The great disturbances of the world market which developed from the first world war, and will again result from the present war, have created immense unemployment. The process of industrial rationalization and transformation has rendered idle six to seven million laborers

in Europe and ten to fifteen million in the United States of Americ
Though France never had much more than five hundred thousand id
workers, because of her still prevailing handicraft economy and sma
individual ownerships, she depends nonetheless on the economies
other nations. If they are weakened in their purchasing power throug
excessive unemployment, France suffers indirectly from the same a
ment. Although the totalitarian states have forced labor into armame
production and have enslaved working populations in conquered neig
boring countries to replace the man power needed for their armi
their labor problem will hit back at them with much greater fiercene
when the war is over. They will be compelled to abandon force ar
slavery in order to organize their labor on a productive and function
basis in collaboration with the outer world.

The guarantee of a minimum of subsistence is recognized as
social obligation by state and society all over the world. One count
after another has introduced a system of unemployment relief an
unemployment insurance and has supplemented these institutions wit
emergency relief measures in critical times.

From the experiences gained in this field, we are drawing conclusio
which point toward certain universal principles in connection wit
the fight against unemployment. Above all, we are becoming consciou
that there is a legal claim to a minimum of subsistence, sustained o
the basis of contributions by workmen and employers with the cooper.
tion of the state and the community. In other words, unemploymei
relief must be supported by the nation as a whole, whose well-bein
depends on successfully coping with such an emergency.

Unemployment insurance is usually combined with a system
employment agencies in order to further the efficient distribution
labor within a regional and national economic area. But experien
indicates that a positive solution of those economic and social deficie
cies cannot be achieved by means of social insurance alone. In o
form or another, we must take care of the *expansion of the market an
the basis of production*. For this purpose, also, an increased supply
money and capital is indispensable. Besides public relief measures, i
creased activity and cooperation on the part of banking institutio
is necessary.

The British Prime Minister, Ramsay MacDonald, always pointed the fact that for this purpose the extension and rationalization of productive enterprise through a modernized banking system is imperative. Gustav Cassel maintained that in times of capital scarcity the performance of unnecessary public work would constitute a misappropriation of capital funds. If such unproductive works are undertaken, not even credit from national banks can help in stimulating production. Such action represents a waste of disposable capital means. In situations such as this, an *international mobility of labor and capital* must be introduced. This can only be accomplished by means of a systematic regulation and organization of world economy. It is not sufficient to supply unemployment relief for citizens of foreign nations, here and there, on the basis of reciprocity. Nor can the international employment agencies of colonization or the migration offices succeed in solving this problem. To ameliorate this problem I suggest the creation of an

INTERNATIONAL LABOR MIGRATION OFFICE

The promising activities of the International Labor Office in Geneva can show us the way in which we must proceed. I propose, in this connection, the establishment of an International Labor Migration Office, directly or indirectly financed by the Bank of Nations. I do not underestimate the difficulties which stand in the way of such an undertaking. In a world of nationalist boundaries, limitations, and restrictions, a rational international distribution of productive labor seems to be an unattainable goal, but what is possible in the realm of large individual countries and empires must be equally possible in an international organization, especially under the present conditions of emergency. An international organization center regulating the labor market of the world must be constantly informed by reports from all countries, indicating the demand for labor in agriculture, industry, mining, etc.

The major tasks of this International Labor Migration Department would be as follows:

1. The systematic distribution of available labor with the aid of a centralized employment agency in cooperation with national labor organizations, employer associations, and governments.

2. The equipment of migrant labor columns with the necessary financial means for transportation to the place of destination, and with the means of transportation and the tools necessary for the performance of their work.

3. The stimulation and support of great productive works serving the progress of mankind; of development and cultivation of backward countries with good prospects.

In order to assure lasting success to these international productive unemployment provisions, the financial cooperation of public and private enterprise is indispensable. In colonies, dominions, or protectorates the management of the organization should remain in the hands of their respective governments, mother countries, or protectors. There are many semicultivated countries with a considerable latent need for capital and labor. These parts of the globe could perhaps be elevated to a higher level of economic development, if the combined capital of the great industrial nations functioned as entrepreneurs. In all these countries, native or domestic labor must be supplemented by a group of experienced laborers acting as planners and leaders to enrich and enlarge their productive forces. In all these pioneering works of colonization and construction the creation of capital must be provided on the basis of durability, continuity, and perpetual reproduction of those capital enterprises. These new productive forces must be considered as counterparts of international capital creation and as counterproducers of the international circulation of products.

The more we proceed in this way the more we recognize that private capitalistic enterprise will not be willing or able to perform this work alone. For these tasks of world economy may not produce immediate profits and are primarily to serve for the benefit of the world as a whole. In most of these undertakings, we may have to depend largely upon public authorities, states, and communities or upon *ad hoc* organized cooperative economic associations. The cooperative form of enterprise will, in fact, be best able to combine private and public initiative. In all instances where producers are identical with consumers, and the entire profit is either set aside as reserve or used for the reduction of the price of the products, this form of enterprise is highly commendable. The greatest success in this respect has been achieved in Sweden.

The Régies Cooperatives of Belgium, organized on the model of the Credit Communal de Belgique, are examples which have produced excellent results. The distribution of electric power, the construction of railroads, waterworks, electric streetcars, homes for workers, etc., supply brilliant possibilities for cooperative planning in Belgium and in other countries. The capital is raised by joint guarantee of the cooperators and is amortized in annuities generally covered by annual earnings. Losses are compensated for from a common reserve fund, without eliminating individual responsibility and self-administration in the separate parts of the enterprise.

Although these cooperatives are based on the cooperation of the public authorities, they can best be compared with the socialistic ideas and projects of great classical social reformers like Saint Simon, Proudhon, and Fourier. The splendid cooperative enterprises of Palestine and Macedonia (repatriation of Greeks formerly settled on Turkish territory) can be characterized as typical cooperative world organizations carried out with remarkable success. All great movements of world migration are in need of such economic organizations for solidarity. No matter if these self-administered community bodies have been organized or are yet to be created, they can easily adapt to their own uses the form of the Régies Cooperatives. The productive forces of individuals will, perhaps, find fertile soil only in the form of cooperative associations for the furtherance of universal cultural purposes.

Statutes and by-laws of the Bank of Nations must provide for long- and short-term credits, to be granted to cooperative associations under conditions which assume real support for these collective welfare undertakings of the present and future. The means necessary for the support of the World Labor Migration Office must be raised by joint contributions from the participating nations. These funds can be periodically or permanently administered by the Bank, which may in turn, if need be, extend credits to the World Labor Migration Department. We in the United States have a parallel national organization in the Reconstruction Finance Corporation.

In the main, we must distinguish primarily between industrial enterprises in prospering national economies and settlements in young countries with new economies. The latter will have to be developed for years to come. They represent the inexhaustible resources of nature, the source of food and raw materials, to be utilized with increasing intensity for the improvement of the standard of living. If we compare this voluntary and dignified form of collective effort on the part of pioneering individuals with the nazi ransom plan for emigrants and refugees, our choice will not be difficult. This cooperative system on a world-wide scale, centralized and organized through the Bank of Nations, is worthy of the efforts of our best world citizens and nations. There is still ample free space on our earth with great inherent treasures of natural capital which could be given gratis to those cooperating settlers who are willing to develop these territories by their labor.

Richard T. Ely and George S. Wehrwein in their book, *Land Economics* (New York: The Macmillan Co., 1940), have presented an enlightened attitude toward the policies of public control over land: "Insofar as land and resources are affected by public interest, no landowner holds title to land to the exclusion of the rights of the public, including future as well as present generations. Our political philosophy must give meaning and content to the vague idea of 'public vs. private rights' to land. The right to control land uses exists and lies in the sovereign power of the state and may be exercised through the police power, eminent domain, and taxation."

The Dominican Republic has lately given a splendid example of this by offering, gratis, fertile and promising soil to a cooperative group of refugees. Surely those nations with virgin territories which open their doors to cooperative settlers, well equipped and financed by the Bank of Nations, will be amply recompensed for their generosity.[6]

But even if soil must be acquired and purchased from private

[6] Cf. the publications of James G. McDonald, Chairman, George L. Warren, Executive Secretary, President's Advisory Committee on Political Refugees: *Concerning Refugee Settlement in the Dominican Republic* (a) Meeting at the Town Hall Club, February 15, 1940; (b) Meeting at the Lawyers' Club, New York City, June 12, 1940. Further, the opinions and publications of the Dominican Republic Settlement Association, Inc., 156 Broadway, New York City; James N. Rosenberg, President, including the economic analysis of Leon Falk, Jr.

Under the supervision of the Brookings Institution of Washington and with the support of the Falk Foundation of Pittsburgh, Pa., an economic, medical, and social research in the Dominican Republic has been initiated. Dana G. Monroe, head of the School of Government at Princeton University, is concentrating the research on the economic potentialities of the new refugee settlement.

nterests, lease or rental estates could be organized by granting advances
n earnings of future labor accomplishments to cooperatives for pro-
uction and settlement.

WORLD BUILDING AND COLONIZATION BANK

It is a well founded fact that there is only one true gilt-edged security
n our capitalistic milieu of today, and that is capital invested in nature,
n promising natural values of soil and other raw material resources.
n order to avoid an undue rise in prices on natural values, we need
he creation and education of efficient settlement associations of general
ervice and benefit to all. These settlement associations organized in
heir mutual relationship can best be supported and fortified through a
World Building and Colonization Bank, which, I hope, will be organized in the near future.

This department of the Bank of Nations is faced with the most vital
problem of our capitalistic system. The more the international relations
of nations gain in influence, importance, and power, the nearer the
ime will come when our present system of competitive, individualistic
capitalism will be supplanted by a system of solidarity. Our present
collective capitalism organized in cartels, trusts, and concerns will be
ransformed into a system that is based on the principle of mutual help
and support. During the last hundred years we have developed a widely
extended system of agreements and contracts concerning international
trade, law, and intercourse. But what is missing are independent unified
nstitutions with their own autonomous right, which must be coordinated with the Bank of Nations.

DEPARTMENT FOR RELIEF AND REPARATIONS

After the present war the migration of international money will be
speeded up by joint loans, reparations, and relief foundations on the
part of creditor nations in the interest of weakened debtor nations
(Finland, Holland, Belgium, Norway, Denmark, Poland, Czecho-
Slovakia, Austria, Greece, Spain, China, etc.). The Bank of Nations
might be the central institution for the regulation of these actions and
organize a special Department for Relief and Reparations.

First it might be helpful in the investment of these and other disposable bank funds for beneficial and utility purposes in the world economy. Subsequently, the Bank of Nations will have the task of gradually bringing order into the present chaos in world markets. The relatively unproductive tasks of money clearing entrusted to the first Bank for International Settlements must be transformed into productive functions of world-wide scope, entrusted to the true Bank of Nations, such as reconstruction and transformation of war and substitute industries into useful peace industries.

INTERNATIONAL SOCIAL INSURANCE DEPARTMENT

Besides world labor migration, world building and colonization, relief and reparations, reconstruction and transportation, we envision the creation of an International Social Insurance Department. There exists, in fact, something like a social conscience in all cultured nations; and this collective sense of social responsibility and duty, in my opinion, demands a growing uniformity in the progress toward socio-ethical goals.

Germany first inaugurated a progressive system of social insurance; England followed, then France at the end of the twenties. The United States enacted the Social Security Act of 1935, which was greatly improved by the amendments of 1939. From *The Origins of the International Labor Organization*, edited by James T. Shotwell (New York: Columbia University Press, 1934), we learn that on all sides, especially on the part of Germany, uniform social insurance provisions have been urged on several occasions. In 1918 Germany proposed as part of the peace treaty (Vol. I, page 227) that:

All governments concerned, which have not already done so, are to introduce compulsory insurance of the workers against sickness, occupational accidents (including occupational diseases), disability, old age and unemployment, insurance of widows and orphans, and maternity insurance. In all these respects foreign and native workers should be treated as far as possible on terms of reciprocal equality.

Unfortunately, the great periodic economic fluctuations against which social insurance must fight everywhere are an insurmountable evil of our private capitalistic system. In so far as we know of remedies, such as social insurance, we usually characterize them as policies of a state socialistic system. But in reality they represent a progressive approach toward economic principles of cooperation and solidarity. Business men usually complain about the absolute and relatively high social burdens imposed upon them by these programs, which also affect their ability to compete with foreign rivals. In this place, however, we are arguing for the *uniform* introduction of social insurance in all countries. Were this done all competitors would fare alike. If social conscience leads to a progressive extension and consolidation of our national unemployment insurance systems, the time is not far distant when we shall wish to establish international standards and principles in this field. Government unemployment insurance measures might then be supplemented by cooperative self-supporting institutions.

INTERNATIONAL UNEMPLOYMENT INSURANCE DEPARTMENT

After this war the world labor organization might crown its work by inaugurating an International Unemployment Insurance Department as a division of the Bank of Nations. In the past every genuine insurance institution has shown the tendency to spread over the entire world economy. Each special risk is dependent upon international reinsurance, and therefore in the future universal cooperation between all national social insurance institutions can and will be brought about to the advantage of all nations.

In abnormal situations of emergency mutual help among nations is not a new and unprecedented phenomenon, and this will not be the first time that insurance has played a great role in such situations. Why should it not be possible to pave the way for an international unemployment insurance system? Are we not faced here with one of the most terrible and depressing maladies of our economic system? If this challenging opportunity is wrecked through lack of unity on the part of international labor or selfish opposition on the part of international enterprise, there might be no other way to stop social world revolution with its disastrous and destructive consequences.

As a student of insurance for several decades I should like to present a few measures which might contribute to the solution of this problem:

To begin with, for the international protection of the security of labor,

I recommend setting aside a percentage from the premium contributions assessed in each country for the purpose of unemployment insurance. In this way a fund can be accumulated to help in cases of extraordinary damage. If and when the coverage of national unemployment risks exceeds a certain limit, these internationally accumulated funds might be drawn upon to meet the national emergency.

WORLD CROP INSURANCE DEPARTMENT

These insurance reserve funds for the purpose of protecting the unemployed will parallel the money reserve system of the Bank of Nations and its raw material reserves to equalize crop deficiencies and other cyclical fluctuations in world economy. A universal crop insurance plan, carried out by a World Crop Insurance Department would round out this comprehensive system.

Insurance protection is not a cure-all and should only supplement all the other progressive devices for productive international labor mentioned above. It is only when the productive and constructive subsidiary reforms are inadequate that international social insurance should be called upon to help.

The absence of organization and planning in our capitalist system and the increasing confusion in international financial relations are becoming intolerable. This condition prevents continuous and equitable production for use and coverage of the needs of the working population. Even the owners of interest-bearing securities, representing productive capital, are driven from one depression to another. If, however, the idea of an organized world economy, of economic planning on a world-wide scale, gains ascendancy, it will mark the rise of a new age in the development and utilization of world productive forces. We can scarcely envision the far-reaching consequences of such a new universal order.

The struggle for raw materials and for the resources of our earth constitutes an actual and potential peril to world peace. The new rational system which must replace the present disorganization, will not be content with a mere national monopoly control and like measures against monopolistic organizations (such as the anti-trust division of the Department of Justice, F.T.C., S.E.C., T.N.E.C., etc.). The world will hardly go so far as to advocate "expropriating the expropriators" or similar repressive measures. But a mere international monopoly control will not solve the situation.

INTERNATIONAL RAW MATERIAL CLEARING HOUSE AND RESERVE BOARD

There is only one genuine solution to this most vital problem, and that is the creation of international agencies of integration, to avoid abuses in the utilization of raw material resources. An international organization of integration is needed, which does not exclusively serve the interests of one-sided capitalist or nationalist factions. Integration and differentiation, supplementing each other, are the two powers of progress in the evolution of our society. All productive forces which have grown and blossomed within local, national, and imperial limits should be relieved of their regional limitations and assigned their rightful place in an organized world economy. Thus, the essence of the problem of coordinating our deranged productive forces lies in the creation of centers of organization for the distribution of raw and subsidiary materials and of other natural products which directly contribute to the well-being of humanity.[7] An International Raw Material Clearing House is considered as an indispensable department of the Bank of Nations for the attainment of this end. Furthermore a Raw Material Reserve Board should be entrusted with the task of setting aside, in good years, reserves of natural, durable goods (such as cotton, corn, grain, coffee, sugar, and rubber), so that the world could draw on these reserves in lean years.

A WORLD INDEX OFFICE

A vigilant body must be constantly informed of crop and agricultural conditions, supported by statistics and index figures. It will add an invaluable service to the functional solution of our problem. The importance of these statistical and research departments cannot be overemphasized. In the draft of the by-laws of the Hemisphere Bank,

[7] In his book, *The International Distribution of Raw Materials* (New York: Harper & Brothers), Herman Kranold has vividly painted the obstacles—not altogether insurmountable —in the way of organization and distribution of productive forces.
See also: Eugene Staley, *Raw Materials in Peace and War* (New York: Council on Foreign Relations); Brooks Emeny, *The Strategy of Raw Materials* (New York: The Macmillan Co.).

interestingly enough, for the first time such powers have been extended to the departments of experts.

A World Index Office will be of great significance with regard to production, distribution, and consumption. For many years, Irving Fisher has propounded a new index doctrine and has shown the world the role that index numbers may play in the credit, gold, and currency structure of the future. All nations have their index institutions and it is only one step further to combine these national index institutions through a world index office. I am inclined to believe that such a World Index Office will some day be preferred to a Fort Knox as a logical place to pool the gold of all nations. The Bank of Nations will provide the necessary credits for this venture designed to help in counteracting the unavoidable cycles and fluctuations in world economy. We shall never achieve lasting results from temporary contractual agreements lacking sound principles and designed only to overcome crises of overproduction and faulty investments. After this war, the cry for an improved organization of our economy will be heard all over the world.

These are but a few, though very important, of the many subsidiary functions that may be integrated in the scope of the Bank of Nations.

In order to utilize to the fullest the immense treasures of our earth for our entire world society, we need a central impulse—a driving force—and above all a financial mechanism to facilitate the most advantageous cultural development of mankind. It is a disgrace to our civilization and culture when, in consequence of a poor harvest, floods, drought, dust storms, soil erosion, or other ravages of the elements, whether in India, China, or Russia, millions of human beings and domestic animals perish from starvation and exhaustion—while in other lands vast surpluses of grain, foodstuffs, cattle, and commodities accumulate.

Under our old capitalist system, the danger of being swept away on a high tide of security capital by cyclical booms and depressions never disappears. After each crash of the stock market a break occurs in the sphere of production, a reversal in the price level, a destruction of productive and real capital, which, in itself, may have had a considerable productive value. Such crises affect not only the small capitalists but also the workers, and such recessions—as we know—increasingly develop into major crises. The time has now come when this primitive amateur method of price jugglery must be replaced by an international system of price regulation.

The Bank for International Settlements has never been more than a hydraulic pump and clearing house for money and an issuing house for securities without substance. It has never contributed to the positive creation of capital. If it remains on this unproductive level, it can never act as a leverage for a superior and uniformly organized world economy. The Bank of Nations, on the other hand, should fulfill an epoch-making task. All great movements have originated in periods of severe crisis. It is unnecessary to reiterate the seriousness of the situation which we are facing. It is the responsibility of the citizens of the world and of their leaders to persevere in striving toward the highest ideals of international well-being and to aim constantly at securing the most efficient and effective operation of our economy.

CHAPTER V

THE EUROPA BANK

WHENEVER, during our era of industrial expansion and capitalist development, a war was waged, the blame for that war was invariably placed on one or the other of the belligerents; arbitrary damages were computed and reparations payments imposed on the guilty party. This spirit of crime and punishment dominated the peace after the Franco-Prussian War and reached its climax after the World War. In the present struggle, we are again running the risk of branding one or more of the belligerents as the bogy who is to blame for all the evil. If statesmen and politicians are to permit themselves to indulge in this fallacy again, the possibility of a fair and lasting peace will be extremely small.

This time, the men who will take it upon themselves to make the peace must realize at the outset that all belligerents are more or less at fault in the present European war and that weaker nations are eventually drawn into the struggle against their will. Without this morally honest and economically sound approach, it would be impossible to create the atmosphere indispensable to a just and lasting peace. I do not underestimate the importance of punishing war mongers; but, in a world of economic wrongs, who is to determine the guilty party and who is to pronounce the verdict? This spirit of revenge and punishment must be replaced by a sincere desire on the part of the peacemakers to correct their mistakes and to cooperate in the reconstruction of the ruins.

Future generations will realize that mercantilist errors lead to the nationalistic upheavals, which were an attempt to wipe out by force the nightmares which these errors created. If we could recognize this now as an undeniable fact, all the nations would have won the war. Unfortunately, such recognition will come only after humanity has passed through the purgatory of the war of wars, the effects and consequences of which are still far beyond our imagination. But I am inclined to believe that this war will be sufficiently horrible to cause men to abandon narrow self-interest in favor of a new spirit more worthy of our human society. Instead of merely preaching the beautiful theories of Christianity and democracy, it would be wiser to devote our endeavors toward the practice of Christianity and democracy.

This time, the problem of reconstruction will consist of more than the simple building up and repairing of destroyed areas, and of reestablishing disrupted international connections. For individual nations have increasingly espoused wasteful and dangerous autarchic ideas. The phantom of self-sufficiency, with all its implications, means a false distribution and application of wealth, which leads but to a dead end. It means a disturbance of both the national and the international economy and the creation of unproductive capital. In the interwar and war periods, those misappropriations served mostly destructive purposes. They ruined world production as much as they did world trade, finally throwing out of gear the already badly unbalanced machinery of the capitalist system.

Among the many phases of international reconstruction and reorganization, we must strive for the gradual elimination of clumsy, restraining customs walls and devastating barter trade, the replacement of substitute enterprises, the gradual reduction of protective subsidies to industry, trade, and agriculture, the general transformation of armament industries into productive peace undertakings, and, finally, housing for the masses and the construction of other utilities.

We know only too well the obstacles and difficulties in the way of such movements as these. We know that a return to orthodox free trade is as impossible as the return to orthodox capitalist individualism. Both free trade and laissez faire capitalism need a new form of organization. For this functional organization no simple cure-all can be found. One thing is certain: A central mechanism must be set up to direct and coordinate this reconstruction. This mechanism will provide us with a relatively simple formula in higher economics, which is as indispensable as simple formulae are in higher mathematics.

Was the first international public banking institution, the Bank for

International Settlements, such a mechanism—a simple but sufficiently comprehensive formula? What was the lesson taught to the world by this world bank which started out with such hopeful potentialities?

One must have witnessed its early origin, organization, and history, in order to understand fully the errors and deficiencies embodied in this instrument of world finance. It represented, in fact, the product of an era of utter misunderstanding of international economic laws, even though it was motivated by many good intentions. In the negotiations concerning the economic problems of the Bank, especially the reparations problem, a spirit of good intentions and understanding on the part of the experts was always evident, frequently conflicting with the political spirit of "payment of reparations" or "liquidation of war debts"—in short, fulfillment of one-sided obligations.

As a persistent worker for a definite settlement of the international debts, from 1920 to 1932, I cannot resist pointing out the paradoxical events of those years: On September 6, 1928, the governments of Great Britain, France, Germany, Belgium, Italy, and Japan made an agreement with regard to the "necessity for a complete and definite settlement of the reparation problem and for the constitution of a committee of financial experts to be nominated for this purpose by the six aforementioned governments."

How badly the results of the agreement, the Young Plan and the Bank for International Settlements were suited to carry out a "complete and definite settlement" of the international debts, has been explained in Chapter II.

But again the reader is invited to review the history of economic developments from 1924 to 1932. If he examines those unfortunate reparations vehicles, he can understand the reason why these institutions failed to put an end to the debts. He will appreciate the difficulties surrounding a mission to bring about a definite understanding and settlement of the international debts between France, Germany, and the world at large. It was the selfish spirit pervading the entire interwar epoch which caused the understanding to break down and culminate in the explosion of 1939.

The first world bank was not an instrument of friendship and collaboration in the reform of our socio-economic world order. Indeed, the foundation of the Bank for International Settlements would never have been proposed as the core of the Young Plan had it not been for two reasons: First, in order to salvage something from the crises and emergencies of the reparations situation, a financial institution of great size and capital power was needed for the future commercialization of war debts; and, second, the Western world still dreamed of a strong instrument with a highly developed issuing technique for large future international loans.

The Bank for International Settlements was never intended to be a democratic institution created out of the urgent necessity of distressed peoples. Its initiators were world-famous bankers, financial experts, and representatives of nationalist advantage, who, in secret sessions, attempted to safeguard their jealous conflicting interests. Public opinion did not play a strong part in this venture. The mass of the people did not understand the technicalities of the proceedings and had been rendered apathetic and indifferent to this significant experiment by the economic consequences of the World War.

In order to understand fully the character and provisions of the Bank for International Settlements, which was the executive organ of the Young Plan, we must explain briefly the tasks of the Dawes Plan of August 30, 1924 (date of the London protocol), and its successor, the Young Plan. The tendency and results of the Dawes Plan provisions clearly show us the motive for the Bank for International Settlements and the reason for the inadequacies of its powers.

When in 1924 the problem of conversion of German currency into reparation "payments," transferable and acceptable to the Allies, was acute, the Dawes Committee urged the selection of five experts, representing the United States, Great Britain, France, Italy, and Belgium, to accomplish this task.[1] These experts were backed by their respective

[1] Part IV, Appendix 6, of the Dawes Report required the "committee of five":

"A. To apply such bank balances as stand to the credit of the Agent General for payments for deliveries in kind and payments under the Reparation Recovery Act, in accordance with the program established periodically by the Reparations Commission, after consultation with the Transfer Committee as to the character and amount of such deliveries;

"B. To convert these bank balances into foreign currencies from time to time, and after conversion, to remit them in accordance with the instruction of the Reparations Commission.

"Both the foregoing powers A and B to be exercised to the extent to which in the judgment

central banks, and the General Agent for Reparation Payments presided over this "committee of five."

We have shown above how the American gold stream stimulated German production and made the task of the Dawes Committee easy at first. But, later, the Transfer Committee was faced with the difficulty of transferring German payments and at the same time maintaining the stability of the mark. We have learned the reasons for the difficulties in the way of German exports, namely, customs barriers set up by receiver countries and their unwillingness or inability to import the highly specialized German goods.

As explained by J. W. Angell, in *Recovery of Germany* (New Haven: Yale Press, 1929), the opinion prevailed in the United States

that for a transition period of 20 or even 30 years, Germany will have to continue to do, what she has been doing since 1924, viz., selling securities and property abroad and negotiating *credits* in order to obtain the funds required *to meet all current obligations.* In other words, during these years, *Germany's capacity to pay abroad will be determined by her capacity to borrow abroad, or to secure the necessary funds from* [italics mine] foreign countries in other ways.[2]

But the more Germany insisted on extending exports in goods and services, the stronger grew the resistance on the other side.

From this unsoluble situation resulted the glorious period of artificially stimulated German exports. Allied nations and importers ardently sought for means to develop additional demand for German products which would not compete with normal imports. These surplus demand products were to be charged to the reparations account, and given as gifts to the receivers of these goods.

In this way the creditors tried to solve the problem of how to avoid

---

of the Committee the foreign exchange market will permit, without threatening the stability of the German currency.

"C. To invest from time to time in bonds or other loans in Germany such amounts as the Committee may deem wise. The Committee shall proceed to make these investments as soon as the amount of the credits exceeds the sum which the Bank will keep on deposit. On the other hand, the Committee may sell the bonds which it has acquired, or liquidate the loans which it has granted, whenever in its opinion the sums may be converted into foreign exchange, or the Bank can accept additional deposits."

[2] Cf. Gideonse, "The International Bank," Rutgers University Bulletin, 1930.

German industrial competition and on the other hand be relieved of tax burdens through German reparation deliveries. On page 18 of the report, *Reparation Payments and Future International Trade*, published by the Committee of Three—Sir Josiah Stamp, N. Pirelli, and U. de Chalandar—we read that

the body of taxpayers and the affected industries overlap and represent the same group of people; [and so long as this was the fact, the import of German payments *in natura* did not conflict with national interests].

The committee further explains:

So long as a special reparation scheme represents merely a method of easing the accumulating fund, and promoting exports from Germany, and to the receiving country appears nothing but a dumping of alien goods in immediate competition with its own labor and capital, so long will the problem be politically unsoluble. But if every scheme owes its genesis to the necessity for a reparation outlet, at the same time creates a demand for home labor and industry which would otherwise be immediately called for, the sting of the opposition for it will be drawn. The two interests must be "married" in each scheme.

At the end of the report a "standing organization" is proposed, to distribute

the German surplus on the widest scale to all the world, and so preventing a localised slump in prices, enlisting the interests of all parties, deciding relative eligibility of schemes, keeping the total not too large or too small, standardizing methods of enquiry and finance, and so preventing the glut of ill-advised and ill-assorted claims which would come from uncoordinated effort with the speculator and promoter rampant.

In short, as stated by Gideonse:

The general idea of this "marriage plan" is, that a certain proportion of their expense should go to home labor and industry, while the balance would be supplied by German imports. The "standing organization" would have as one of its main functions to select only those proposals which could ultimately be placed on the investment market on an independent basis.

Or, in the words of Sir Josiah Stamp:

No problem ought to be worse, but rather the better, for systematic and orderly regulation and coordination in place of blind and unrelated force

This moreover was not a new idea, for as far back as 1922 the Credit Committee of the Genoa Conference had also recommended an international institution for "the examination of opportunities for undertaking work in connection with European reconstruction and assisting in the financing of such undertaking."

This proposal [Gideonse states] which had been endorsed by the Supreme Council in a resolution of Jan. 10, 1922 [Cf. Cmd. 1621/1922, pp. 5-6] was the first indication that the Creditor Nations were growing aware of the fact, that the reception of large payment on reparation account might involve sacrifices which could conceivably be handled *more efficiently through a international semipublic body* [italics mine] than through the separate public authorities themselves.

However, although under the Dawes Plan some of these assisted projects had been performed, there was no general authority for these assisted schemes.

As a result, on the basis of the report of the Committee of Three headed by Sir Josiah Stamp, and on the recommendation of the Transfer Committee of the Dawes Plan, a permanent apparatus for the financing of reparations schemes and payments was created in the Bank for International Settlements. The B.I.S. was authorized to transform the Transfer Committee of the Dawes Plan into a permanent clearing and assisting institution.

In my book, *The World Credit and Finance Reform,* and in the memorandum on the Bank of Nations of 1922 (proposed to the Genoa Conference—see Appendix) a joint Franco-German reparations system was proposed, to build up the destroyed areas of France and Belgium. However, by the time the Bank for International Settlements was organized, these countries had already rebuilt their ruins on their own account, and the German "reparation" payments were unable to fulfill their original purpose. But, instead of putting an end to these payments, a new era of huge public and semipublic works for coordinated use of reparations payments, the so-called "assisted schemes," was started. In France and the French colonies, electric power enterprises and railroad and harbor constructions were planned and partly carried out. But, as Gideonse states: "The greatest obstacle to wide employment of the idea of the 'assisted schemes' lies in the relatively small number of appropriate projects that have been found to be commercially attractive."[3]

Between 1929 and 1932, hundreds of such propositions were "discussed" in Paris. I had the privilege of examining the most fantastic projects born out of the spirit of "let Germany pay" (but never performed), which the German Embassy in Paris placed before me. The following are a few examples: Automobile highways through the Sahara Desert connecting visionary winter resorts with paradise-like oases, sponsored by the Citroën Motor Company; Senator Mahieu's Trans-Sahara Railway; a "Golden Gate" bridge spanning the Straits of Gibraltar as part of an Europa-African railway system; irrigation of the Sahara Desert so as to make it navigable, with ports and harbor construction; horticultural projects in the Sahara Desert for the French perfume industry; a huge gambling casino project to construct casinos for the Côte d'Azur, Côte Basque, Normandy, and Brittany; the "Eurafrica" Company for the exploitation of the African continent; and other very inviting mirage-like fantasies to cost billions of francs. It was a rare experience.

Finally, there was the possibility of endowing foreign countries—China, Russia, in South America, and elsewhere—with German reparation works. Of this search for worth-while ventures, Gideonse writes:

Here political difficulties and possibilities of conflict with industries which are beyond the control of the reparation creditors, increase—and here precisely is where the new Bank for International Settlements will have to perform its functions in welding together still broader interests than those of the industrial groups and the taxpayers of the creditor nations.[4]

[3] The following is an example of how the scheme worked: "The plans for the construction of railroads and waterworks in Indo-China provide the use of large shipments of German goods, in payment for which the Indo-Chinese government signs 5 per cent bonds to the Paris government. The German products are paid in reichsmarks from the French share in the reparation annuities. In this case the advantages of both parties are quite clear. Paris received a series of bonds which are particularly acceptable to its bondbuyers in return for its German credits, and Indo-China enjoys very much more favorable treatment than it would receive in negotiating credits under ordinary circumstances. . . ." (Gideonse, *op. cit.*)

[4] *Ibid.*, p. 14.

PLAN FOR PERMANENT PEACE

We know how the crash of 1929 and the depression which followed brought the entire reparations dream to a deadlock. In the light of the aforementioned experiences, the reader will be able to realize that the absurdity of the whole reparations system will probably never be surpassed.

Let us now go on to the functions of the Bank for International Settlements itself. We may divide them into reparations and credit, banking and clearing.

A. REPARATIONS AND CREDIT FUNCTIONS

The Young Committee, as it emphasizes in its report, intended

to set up an institution whose direction from the start shall be *cooperative and international* [italics mine] in character; whose members shall engage themselves to banish the atmosphere of the war, to obliterate its animosities, its partisanships, its tendencious phrases, and to work together for a common end in a spirit of mutual interest and good-will.

What a lovely melody and how aesthetic its qualities! Why did it have to be played upon so discordant an instrument as "reparations"?

When the Young Plan was formulated, the obligations of Germany were still gigantic. Under the Dawes Plan, she was still paying an annuity of two billion, five hundred million reichsmarks and, in addition, an undefined amount dependent upon a prosperity index. The Young Plan modified this payment and divided the annuity into two parts: (a) six hundred and sixty million reichsmarks which were unconditional, and (b) more than one billion which were conditional under certain circumstances.

The unconditional part of the six hundred and sixty million was "payable without any right of postponement of any kind in foreign currencies," and was guaranteed by the income from the German Railway Company and paid directly to the Bank for International Settlements via the Reichsbank. A special right of "mobilization" of the unconditional part of the annuity was granted to the creditors.

As for the conditional part of more than one billion, the Young Plan provided that the German government should give at least 90 days' prior notice of the right to suspend the transfer of the postponable part of the annuities, in case an exceptional emergency interrupts the normal course of economic life, to which the scheme is adapted. Germany will thus be enabled, under certain circumstances, temporarily to relieve her balance of payments and will, in fact, enjoy the advantages of a form of transfer protection without its attendant limitation.

In case notice was given an Advisory Committee had to

consider the circumstances and conditions which had led up to the necessity for postponement. [This was a lengthy process and these precautions were only intended] to protect Germany against the possible consequences of a *comparatively short period* [italics mine] of depression.

But, even if Germany were to give notice, the entire sum was first to be paid into the Reichsbank, to the account of the Bank for International Settlements, and its larger part actually transferred.

The right to postpone payments was only to arise *after* the right to withhold transfer had been in force *for one year*; [and this was to apply to only] 50 per cent of any sum the transfer of which shall then be susceptible of postponement under the conditions stated above.

These provisions did not foresee the crash of 1929 and the lasting depression which followed. And, when in 1931 the disaster began to move with amazing rapidity, Germany was unable to wait one year (and ninety days) for the relief to her budget. Germany did not call in the Special Advisory Committee. The nationalists—for political reasons and for reasons of credit prestige—thereby circumvented the right of this Committee to investigate. It was at a time when "the Young Plan had become extremely unpopular." As Lansing Dulles correctly affirms: "Any further official recognition of it, even to ask postponement, might lead to an overthrow of the Government. For these reasons Germany appealed instead through her ambassadors and high officials for more immediate and substantial relief."

This need for relief resulted in the "standstill" agreement first outlined by the Wiggin Committee. This standstill agreement has been prolonged ad infinitum. And the German Railway Company, the income of which was to guarantee the payments, was taken over by the nazi government in May, 1940.

Gideonse summarizes the reparation functions of the Bank for International Settlements as follows:

1. Service as a trustee to whom the payments in foreign currencies and reichsmarks are to be made by Germany and by whom the distribution to the appropriate recipients is to be managed.

2. Service as a common centre of action and authority in the problems of mobilization and commercialization for the purpose of coordinating and controlling the arrangements—a service which requires an authority of a continuous and permanent character in order to obtain the confidence of prospective bond buyers.

3. The Service in directing and controlling the continued existence of deliveries in kind, at any rate for a period of years, and perhaps—through the operation of the Advisory Committee in case of difficulties with the postponable part of the annuity—for the entire duration of the plan.

4. Authority to take the necessary action in connection with a declaration of postponement of the postponable part of the annuity, including the convening of an Advisory Committee—international in character and existing as a constituent part of this central authority—to consider the situation which had brought about a necessity for a postponement or the situation which a postponement itself created.

5. Authority to arrange for the discharge, either exceptionally or regularly as part of the plan, of payments in marks within Germany (for instance in case of postponement of transfer or of purchases of German goods) and authority to dispose of such funds and assets in the interests of the creditors by arrangement with the Reichsbank or other German authority.

So much for reparations—now what about credits?

Moreover [the Young Committee stated], in so far as the task of transferring the payments into foreign currencies is involved, besides a restriction of imports, an extension of German export trade, we envisaged the possibility of a financial institution that should be prepared to promote the increase of world trade by financing projects, particularly in undeveloped countries, which might otherwise not be attempted through the ordinary existing channels.

In Part 6 of the Young Report, on the functions of the Bank, we also find that

by judicious non-competitive financial development the bank should prove a useful instrument for opening up new fields of commerce, of supply and of demand, and will thus help to solve Germany's special problem without encroaching on the activities of existing institutions. . . . These new facilities should augment and perfect existing arrangements for carrying through international settlements. . . . *The Bank will be in a position to open up to trade new possibilities of development* [italics mine].

Meanwhile, the world has learned how little the Bank for International Settlements was able to live up to these expectations.

One of the greatest disappointments of the Bank for International Settlements, especially for Germany, was its negligible short- and long-term credit policy. In the Young Plan discussions in Paris, the extension of short-term credits for the stimulation of exports and trade was frequently urged. Later, in 1931, the Bank for International Settlements favored the conversion of short-term into medium- or long-term credits. Further, the extension of long-term credits to China, Russia, the Balkan countries, and others and the financing of mortgage banks were planned. But none of these laudable intentions materialized. In one case a bond issue of an international mortgage bank was bought, but no creative credit activities were performed at all.

As Lansing Dulles states:[5]

The decision in all such matters was definitely influenced by the two schools of thought which had existed since the origin of the Bank. One represented by the Germans and Belgians urged the creation of credit, the development of backward countries, and stimulus to export trade; the other, represented by the French and Americans, urged that the Bank was not equipped for such work, and that it would be going counter to sound finance if it moved in this direction. The Italians were against such a development, while the English were divided in their views . . . some were eager to develop the lending side of the Bank's potentialities, and others its rescue work, advisory functions, and technical studies.

For Germany this unproductiveness of the Bank for International Settlements was very discouraging. German youth openly revolted.[6] Lansing Dulles gives a vivid presentation of this general disillusionment and ill-feeling:

[5] *Op. cit.*, p. 203.
[6] *Op. cit.*, pp. 300-302.

The Bank was bound in the interests of cooperation and constructive banking to help German credit and exchange. Within the limits set by its resources it did so, constantly. For two reasons, however, this accomplishment failed to satisfy German desires. One was that the efforts of the Bank in this respect were not given wide publicity. The other was that the Bank did not, or could not, carry out some of the more ambitious suggestions in the Young Plan.

In the first place, the Young Plan envisaged an institution that would promote world trade by financing large projects, particularly in undeveloped countries, and thus serve the interests of German trade. Then in the second place, the Plan indicated that real cooperation called for a reduction of obstacles in the free working of economic forces. These two hopes were grievously disappointed. The Plan could not, of course, bind the nations to a liberal policy, but it implied efforts in this direction, either through the activities of the Bank in particular or through other efforts of the nations subscribing to the Plan.

A third reason for claiming that Germany had been deceived by false hopes was that the financial relief offered by the reduction of annuities was wiped out by the rapid fall in prices that took place in 1930. This meant that the monthly payments were equal to or greater than the Dawes schedule in terms of gold or goods. Thus, in three respects, the Young Plan seemed to bring disillusionment—it did not extend Germany's export trade, it did not lessen tariffs and other international obstacles, and it did not offer as much direct relief as its authors had intended.

Germany had counted on these things and more from the Paris Conference. The first offer which they made was much below the figures finally accepted. While it is true that they would naturally offer much less than they might expect as a final settlement, nevertheless, the way in which the offer was made and the attitude of the press indicate that they hoped for extensive gains. The flight from the mark, a very alarming episode during the course of the long negotiations, indicates disillusionment in Germany as well as bearish sentiment outside. It is probable that they would not have been willing to have revision at this time if they had not expected a larger concession, although a categorical statement is unwise in so complex a situation. A final agreement was made possible partly by the hopes which Dr. Schacht entertained that there would be an increase of exports through the new Bank. This might, in fact, have been possible had not future economic troubles, combined with limitations placed on the Bank's activities, effectively stopped efforts along this line.

While attention was being focused on this matter the whole complexion of economic life altered. All nations were faced with declining production. This was first observable in the United States in July, 1929, although it was not generally recognized for several months. The recession in other countries came a little later. They were all faced with the political and economic necessity of trying to preserve the standard of living, export trade, budget balance, and social stability. In so doing they resorted to measures which intensified national rivalry and ill feelings.

In Chapter II we have explained the fatal economic consequences of this bitter disillusionment, violently encountering the grave world depression, and how these conditions were exploited for political propaganda purposes in pre-nazi Germany.

B. BANKING AND CLEARING FUNCTIONS

In the January, 1930, number of the Parisian journal, *Evolution,* in an editorial, "La Banque des peuples, instrument économique de la paix," designed to serve the international appeasement and rapprochement of nations, I stated:

We should not fail to recognize the possibility of progressive organization offered by the Bank for International Settlements. . . . Whether, however, the ultimate goal of its functions can be attained, namely, the control and equalization of business cycles and the constant progress of capital accumulation in a capitalistically organized world economy, is extremely doubtful.

From the anarchic world of individualistic competitive economy, which is only insufficiently regulated by separate trust and cartel monopolies, suddenly a peak banking organization emerges. The world predicts for it a splendid future, with development of tremendous powers. But nobody is certain of the beneficial effects of its future financial activities.

Many different opinions were heard. Some believed the Bank for International Settlements was quite harmless, others feared the birth of a capitalistic vampire which would bleed the world, or, as Gideonse puts it, "destroy national sovereignty in economic and financial matters and replace the government of the world by democratic institutions with oligarchical control of a small group of mutually interdependent banking interests";—or, to quote Chairman McFadden of the House Banking and Currency Committee, "make a new epoch in world financial history and to be the basis of the greatest danger free government has had to fear in centuries." There are many similar utterances which can be heard and read today about the Hemisphere Bank.

We can really appreciate the banking functions of the Bank for International Settlements only if we look at the postwar gold situation. What was the general consensus with regard to the gold problem of 1930?

In the capitalist world, during the gold standard era, the increase in gold production was always thought to be one of the most important conditions for progress in the production of goods. According to the logic of the gold standard an increase in the media of exchange proportionate to the volume of the rise in commodity production was necessary, the basis of the media of exchange, naturally, being gold. It was believed that only under that condition would steadily increased and enlarged reproduction of capital, *the very basis of all economic progress,* take place.

During the twenties, although the gold standard was reintroduced in most countries, gold had become such an expensive medium of circulation that nations were forced to use it generally only as coverage for national paper money and to store it for this purpose in the vaults of their central banks. If the increase in gold coverage was not possible in the customary degree, it was assumed that immediately a deadlock in the progress of world production would set in. Keynes estimated an average annual progress of three per cent in the volume of the world's economic production. The demand for gold in the world would rise in the same proportion if we would everywhere maintain our gold currency on the traditional basis.

In the late twenties, however, gold production in the leading productive countries began to show a remarkable decrease. The estimates of Robert Kotze, the expert of the Government of the Union of South Africa, were so pessimistic that he predicted in 1930 that in ten years our gold production would amount to only 18 per cent of the 1930 level.

With South African mines producing about 50 per cent of the world's gold and no other important discovery of gold mines (except in Siberia) in sight, the danger of a strong international shortage of gold seemed evident. Such shortage of gold would bring about a rise in the price of gold by leaps and bounds, and a decline in the price level of goods.

These changes in prices—according to gold stocks in the various countries—would then occur quite irregularly and cause considerable disturbance of world trade. It was the anticipated scarcity in gold, therefore, that forced the nations more and more to take definite steps in the control of the application of gold for monetary purposes. An important activity was in sight for the Bank for International Settlements, namely, to take direct steps toward a restriction in the use of gold for monetary purposes. It was further believed that only a unified systematic regulation in the supply and distribution of gold could help in this case.

As we know, Mr. Kotze's historic statement and prediction have not proved to be correct. The high price put on gold has given a great incentive to gold production all over the world. The League of Nations statistics show that world gold production (in terms of kilograms) increased from six hundred and ten thousand kilograms in 1929 to one million, eighty thousand kilograms in 1937, and keeps on increasing at an approximate rate of 3½ per cent. (Russia has not disclosed its figures since 1938.)[7]

In 1929, one kilogram of gold was valued at $664.55, and ever since January 1, 1934—following the devaluation of the dollar—one kilogram of gold has been valued at $1,125.27; so that the dollar value of new gold production is now roughly three times what it was in 1929. But the fear of inadequacy in gold production was a deciding factor in the abandonment of the gold standard in leading countries in the early thirties.

In the prevailing opinion, one of the major tasks incumbent upon the Bank for International Settlements was the safeguarding and control of the entire system of gold currencies, upon which the largest part of world trade depended. At the outset, countries with paper and silver currency were excluded from participation in the Bank. The Bank for International Settlements was supposed to give support to central banks in their endeavor to maintain their national gold currency. Furthermore,

[7] Littlepage has disclosed much of what the Russian government has hidden: Russia is the second strongest gold-producing country in the world, with substantial unknown gold funds and mines. It may be that the new European war or peace will bring much of these undisclosed gold sources to the surface and that in that event other reasons than those of currency technique alone, namely, reasons of Russian or international politics, may bring the world back to the gold standard. (See Chapter III, pp. 96 ff. for a fuller discussion of the gold problem today.)

the B.I.S. was to extend short-term gold credits for this purpose or to supply the necessary foreign currency in case of rising rates of exchange. The Bank was therefore expected to dispose of its own funds of gold and media of exchange. It had to accept gold deposits from the leading central banks and open up a clearing intercourse on this basis. It was expected that in this way unnecessary gold shipments *in natura* could be avoided and that at the right time each individual country could dispose of the gold necessary for currency purposes.

Each central bank was given the right to reject such measures taken by the Bank for International Settlements as were apt to influence their individual currency disposition. The entire system of regulations could therefore only be performed by means of voluntary agreements. Any future regulation by force was excluded.

Authorized Banking Functions

The banking functions of the Bank for International Settlements are set forth in Art. 22-26 of the Statutes as follows:

The Bank may in particular:

(a) Buy and sell gold coin or bullion for its own account or for the account of central banks;

(b) hold gold for its own account under earmark in central banks;

(c) accept the custody of gold for account of central banks;

(d) make advances to or borrow from central banks against gold, bills of exchange and other short-term obligations of prime liquidity or other approved securities;

(e) discount, rediscount, purchase or sell with *or* without its endorsement bills of exchange, cheques and other short-term obligations of prime liquidity, including Treasury Bills and other such Government short-term securities as are currently marketable;

(f) buy and sell exchange for its own account or for the account of central banks;

(g) buy and sell negotiable securities other than shares for its own account or for the account of central banks;

(h) discount for central banks bills taken from their portfolio and rediscount with central banks bills taken from its own portfolio;

(i) open and maintain current or deposit accounts with central banks;

(j) accept:

(1) deposits from central banks on account or deposit account;

(2) deposits in connection with trustee agreements that may be made between the Bank and Governments in connection with international settlements;

(3) such other deposits as in the opinion of the Board come within the scope of the Bank's functions.

The Bank may also:

(k) act as agent or correspondent of any central bank;

(l) arrange with any central bank for the latter to act as its agent or correspondent. If a central bank is unable or unwilling to act in this capacity, the Bank may make other arrangements, provided that the central bank concerned does not object. If in such circumstances it should be deemed advisable that the Bank should establish its own agency, the sanction of two-thirds majority of the Board will be required;

(m) enter into agreements to act as trustee or agent in connection with international settlements, provided that such agreements shall not encroach on the obligations of the Bank towards third parties; and carry out the various operations laid down therein.

The following provisions with regard to profits were made:

a. Five per cent of the yearly net profits shall go to the legal reserve fund until it reaches ten per cent of the paid-in capital stock.

b. After this provision has been fulfilled, a cumulative dividend of six per cent on the paid-in share of the capital shall be paid.

c. Twenty per cent of the remainder is to go to the dividend until a maximum of twelve per cent is reached. The directors may decide to reserve this for use in maintaining the cumulative dividend.

d. After making the foregoing provisions one-half of the balance of the profits are to go to the general reserve until it equals the paid-in capital. Thereafter the contribution to the general reserve is to decrease gradually from forty per cent to five per cent, according to a series of proportions between the paid-in capital and the general reserve set up in the plan.

e. The remainder of the profits will be divided as follows:

(i) Seventy-five per cent to the government or central banks which maintain time deposits at the Bank withdrawable in not less than five years from the time of deposit, and after five years, on not less than one year's notice. This shall be divided annually in proportion to the size of the deposits maintained.

(ii) Twenty-five per cent to be used to aid Germany to pay the last twenty-two annuities provided the German Government elects to maintain a long-term deposit—amounting to the minimum sum of 400,000,000 reichsmarks. If the deposit is smaller, the participation is to be in proportion and the balance of the profits will go to the purpose described in (i) above.[8]

With untiring efforts, Lansing Dulles has ably preserved the history and experiences of the first three years of operation of the Bank for International Settlements, invaluable for similar future creations, such as the Hemisphere Bank or the Bank of Nations.

The banking revolution of the thirties, with its holidays and moratoria, standstill agreements, etc., have forced the Bank for International Settlements to change its gold and banking prescriptions and usages. While far from stabilizing the world credit structure, the Bank for International Settlements has, however, weathered the storms of depression, totalitarian revolution, and war.

It was clear from the outset that the functions of centralized gold settlements and clearing would attract the cooperation of the United States, because the Federal Reserve System has in many respects been a model for the Bank for International Settlements' banking functions.[9]

THE BANK FOR INTERNATIONAL SETTLEMENTS DURING THE SECOND
WORLD WAR

During the present war, as Jules Sauerwein has stated in his interview[10] with the American banker, Thomas McKittrick, Chairman of the Board of the Bank for International Settlements, the bank has carried on its work with remarkable perseverance:

The peculiar thing about the Bank for International Settlements is that it is one international institution that has not retired to the sidelines but has successfully stayed in the running throughout these catastrophic months which marked the collapse of the very structure of European nations. It offers the unique spectacle of a meeting ground of high-ranking representatives of warring countries who collaborate daily without a single hitch in the name of their respective national banks.

[8] Cf. Statutes, Art. 53.
[9] For the theoretical results of an ideal clearing system, see Lansing Dulles, *op. cit.*, pp. 274-75.
[10] *New York Times*, Sept. 30, 1940.

THE EUROPA BANK

To see this remarkable outfit at work one might almost get the impression of being on another planet out in space, remote from terrestrial squabbles, and in the presence of an organism having nothing to do with the life of nations—unless as an example of what might have been had the world been a good deal wiser. But when closer observation reveals that such down-to-earth realities as dollars, gold and a portion of every country's monetary resources are involved, one becomes aware that the Bank for International Settlements is far from being a mirage, and is worth an examination, not simply as an ephemeral curiosity but as an institution definitely here to stay. It is no phantasmagoria bound to vanish in the Alpine mists.

The substantial individuals directing that body certainly bear no resemblance to mythical beings. Until May, 1940, the administrative council was presided over by the British banker, Otto Niemeyr, with a Belgian and a Japanese vice presidents. Three of the administrators are Walther Funk, Reichs Minister of Economics; Montagu Norman, Governor of the Bank of England, and the Marquis de Vogue, outstanding French financier. Among the directors we find Roger Aubouin of France, Paul Hechler of Germany, Dr. Raffaele Pilotti of Italy and Marcel van Zeeland, brother of the former Belgian Prime Minister. . . .

. . . Back of the faith which keeps them going is the certainty that, no matter what the nature of the peace treaties that will put an end to the military and political hostilities, there will have to be a cessation of economic hostilities in their wake, and that such an economic peace must be world-wide if it is to exist at all. A good omen, though it is insufficient, to justify any naive optimism, is the fact that there has been no objection formulated from any quarter regarding the activities of the bank, that the monetary restrictions imposed by the various States were raised on its behalf and that the interest on the bank's peace-time loans has been scrupulously and regularly paid. Here we are in the presence of facts and not merely wishful thinking. The directors of the B.I.S. find a source of encouragement in their own experience of the last ten years, but above all in that of the last twelve months, for their confidence in the coming reconstruction of European and world economy.

With regard to the future of the Bank for International Settlements, Mr. McKittrick makes an encouraging statement in the conclusions presented at the end of his report to the general shareholders' meeting of the bank on May 27, 1940:

PLAN FOR PERMANENT PEACE

In a great part of the world the needs of war have overshadowed the financial and economic considerations of normal times. A large part of the controls imposed by the governments as well as the crisis in trade and in the economic and financial systems will be, we may hope, of a temporary nature But under the troubles of war there is no doubt that basic changes are taking place, that they are due to have repercussions on the future of Europe and the world and that the post-war generation will have to face not only the consequences of the conflict but also the effects of these hypothecary and permanent changes.

It is of capital importance that there be, at the close of the hostilities, an exact picture of the situation and of its urgent problems. The delays due to incompetence must be reduced to a minimum. Post-war regeneration through the means and resources at the world's disposal should not be an impossible task, deplorable as the ruination may have been. Thanks to the experience of the past twenty-five years, we understand monetary and trade problems much better than at the close of the last war, and we are much better equipped for solving them. Men in practically every nation have been devoting themselves much more than formerly, to questions of this kind. The information from every country, aside from certain details kept secret for military reasons, forms an imposing collection. With the help of national institutions there should be satisfactory possibilities for a correct analysis of the international situation as soon as the war ends.

Naturally the deciding factor without which no amount of competence could be effective is the desire of the nations to cooperate and reorganize the world reasonably. But if this good-will exists we shall have adequate means at our disposal for the urgent work of reconstruction.

And after this war? Will the world have learned a lesson? Will the international war debts be eliminated, or new war debtors created? In the present war, we have harvested the fruits of the old method of reparation settlements; in the future a mutual enterprise must guide us to heal the wounds and losses of the greatest disaster in the history of mankind. We must change an economic system which has been proved to result periodically in financial catastrophes and human tragedies, a system which mercilessly leads to peaks and depressions whose ultimate correctives are nothing but wars and revolutions.

It is not necessary to "toss out the baby with the bath." The problem can be solved on the basis of a reformed capitalist system, if the leading spirits of our present capitalist society are willing to cooperate and to give up their passive or active resistance. If, on the continent of Europe, miracles of organization for destructive purposes have arisen out of distress, we can and must create and organize constructive works to the best of our abilities when peace is in sight.

A EUROPA BANK?

The constant cooperation of the leading central banks for the purpose of arriving at international settlements has proved to be very useful and will probably never be given up. A central banking mechanism will be the minimum of future world financial cooperation. The Bank for International Settlements has laid the groundwork for the future organization of a true Bank of Nations, to stabilize and safeguard the credit structure of the world and to create international money and credit.

If, after the present war, continents or groups of nations demand their own continental or group banks, such as the Hemisphere Bank or even an Oriental Bank, the Bank for International Settlements might well be transformed into a Europa Bank. The extent of functions of this Europa Bank largely depends upon the domestic and foreign monetary policy of the United States and other nations. If, for instance, the United States agrees with the twenty-one American republics on issuing a common inter-American currency by means of the Hemisphere Bank, the Europa Bank would probably have to balance this action by creating a European medium of exchange, and so, logically, a proposed eastern Asia bank would create its own oriental currency. This question will be treated in Chapters VI and VII on the Inter-American and Oriental Banks. Large empires would, perhaps, prefer to maintain their own currency for their respective empires, or currency unions might be formed among blocs of nations or empires. England and France had unified their economies as a wartime expediency,[11] and similar policies may be applied to a permanent European economic union or federation when the war is ended.

The extent of the long- and short-term credit policy of the Europa

[11] The Pétain government has "pegged" the franc to the dollar.

Bank again is dependent upon the question of whether—first through the establishment of group banks—a transition period of group and empire economies is brought to life, or if a complete world solution is preferred at the very outset. The powers of the proposed Hemisphere Bank represent only one of the various possibilities of assorted potentialities and functions for such continental or group banks. This question must be carefully examined and adjusted to the individual circumstances. But the various group or continental banks could certainly not dispense with a true World Bank as central economic world authority.

EUROPA BANK OR BANK OF NATIONS?

The future of the Bank for International Settlements depends entirely upon the mentality of the peacemaking powers at the end of the present world war.

In a discussion following one of my recent lectures, condemning the contradictory policies of the Reparations and Transfer Systems and the unbearable burdens imposed on Germany by the Allies, a member of the audience raised this very significant question: "What would Germany have done, had she been victorious in World War I?" I had never been asked such a question before, but I answered instinctively "She would probably have made exactly the same mistakes as did the Allies." My reply was evidently an unexpected surprise, because it aroused the spontaneous applause of the audience.

Since that time I have often pondered what Germany would really do if she were victorious in World War II. Reparations? Contributions. Who would be the debtors or contributors? Would she repeat or reverse the psychology of 1919? Or, would Germany remake history. This question greatly depends upon a one-sided victory, in which cannot as yet believe.

But there are hopeful signs, experiences of the last twenty years which make me believe that we need not be too pessimistic about the next peace. There was Count Coudenhove Kalergi, the distinguished Austrian-Japanese writer of *Pan-Europa* and editor of the magazine of the same name, who, like Clarence K. Streit, supporter of the demo cratic *Union Now*[12] idea of 1939, promoted a Pan-European movement, displaying his brilliant talent of oratory before a faithful community of European intellectuals. There were Loucheur, Herriot, and Briand in France; Schacht, Stresemann, and many other prominent statesmen in Germany; Sir Arthur Salter, Lloyd George, and Neville Chamberlain in England, all commenting favorably on a "United States of Europe." While Count Coudenhove Kalergi stressed the necessity of an economic union of western European nations as a balance against such gigantic capitalist powers as the United States, the British Empire, the state capitalist Soviet Russia, and the future eastern Asia bloc, Briand conceded the economic task of Pan-Europa a secondary place. Briand conceived of a federal union of separate states with sovereign rights and believed that international cartels would be able to reorganize and nationalize the economic system of Europe. The 1930 Briand "Memorandum on the Organization of a Regime of European Federal Union" provided for representation of all European governments which were members of the League of Nations. In addition a Permanent Political Committee was to be formed, to prepare a program including the study of political, economic, social, and other questions of European interest not yet handled by the League of Nations. A permanent secretariat in Geneva was to deal with the administrative functions of the organization.

Briand's plan was supported by the Belgian Foreign Minister, Paul Hymans, and by Salvador de Madariaga, a Spanish representative at the League of Nations. One of the most fervent supporters of the Pan-Europa idea up to the present day has been Edward Beneš, former President of Czecho-Slovakia. In Germany, Austria, and Scandinavia the Briand movement was matched by local committees, and in Stockholm the joint Scandinavian committee drafted the first constitution for a Federation of Europe. Later the idea of Federation was further developed, and a professional army, an international police force, an international tribunal, and other interstate organizations proposed.

In June, 1930, Winston Churchill published an enlightened article

---

[12] Clarence K. Streit, *Union Now*. (London: Jonathan Cape, Ltd.) A useful bibliography on the various proposals for international organization, is that prepared by the Carnegie Endowment for International Peace, "The New World Order," Select Bibliographies No. 10, (Washington, D. C.).

in *Nord und Süd,* edited by Professor Ludwig Stein, in the same issue
in which my first pamphlet on "The future economic and social tasks
of the World Bank" was published. In 1935, Lord Davis and Winston
Churchill founded "The New Commonwealth," sponsored by British
Tories, without much practical consequence.

In his highly stimulating book, *The United States of Europe,*[13] Alfred
Bingham has done more, perhaps, than anyone else to clear the way and
to explain the basis for a 1940 Pan-Europa movement. He draws our
attention to the particularly timely words of Winston Churchill spoken
before the "New Commonwealth" on November 25, 1936.[14]

Churchill addressed the "New Commonwealth" as follows: "Where we
differ from other peace societies is that we contemplate and advocate the
use of force against the aggressor in support of law. We think it utterly
futile to have a League of Nations or an international Court unless behind
that there is an armed organized force capable of procuring respect for
their decisions."

Churchill was one of the first to see that the airplane had ended Britain's
insular security. In calling for a "reign of law in Europe" he said:

"In all this there stands first and foremost the interests and safety of Great
Britain and the British Empire. . . . It seems very unlikely that the world
will be able to preserve any semblance of civilization unless bombing air
power is brought under complete control of an international organization."

During the last half dozen years [Bingham points out], as Japan, Italy,
and Germany successively set out on careers of conquest and reduced the
League to a powerless "front" for the "have" nations, collective security
against aggression came to depend not on any international machinery but
on military alliances between Britain and France and such other powers,
including the Soviet Union, as they might secure from time to time. With
the possible exception of the New Commonwealth almost the only voices
that kept alive the idea of an inclusive international organization during this
final grim period were those of the peace societies.

It was they or their precursors who had made the ground fertile for the
League of Nations idea in the last war. It was the League of Nations Unions
and Societies that built up such loyalty as there was toward the infant world
government during the 1920's. It was such bodies as the Women's International League for Peace and Freedom, the War Resisters League, the

[13] Alfred Bingham, *The United States of Europe.* (New York: Duell, Sloan and Pearce, 1940.)
[14] *Ibid.,* pp. 62-63.

Fellowship of Reconciliation, which kept drilling into millions of minds in various countries not only that war was stupid and horrible, but that peace must be *built*, and that it required effective international institutions.

As brave thinkers in many countries face today the task of a comprehensive attack on all the basic economic and political problems of Europe and the world, they can build where others have already built. For generations, while some people have waged war, others have thought and planned and worked for human unity.

The main reasons why I so far have never wholeheartedly supported the Pan-Europa idea are these: During Count Coudenhove Kalergi's admirable efforts, I strongly felt that without the inclusion of at least its fertile hinterland, Soviet Russia, the European continent would remain economically a torso, and the economic solution of the Pan-Europa problem was obviously the decisive prerequisite to its success politically. This solution was dependent upon a creative Europa Bank of partners with equal rights. Here the first difficulties arose, because the League of Nations was far from encouraging equality among European nations.

The Briand proposals neglected the economic solution to an unsupportable degree. He insisted, for instance, that "a customs union could not be a first step but must be one of the last," as Bingham states, "and he was among the clearest exponents of the theory that publicly supervised international cartels provide the readiest machinery for rationalizing Europe's economic system."

Last, but not least, the exclusion of England, involuntarily or by preference, from a European federation did not agree with my concept of an efficient European economic organization. Instinctively, I have always tended toward a more comprehensive and possibly world-wide solution.

For political and economic reasons the idea of union among European nations is very sound in principle. Such union offers a possibility to do away with the mutually exclusive trade barriers and disturbing nationalist and political ambitions. The combination and welding together of the overpopulated industrial nations of Europe with the underpopulated agricultural nations into an enlarged market is vital for the peace of Europe and of the world. To exclude Russia from this enlarged European market would be as illogical as the exclusion of a European federation from the outer world market.

With the inclusion of France in the economic union of European nations, it would be possible to solve the two main problems which until now have prevented a sensible solution of Pan-European plans:

1. The colonial question. If the French colonial empire and the former German colonies became part of the new European union, a main obstacle for appeasement would be eliminated.

2. Definite disarmament of Europe. This could be accomplished and security for all European nations cemented in European economic security. It is needless to explain how this would improve the world disarmament and peace situation. Only an economic European union can bring freedom to its members.

The most powerful instrument and the most vital motor for all these developments toward a socio-economic, as well as a political, peace in this most belligerent and revolutionary part of the world would be the transformation of the Bank for International Settlements into a creative Europa Bank or—if possible—a Bank of Nations. The *furor teutonicus* may find the fulfilment of its "mission" in having unwittingly laid the ground for a constructive work of peace.

A NAZI EUROPA BANK?

Although Schacht was relieved of his post at the head of the Reichsbank, and thus is no longer in control of nazi finances, it has long been rumored that he was commissioned by Hitler to draw up post-war plans. In Chapter III it was also pointed out that the Goering Brain Trust, the Goebbels-Ley-Himmler trio, and the Army have ideas of their own on this subject. There has been published in *The Nation* an outline of Schacht's plan which is worthy of our attention.[15]

If *The Nation's* correspondent is correctly informed Schacht's plan is as follows:

[Under the presumption that] Germany and Italy will reorganize the entire

[15] At this time the Schacht plan has as yet not been released, but *The Nation*, Sept. 7, 1940, has published a statement from a prominent Swedish journalist based on an interview with Schacht himself, and vouches for its authenticity. Even if this report is not fully accurate or complete, we can clearly recognize what we may have to expect under certain circumstances. Other reports confirm that this document is accurate enough. In any case, the plan may never be published as long as the Goering-Funk group is in the saddle.

economic system of Europe, including the former colonial possessions of the defeated countries [Schacht holds, according to *The Nation*], the foundation of a European Export and Import Syndicate has been decided upon. This syndicate will fix the regulations for export trade with the United States, Japan, and Russia. Similar or equivalent organizations would have to be created in those countries, to guarantee successful collaboration. Negotiations with individual firms or groups will be replaced by negotiations with government agencies. Prices, quotas, conditions of delivery and payment will have to be fixed by the E. and I.S. in Europe and by corresponding organizations in the United States, Russia, and Japan. All countries in the Pacific Ocean will be considered European, Japanese, or Russian spheres of influence. The distribution of quotas in Central and South American markets will be arranged between the E. and I.S. and the United States.

The distribution of raw materials is to be regulated by an agreement between Germany, Italy, Russia, Japan, and the United States, according to a fixed plan. Germany will, even after the war, continue to develop its artificial raw-material production. It will do so for two reasons: defense of the country, and quicker and less expensive sources of supply. Dr. Schacht is convinced that in eight or ten years artificial raw materials will be better and cheaper than natural ones.

A conference of the banks of issue of the world to be established as a permanent institution. The question of the gold standard is of secondary importance. An agreement on this question with the United States will be aimed at. By seizing South Africa, Germany will become a gold producer too. Besides, the gold shipped to the United States by England and France will be utilized by Germany, Italy, and other states.

The Nation has not commented on the plan, but Dorothy Thompson in one of her famous columns points out:[16]

Dr. Schacht announces quite simply that the real objects of this war are the breaking of the "plutocracies"—namely, Great Britain, and the United States. The Japanese angle reveals itself in the plan that after this war the United States is to have no interests whatsoever, commercial or otherwise, in the Pacific. We are to be allowed to trade exclusively with Europe—which needs some of our products—and with South America, where, far from having a "Sphere of Influence," we are to be apportioned "quotas." We are to be allowed to trade only through a monopolistic import-export syndicate, to be set up for the whole continent of Europe, necessitating the end of individual trading in this country and the establishment of a similar

16 *New York Herald Tribune,* Sept. 30, 1940.

government monopoly here. We shall be invited to stabilize our currencies together with Japan, Russia, and pan-Fascist Europe, and merge the banking systems; but Germany will keep the rubber mark for merchandise and tourist trade. The debts of all Germany's vassals will be recognized in principle, but will be paid in goods.

For Latin America, which lives by exports, this system will mean economic strangulation or collaboration, and we shall eventually have the Axis at our gates.

If Hitler wins, Miss Thompson may not be far wrong. If, however, there should be no final Axis victory, only a part of Schacht's plan will come into its own. Export- and import-controlling institutions may not be avoidable among nations, at least for a transition period. A conference of the banks of issue of the world, as a permanent institution, will be the minimum of accomplishments.

In any event, should Hitler conquer and maintain his conquest of all Europe, there is no question but that he will create a Europa Bank[17] having as one of its functional aims an exporting-importing cartel, under the thumb of Berlin. In that case, the rest of the world must create similar institutions. Obtaining this power, Berlin will play a monopolist's role in all parts of the world. It will invade South America and other parts of the world with goods at sacrifice prices in order to make those markets economically dependent upon it. The only measure capable of counteracting such dumping practices is comparable monopolist powers.

Thus it is obvious that we in the Western Hemisphere, whether in a world at peace or war, must be prepared with a Western Hemisphere Bank, a defensive and creative instrument for the enhancement of a practical democracy. It is to this we now turn out attention.

[17] Germany has in recent years made itself, by conquest, by far the largest stockholder in the B.I.S. Starting off with 19,772 shares, the same amount subscribed by Britain, France, Belgium, Italy, Japan, and the United States, Germany has gained possession, or presumptive control, of the 19,772 Belgian shares, the 19,772 French shares, the 4,060 Austrian shares, the 4,000 Dutch shares, the 4,000 Danzig shares, the 4,000 Danish shares, the 4,000 Polish shares, the 4,000 Czech shares, and the 4,000 Norwegian shares, or 87,316 out of a total of 200,000 shares.

With nearly 44 per cent of the bank's stock under German control, the B.I.S. has become more of a German and less of an international institution. But the bank has always kept a considerable amount of its funds in this country and hence the United States may be in a position to prevent Germany from gaining access to the shares of the bank's assets held by the invaded countries. But the control would remain in her hands.

CHAPTER VI

THE INTER-AMERICAN BANK (HEMISPHERE BANK)

THE creation of an American Hemisphere Bank must be considered as one of the greatest national and inter-American movements in the history of our continent. It represents one of the most significant and decisive steps toward an active American foreign economic policy.

Whether or not it is approved by Congress in 1941, the originators of the plan, President Roosevelt and his advisers, Sumner Welles and A. A. Berle, Jr., will, I hope, find a way to bring this venture to life. Jesse Jones might be able to finance it via the Reconstruction Finance Corporation or the Export-Import Bank in Washington, and Cordell Hull, we can be sure, will make it one of the most important instruments of our foreign policy.

What can we expect from this new and still problematic venture? More business with South America? Security against military aggression, invasion, and fifth-column activities? Establishment of a system of central banks, and a sound system of stable currencies? Increased production, population, colonization; a higher standard of living, increased buying and selling capacity? New funds for the development of backward regions? A policy of planned production, stimulation or restriction; reserves built up through valorization of raw materials? Or, does this system involve a more autarchic and exclusive policy, for protection against dumping and barter-blackmail methods?—a system which cannot be ruined by a buyers' strike or price pressure from European countries, but which is, on the other hand, dependent upon the outer world for the export of large quantities of goods and products?

Broadly speaking, the purpose of this Bank is two-fold:

If our Western Hemisphere, by reasons of totalitarian or imperialist pressure from the other sides of the Atlantic and Pacific, is forced to exercise a more positive and active foreign economic policy for the safety and welfare of the Americas, the Hemisphere Bank must be our financial *spiritus rector*. If European dictators force our Hemisphere to build an empire-federation or customs union on our Western Hemisphere, we must do it with full conviction and courage. We must answer aggression with positive defense measures and with a very strong foreign policy.

The second and no less important task of the head of our Bank is participation in the building up of the new economic structure of the world. Each step, each phase of activity, of the Hemisphere Bank should be undertaken with an eye toward its future coordination with and adjustment to the Bank of Nations as the only possible and ultimate functional world solution.

There is a great difference between the conditions which the Bank for International Settlements had to face in Europe at the end of the first world war and those with which the Hemisphere Bank is now concerned. Further, the Europa Bank is a banking instrument projected for highly developed and industrialized member countries, which after the war may be shattered and weakened, but which nevertheless represent more or less mature economies.

The Hemisphere Bank is faced with much less advanced economies and will have to deal with partly undeveloped nations. A fruit of Pan-Americanism and the United States Monroe Doctrine, the Bank has its roots primarily in political considerations and security, and not in economic and commercial motives. Of all the Pan-American nations, the United States certainly has the greatest export-import volume, but Germany and England enjoy a greater share in Latin American trade than does the United States. Italy and Japan have also, in the past, traded more aggressively than we have with our southern neighbors. The reason is simple: South American nations are, to a great extent, dependent upon the demand of other nations for their raw materials, while the United States is a producer of most of the same raw materials and therefore not very dependent upon South American exports.

Before the war, these ties with countries other than the United States

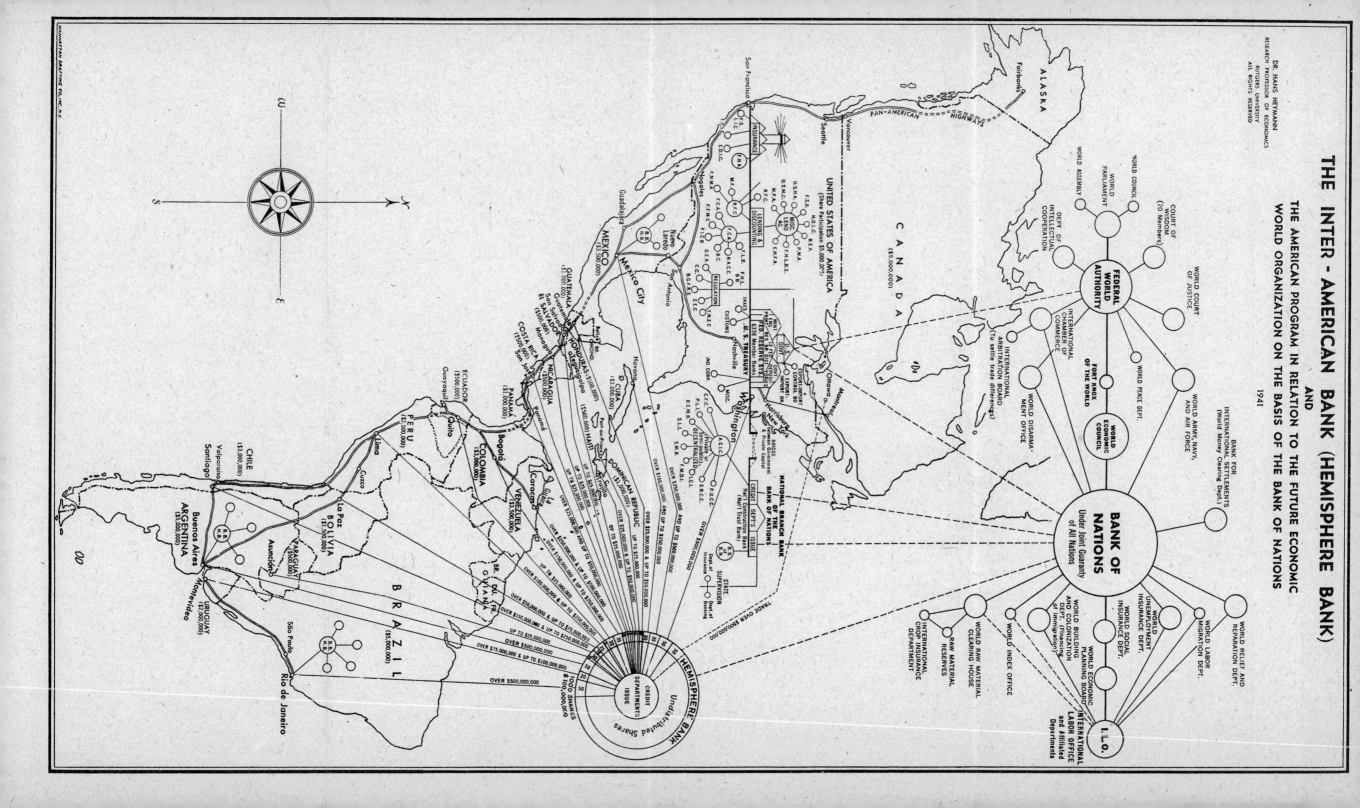

THE INTER-AMERICAN BANK (HEMISPHERE BANK)

AND

THE AMERICAN PROGRAM IN RELATION TO THE FUTURE ECONOMIC WORLD ORGANIZATION ON THE BASIS OF THE BANK OF NATIONS

1941

greatly affected the foreign policies of Latin American nations. They avoided too great a dependency upon their mighty northern neighbor and were split by numerous arbitrary ties with other continental powers. Culturally, Latin America is influenced more by those European countries whose language and customs it has inherited, while the United States has more in common with those countries in Europe which are now, or are destined to become, partners in the Europa Bank. Even politically, some of the Latin American nations have tended toward fascist rather than democratic doctrines. During and after this war, however, a great change may develop as a result of the community of interest among all nations of our Hemisphere. The traditions which bind these nations to the belligerents and neutrals of Europe may be overshadowed by a strong desire for independence from Mother Europe and for a common unity within their own realm.

These are the evolutionary developments which the Hemisphere Bank must face and support with its creative and constructive financial functions, and here active United States foreign economic policy must step in.

For.fifty years this American policy has been prepared through the work of the Pan-American Union, located in a splendid marble palace, the gift of Andrew Carnegie, in Washington, D. C., and its eight Pan-American Congresses, as well as through innumerable other conferences and comprehensive commercial, scientific, and political activities. In 1940, when the Pan-American Union celebrated its fiftieth anniversary in Washington, many of the inhibitions of Latin American nations against a common brotherhood with the United States had been removed and the fear of United States sovereignty in this hemisphere had disappeared. The policy of President Roosevelt and Cordell Hull, their assurances that economic and territorial rights will be respected and that no "policing" of Latin American nations by the United States is intended, have exercised a very favorable influence.

The Hemisphere Bank has the laudable task of giving those nations financial assurances, of tying those nations more firmly together economically, and, by helping them and strengthening their buying power, of developing in those countries new economic opportunities for the United States and an outlet for our export goods, gold, and labor.

Today, in fact, one-third of our regular export trade is directed toward Latin America, and our exporters are beginning to appreciate the policies of our government in increasingly helping to finance or subsidize imports from Latin America, because of the emergency situation with which these countries are faced if Europe cannot relieve them of their surplus raw materials. Without increasing our imports from Latin America, we shall hardly be able to increase our exports substantially. Here a great public task awaits the Hemisphere Bank; by valorizing goods or subsidizing imports from South American nations and by regulating their price level, we have a powerful weapon which can be wielded for the benefit of those nations, of our own country, and of the world at large.

Our administration's policy of lowering trade barriers can greatly help in the present emergency situation. The progressive spirit of Cordell Hull will finally triumph over high-tariff enthusiasts. While it is true that pure free trade may be a hopeless ideal in our present world situation, better organized trade relations and planned commercial policies will soon become imperative.

The tasks designed for the Hemisphere Bank are numerous. Besides stabilizing currencies and promoting monetary equilibrium, and serving for liquidating payments in international exchange, it would above all stimulate trade and investments, promote industries and travel, and examine and give advice in matters of public finance. The granting of loans to governments, the sale and purchase of government obligations, the reinforcement of government guarantees, and the underwriting of government loans would be included in its powers. The Bank, moreover, would act as agent for government fiscal bodies.

What is the Inter-American Bank? What is its history, its functions and organization?

Inter-American Bank[1]

History of the Project[2]

The present project for the establishment of an Inter-American Bank is the result of several months of intensive work in the Inter-American Finan-

[1] *Federal Reserve Bulletin*, June, 1940.
[2] The convention for the establishment of the Inter-American Bank was signed on behalf of

THE INTER-AMERICAN BANK

cial and Economic Advisory Committee and is the outcome of many years of discussion of the desirability of creating such an institution. The first International Conference of American States discussed the matter of providing adequate inter-American banking facilities, and on April 14, 1890 adopted a resolution recommending that the governments grant liberal concessions to facilitate inter-American banking and especially such as might be necessary for the establishment of an International American Bank. This resolution was approved by a vote of fourteen to zero, Argentina, Bolivia, Brazil, Chile, Colombia, Costa Rica, Guatemala, Honduras, Mexico, Nicaragua, Paraguay, Peru, the United States and Venezuela all indicating their concurrence. The Secretary of State, James G. Blaine, in transmitting the resolution to President Harrison indicated his approval of passage of a law by the United States incorporating such an International American Bank, and President Harrison transmitted the resolution and letter of Secretary Blaine to the Congress for appropriate action.

The second International Conference of American States on January 21, 1902 recommended that a powerful Inter-American Bank be set up in New York, Chicago, San Francisco, New Orleans, Buenos Aires, or any other important mercantile center and that it be assisted in every manner compatible with the internal legislation of each of the American republics. This resolution was signed by Argentina, Bolivia, Colombia, Costa Rica, the Dominican Republic, Ecuador, El Salvador, Guatemala, Haiti, Honduras, Mexico, Nicaragua, Paraguay, Peru, the United States and Uruguay.

The provision of inter-American banking facilities, especially in view of the dislocations occasioned by the European war, was discussed at length at the first Pan American Financial Conference which met from May 24 to 29, 1915.

In 1933 the Seventh International Conference of American States, upon the initiative especially of the delegations of Peru and Uruguay, unanimously

the United States by the Under-secretary of State, the Honorable Sumner Welles, on May 10, 1940, at the Pan American Union in Washington. Representatives of Colombia, the Dominican Republic, Ecuador, Mexico, Nicaragua, Paraguay, and Bolivia also signed the convention on May 10, and it was signed by a representative of Brazil on May 13.

Ratification of the convention by all these countries would insure sufficient participation to bring the convention into effect, since these nine countries represent a minimum of 205 shares in the Bank, and Article VI of the convention provides that it shall come into effect between the ratifying parties when it has been ratified by at least five countries who have agreed to subscribe for at least 145 shares.

Ratification of the convention by the United States will depend on the advice and consent of the United States Senate by a two-thirds vote. In addition, since the proposed Bank would be set up under a charter granted by the United States, the Department of State has indicated that Congress will be requested to issue such a charter in accordance with the convention.

153

adopted a resolution recommending the creation of an Inter-American Bank to establish and promote inter-American credit and the interchange of capital, to collaborate in the reconstruction of national monetary conditions, and to perform such other tasks as the Third Pan American Financial Conference might entrust to it. The Third Pan American Financial Conference did not take place, and the Eighth International Conference of American States in 1938 considered a number of resolutions which had been presented to the Seventh Conference and to the Inter-American Conference for the Maintenance of Peace. It resolved to request the Pan American Union to study the possibilities of establishing an organization to carry out the purposes envisaged.

In 1939 the Meeting of the Foreign Ministers of the American Republics at Panama adopted a resolution creating the Inter-American Financial and Economic Advisory Committee to study, among other things, the need, form and conditions for the establishment of an inter-American banking institution. Later in the same year the First Meeting of Finance Ministers of the American Republics at Guatemala recommended to the urgent attention of the Inter-American Financial and Economic Advisory Committee a study of the desirability of creating such a Bank.

The Inter-American Financial and Economic Advisory Committee began its work in Washington on November 15, 1939, and immediately turned its attention to the matter of an Inter-American Bank. After several months of intensive effort in which the delegates representing the twenty-one American republics were assisted by a group of experts from the United States Departments of State and Treasury, the Board of Governors of the Federal Reserve System, and the Federal Loan Agency, the Inter-American Committee on February 7 adopted a resolution recommending to the governments of the American republics the establishment of such a bank, and submitted for their consideration drafts of a convention, charter and by-laws for its establishment. Comments and suggestions were received from a number of the governments and were carefully studied, and on April 16 the Inter-American Committee approved the final texts mentioned above.

Motives for and Purposes of the Proposed Bank

The establishment of an Inter-American Bank would be a step of major importance in the development of inter-American financial and economic cooperation and the economic implementation of the Good Neighbor policy. It has been apparent for some time that there existed a wide zone of economic and financial activity among the American republics for which the existing machinery of cooperation has been inadequate.

The Bank, generally speaking, is designed to promote the fuller exploitation of the natural resources of the Americas, to intensify economic and financial relations among the American republics, and to mobilize for the solution of economic problems the best thought and experience in the Americas. The purposes of the Bank are enumerated in more detail in Section 5 A of the by-laws.

Organization of the Bank

The charter and Sections 2 and 3 of the by-laws provide in considerable detail for the organization of the proposed Bank. The Bank is to be an intergovernmental organization. All of the shares are to be subscribed by governments of the American republics, and none of the shares may pass to others than governments of the American republics. The minimum number of shares to be subscribed by each of the American republics in order to participate in the Bank is specified in Section 2 B of the by-laws; this schedule is based upon the foreign trade of each of the American republics in the year 1938. According to this schedule the United States is in Group H with Argentina and Brazil; the members of this group are required to subscribe to a minimum of fifty shares, or 5,000,000 each. The liability of shareholding governments on their shares is limited to the issue price thereof.

Voting among participating nations is distributed as follows, in accordance with Section 2 H of the by-laws: twenty votes for each government for its minimum shares, and one vote for each additional share which it may subscribe. Important decisions require a four-fifths vote. It is thus possible that one or more governments may acquire sufficient shares to possess more than twenty per cent of the total vote and thus be able to exercise a veto power on important decisions.

The directors of the Bank are all to be appointed by the shareholding governments, and are to be responsible to them alone. Generally speaking, moreover, the Bank may take no action which may affect a particular nation until after that nation has been given an opportunity to object to, or to give its consent, approval or guarantee to the operation. This safeguard of the interests of individual nations is inherent in the entire plan, and appears throughout the drafting. In addition, it is specifically provided in Section 5 C that:

"The operations of the Bank shall at all times be conducted in conformity with the laws of the territory where the Bank is acting and, so far as possible, be conducted in conformity with the policies of the participating government directly concerned."

United States Participation in the Establishment of the Bank

The appropriate convention [was] signed on behalf of the United States on May 10, 1940. Ratification of this convention by the United States will of course depend on the advice and consent of the United States Senate by a two-thirds vote. In addition, since the proposed Bank would be set up under a federal charter granted by the United States, Congress will in accordance with the convention be requested to issue such a charter. Moreover, certain additional legislation will be necessary in order to permit the participation of this Government in the Bank. Specifically, the United States must subscribe to at least the minimum number of shares required for participation by a country in Group H. Consideration of all these matters in the Senate and the House of Representatives will provide ample opportunity for a full discussion of the proposal.

Section 4 of the proposed charter provides that the Bank shall have succession for a period of twenty years, which may be extended, or until such earlier time as it shall be lawfully dissolved, in accordance with the terms of the by-laws, and that the United States agrees not to repeal or amend the charter except upon the request of the Bank pursuant to a four-fifths majority vote of the Board of Directors of the Bank. This charter and the by-laws of the proposed institution are to be annexed to the convention and to be integral parts of it. It is obviously not feasible to permit one party to an international convention ratified in each country according to its constitutional procedure to be free to change an integral part of the convention without the agreement of all of the other parties thereto.

Powers of the Bank

The powers with which it is proposed to endow the projected institution are specified in Section 5 B of the by-laws. In general it may be said that the Bank is given rather broad powers, subject to restrictions which will be mentioned immediately below, to engage in all usual banking operations. In keeping with the intergovernmental character of the institution, it is specified that all extensions of credit by the Bank, either direct or indirect, must be to a participating government or to a fiscal agency, central bank, political subdivision or national of a participating government with the guarantee of that government, or, in the case of extensions of credit having a maturity not exceeding two years to any such fiscal agency, central bank, political subdivision or national, only if the government thereof does not make a timely objection. In this way, and in accordance with the provisions of Section 5 C of the by-laws, which was quoted above, special care has been taken to ensure to each country the ability to bar any activity of the Bank within its territory which such country may deem undesirable.

While the purpose and powers of the projected Bank have been stated in fairly broad and elastic terms, as is both customary and essential in the organic laws of such institutions, discussions during the drafting of the convention and by-laws indicated that it was the intention of the Inter-American Financial and Economic Advisory Committee to complement existing financial institutions rather than to provide a substitute for them.

Rights, Privileges, Immunities and Exemptions Granted to the Bank

In view of the intergovernmental character of the Bank, arising especially from the fact that all the participants are sovereign governments, Article II of the convention would grant to the proposed Bank certain rights, privileges, immunities and exemptions which would permit the Bank to carry on any operations to which the governments concerned have indicated no objection without being liable to subsequent unilateral action against the Bank by any of the governments. Special care has been taken in the drafting to concede such rights, privileges, immunities and exemptions which are essential to the proper functioning of the Bank without permitting abuses to occur. Thus Article II, A and D of the convention permits legal action in regard to adjudicated claims against the Bank and its depositors. Similarly, Article II, C specifically excludes general non-discriminatory taxation, such as income taxation, upon individuals dealing with the Bank from any tax exemption accorded by the convention. Moreover, Article II, B assures the Bank that, where exchange restrictions or controls exist, it shall be accorded facilities for transferring out from a country, on the most favorable basis, amortization, interest, and other returns only from loans and investments of funds to which the government concerned had not previously made the timely objection which it is privileged to make.

CONVENTION

FOR THE ESTABLISHMENT OF AN
INTER-AMERICAN BANK

Pan American Union, Washington, D. C., April 17, 1940

The Governments of the American Republics

CONSIDERING

First, that economic and financial cooperation among the American Re-

publics is an essential factor in fostering the welfare of and maintaining
solidarity among these Republics;

Second, that such cooperation would be greatly facilitated by the establish
ment of an Inter-American Bank;

have resolved to conclude a Convention as follows:

Article I

The High Contracting Parties agree to the creation of an institution to be
known as the "Inter-American Bank" for the purposes and with the power
stated in the proposed Charter and By-Laws annexed hereto. The High
Contracting Parties agree that the Bank shall be accorded the powers, right
and privileges to engage in the various activities, transactions and operation
envisaged in such Charter and By-Laws and further agree to enact any
legislation and to take any other action necessary to effectuate and protec
such powers, rights and privileges to the Bank. The United States of America
also agrees to grant to the Bank a Charter substantially in accordance with
the proposed Charter annexed hereto. Each High Contracting Party hereby
agrees to subscribe for the minimum number of shares required of such
Party for participation in the Bank as provided in the annexed By-Laws.

Article II

The High Contracting Parties grant, within their respective territories
in time of peace or war and in any period of emergency and in any other
situation, the rights, privileges, immunities and exemptions enumerated in
this Article; and agree also to enact any legislation and to take any other
action necessary to effectuate and protect such rights, privileges, immunities
and exemptions.

A. The Bank, its assets, obligations to it and its real and personal
property of whatsoever nature, including any property deposited with
it on a custody basis or otherwise, shall wheresoever located and by
whomsoever held, be exempt and immune from (1) requisition, seizure
attachment, execution, confiscation, moratoria and expropriation; (2) pro
hibitions, restrictions, regulations and controls of withdrawal, transfer
or export; and (3) currency, monetary, exchange and debt regulation
and control, by the High Contracting Parties or any political subdivision
thereof, whether or not compensation is offered; provided, however, that
nothing in this paragraph shall prevent a High Contracting Party or

political subdivision thereof from attaching or levying execution, subject to any prior lien or claim of the Bank, upon admitted or adjudicated claims of its nationals against the Bank or upon property admitted or adjudicated to be held by the Bank for such nationals.

B. Where restrictions, regulations, prohibitions or controls exist or are hereafter imposed in the territory of a High Contracting Party in regard to the conversion or exchange of its currency into foreign currencies, the High Contracting Party shall make available to the Bank, by sale or otherwise, as provided in the next sentence, foreign exchange and precious metals, requested by the Bank, for such local currency acquired by the Bank as a result of loans, discounts, extensions of credit (including those in the form of deposits), guaranties thereof, or investments, made by the bank to such High Contracting Party, in its securities and obligations, or with its guarantee, express approval or consent, or to which it has made no timely objection as defined in and when expressly provided for by the by-laws of the Bank, including principal, interest, and other returns, thereon. Such foreign exchange and precious metals shall be so made available to the Bank on a basis, as to amount, rate, and all other factors, no less favorable than the most favored treatment extended under any circumstances by the High Contracting Party to any government including its own or to any political subdivision, individual, partnership, association, corporation or other organization or entity of whatsoever nature.

C. The Bank and its assets and real and personal property of whatsoever nature, including without limitation of the foregoing, its Charter, franchise, capital, reserves, surplus, income and profits; its activities, transactions and operations; its shares of stock and all notes, debentures, bonds and other such obligations issued by the Bank, including dividends and interest thereon, by whomsoever held; any remunerations or salaries paid by the Bank; and any individual, partnership, corporation, association or other entity in its dealings and relations with the Bank in any of the foregoing matters and in its acquisitions, holdings transfers or dispositions of any such shares and obligations of the Bank, shall be exempt and immune from all taxation by a High Contracting Party or a political subdivision thereof now or hereafter imposed and by whatever name described, including, without limitation of the foregoing, excises, duties and imposts; provided, however, that the foregoing shall not be construed as preventing the imposition by a High Contracting Party or any political subdivision thereof of non-discriminatory taxes upon nationals of such High Contracting Party with respect to any of the foregoing. Notwithstanding any of the foregoing, neither a High Contracting Party nor any political subdivision thereof shall impose any tax on or measured by salaries or remunerations paid by the Bank to its officers or employees who are citizens of any other High Contracting Party. Nothing in this paragraph shall make the Bank or any other party referred to above exempt or immune from any customs duties or imposts or other taxation imposed on or in connection with the importation or exportation of any article; provided, however, that the exportation of (1) coin, currency and of intangible property, including, without limitation of the foregoing, shares of stock, credit instruments, securities, and evidences of indebtedness, and (2) precious metals, other than precious metals produced in the territory of the High Contracting Party and being exported for the first time, owned or held by the Bank, or deposited with it on a custody basis or otherwise, and by whosover held, shall be exempt and immune from any customs duties or imposts or other taxation. The provisions of this paragraph shall not be construed to restrict in any manner any exemption, deduction, credit or other allowance accorded by the laws of any of the High Contracting Parties in the determination of a tax imposed by such party.

D. The Bank, its assets, obligations to it and its real and personal property of whatsoever nature, shall, wheresoever located and by whomsoever held, be subject to attachment or execution by a private party only after final judgment or decree in a suit, action, or proceeding in a court of a High Contracting Party or political subdivision thereof.

E. The shares of stock and the notes, debentures, bonds and other securities and obligations issued by the Bank shall be exempt and immune from prohibitions, restrictions, regulations, or controls now or hereafter imposed by any High Contracting Party or any political subdivision thereof, with respect to the registration, issue and sale of stock, notes, debentures, bonds and other securities and obligations; provided that notes, debentures, bonds and other securities and obligations issued by the Bank shall not be issued or sold by the Bank in the territory of a High Contracting Party which makes a timely objection, as provided in the By-Laws of the Bank.

Article III

As used in this Convention and the annexed By-Laws of the Inter-American Bank "nationals" of a High Contracting Party or of a participating country or government shall include any person who is domiciled in, or a citizen or resident of, such High Contracting Party or such participating country or government; and shall also include any individual, partnership, association, corporation or other entity organized under the laws of such High Contracting Party or such participating country or government or political subdivision thereof or having a permanent establishment, such as a branch, office, agency or other fixed place of business, in the territory of such High Contracting Party or of such participating country or government; but shall not include the Bank.

As used in this Convention and the annexed By-Laws of the Inter-American Bank, "political subdivision" shall include territories, dependencies, possessions, states, departments, provinces, counties, municipalities, districts, and other similar governmental organizations and bodies and agencies and instrumentalities thereof.

Article IV

The original of the present Convention in English, Spanish, Portuguese and French shall be deposited in the Pan American Union, in Washington, and opened for signature on behalf of the American Republics.

Article V

The present Convention shall be ratified and effectuated by the High Contracting Parties in conformity with their respective constitutional methods. The Pan American Union shall transmit authentic certified copies of the original of the Convention to the High Contracting Parties for the purpose of ratification. The instruments of ratification shall also be deposited in the archives of the Pan American Union, which shall notify the signatory governments of such deposit. Such notification shall be considered as an exchange of ratifications.

Article VI

The present Convention shall come into effect as between such ratifying High Contracting Parties if and when ratifications of this Convention shall have been deposited with the Pan American Union by at least five of the High Contracting Parties which have agreed to subscribe for at least a total of 145 shares of stock of the Bank. Each deposit of ratification shall be accompanied by the designation of a person to serve on the Organizing Committee of the Bank, which Committee shall meet forthwith after the Convention shall have come into effect as provided herein and proceed with all arrangements necessary for prompt organization of the Bank.

PLAN FOR PERMANENT PEACE

Article VII

Each High Contracting Party shall remain bound under this Convention for one year after such Party ceases to participate in the Bank and ceases to be in any way obligated to the Bank.

Article VIII

This Convention shall remain open to the adherence of American Republics which are not original signatories. The corresponding instruments shall be deposited in the archives of the Pan American Union which shall communicate them to the other High Contracting Parties.

In Witness Whereof: the undersigned plenipotentiaries, having deposited their full powers found to be in due and proper form, sign this Convention on behalf of their respective Governments, and affix thereto their seals on the dates appearing opposite their signatures.

Proposed Charter of the Inter-American Bank

(Such Charter would be granted by an Act of the Congress of the United States of America)

Sec. 1. There is hereby created a body corporate with the name "Inter-American Bank," hereinafter referred to as "the Bank."

Sec. 2. The structure, operations and activities of the Bank shall be as defined by the By-Laws, which are annexed to the Convention relating to the establishment of the Bank. The Bank shall also have all incidental powers necessary and proper to carry out the powers now or hereafter expressly authorized herein or in the By-Laws of the Bank.

Sec. 3. The Bank may begin operations when at least a total of 145 shares of stock of the Bank are subscribed for by at least five governments which have also deposited their ratifications of the aforementioned Convention with the Pan American Union.

Sec. 4. The Bank shall have succession for a period of twenty years from the date of enactment hereof or until such earlier time as it shall be lawfully dissolved. The United States agrees not to repeal or amend this charter except upon the request of the Bank pursuant to a four-fifths majority vote of the Board of Directors of the Bank. The United States may extend the charter for additional twenty years period upon the request of the Bank pursuant to a four-fifths majority vote of the Board of Directors of the Bank.

Sec. 5. Amendments to the By-Laws of the Bank, consistent with the aforementioned Convention, this Charter, and the purposes of the Bank as now set out in Article 5 A of the By-Laws of the Bank, may be adopted by the Bank pursuant to a fourth-fifths majority vote of the Board of Directors, provided, however, that Article 5 A of the By-Laws may not be amended, and provided further, that a unanimous vote of the representatives of all the participating governments (and not merely unanimity of the votes cast) shall be required to increase or decrease the minimum holdings of participating governments in the stock of the bank and to amend the provisions of the By-Laws relating to the manner and effect of the making of a timely objection by a participating government. As used in this act four-fifths majority vote of the Board of Directors shall mean four-fifths of the votes cast.

Sec. 6. The Bank shall have power to adopt, alter and use a corporate seal; and to make such contracts and to acquire, own, hold, use or dispose of such real and personal property, as may be necessary for the transaction of its business.

Sec. 7. The Bank may sue and be sued, complain and defend, in any court of competent jurisdiction. Any civil suit at law or at equity, brought within the United States, its territories and possessions, to which the Bank shall be a party shall be deemed to arise under the laws of the United States, and the district courts of the United States shall have original jurisdiction of all such suits; and the Bank in any such suit may, at any time before the trial thereof, remove such suit into the district court of the United States for the proper district by following the procedure for the removal of causes otherwise provided by law.

PROPOSED BY-LAWS OF THE INTER-AMERICAN BANK

Pan American Union, Washington, D. C., April 17, 1940

DRAFT OF BY-LAWS OF THE INTER-AMERICAN BANK

1. Location

The principal office of the Bank shall be in the United States of America and at least one branch or agency of the Bank shall be established in the territory of every other participating government. Additional branches and agencies may also be established.

2. Capital Structure and Participation

A. The capital stock shall be expressed in United States dollars (hereafter referred to as dollars) and shall be authorized in the amount of $100,000,000 consisting of 1000 shares having a par value of $100,000 each, to be paid for in gold or in dollars. Fifty per cent of the issue price of each share shall be paid up at the time of subscription for such share and the balance may be called up at a later date or dates at the discretion of the Board of Directors of the Bank; Provided, however, that with respect to the minimum shares of governments in groups A, B, and C, 25 per cent of the issue price of each share shall be paid up at the time of subscription, an additional 25 per cent of the issue price shall be paid up within 12 months thereafter, and no calling up of balances shall require any government in such groups to pay more than 25 per cent of the issue price of such minimum shares within any 12-month period. Three months' notice shall be given of any calling up of any balance on any shares. Upon the formation of the Bank the shares of stock shall be sold at par. Thereafter the issue price of shares shall be fixed by a four-fifths majority vote of the Board of Directors.

B. Stock shall be available for subscription only to the Governments of the American Republics which have subscribed or adhered to the Convention relating to the Bank. For a Government to participate in the Bank it must subscribe for a minimum number of shares, determined in relation to the dollar value of the total foreign trade of each of the American Republics during the year 1938, as follows:

Group A: Up to 25 million dollars:
Costa Rica, Ecuador, El Salvador, Haiti, Honduras, Nicaragua
and Paraguay . . . . 5 shares
Group B: Over 25 million dollars and up to 50 million dollars:
Dominican Republic, Guatemala and Panama . . . . 10 shares
Group C: Over 50 million dollars and up to 75 million dollars:
Bolivia . . . . 15 shares
Group D: Over 75 million dollars and up to 100 million dollars:
Uruguay . . . . 20 shares
Group E: Over 100 million dollars and up to 150 million dollars:
Peru . . . . 25 shares
Group F: Over 150 million dollars and up to 250 million dollars:
Chile, Colombia and Cuba . . . . 30 shares
Group G: Over 250 million dollars and up to 500 million dollars:
Mexico and Venezuela . . . . 35 shares
Group H: Over 500 million dollars:
Argentina, Brazil and United States of America . . . . 50 shares

Each participating government may subscribe for stock in addition to the minimum. Where the demand for such additional stock exceeds the amount available for issue by the Bank, such demand will be met on an equal basis from such available shares.

C. Governments of American Republics which do not participate in the Bank at the time of its formation or which shall have at any time ceased to participate in the Bank, shall be permitted to participate in the Bank upon adhering to the Convention relating to the Bank, subscribing for the minimum number of shares, and complying with any other terms and conditions designated in regulations of the Bank.

D. Liability of a shareholder on its shares shall be limited to the issue price of the shares held by it.

E. (1) The shares of stock held by each government shall be security for all the obligations of such government to the Bank and shall not be otherwise pledged or encumbered by the shareholder.

(2) If a government fails to make payment on a share on the day appointed for such payment, the Bank may, after giving reasonable notice to such government, vest in itself title to such share, paying to the defaulting shareholder an amount equal to the fair value of such share as determined by the Bank less any amount which the Bank considers necessary as additional collateral for any outstanding obligation or liability of such government to the Bank. Failure to make payment on a share on the day appointed for such payment shall deprive the defaulting government of its right to exercise a vote in respect of such share so long as such government remains in default, provided that the failure of a government to make payment on the minimum number of shares required to be subscribed by it shall deprive such government of the right to exercise any voting power during the period of default.

(3) If a government defaults on any other obligation to the Bank, the Bank may, after taking reasonable action to realize on any other collateral given to secure such obligation and after giving reasonable notice to such government, vest in itself title to an appropriate number of shares belonging to such government and apply to the defaulted obligation the fair value of such shares, as determined by the Bank. Any amount remaining, less any amount which the Bank considers necessary as additional collateral for any outstanding obligation or liability of such government to the Bank, shall be paid by the Bank to the defaulting government.

(4) If, after a government has had a reasonable opportunity to present its position to the Board of Directors, the Board by a four-fifths majority vote finds that such government has violated any provision of the Convention relating to the Bank, such government shall cease to participate in the

Bank, but its obligations and duties with respect to the Bank shall continue and the Bank may vest in itself title to an appropriate number of shares belonging to such government and apply the fair value of such shares as determined by the Bank to compensate the Bank for such damages as the Bank determines it suffered by reason of such violation. Any amount remaining, less any amount which the Bank considers necessary as additional collateral for any outstanding loan or liability of such government to the Bank, shall be paid by the Bank to such government.

F. Shares of stock may be transferred only to the Bank or to other participating governments at a price to be agreed upon between the parties and upon the approval of the transfer by a four-fifths majority vote of the Board of Directors. If, as a result of the transfer of shares of stock or acquisition by the Bank, or for any other reason, a government holds less than the minimum amount of shares of stock required of it, such government shall cease to participate in the Bank, but its obligations and duties with respect to the Bank shall continue.

G. The capital structure of the Bank, including the number and par value of shares may be increased or decreased by a four-fifths majority vote of the Board of Directors, except that a unanimous vote of the representatives of all the participating governments (and not merely unanimity of the votes cast) shall be required to increase or decrease the minimum holdings of participating governments.

H. The voting power of the participating governments on the Board of Directors shall be distributed as follows: 20 votes for each government for its minimum shares, and 1 vote for each additional share. However, regardless of the amount of stock owned by it, no government shall have a voting power in excess of 50 per cent of the total voting power of all the other participating governments.

3. Management

A. The administration of the Bank shall be vested in the Board of Directors composed of one director and one alternate appointed by each participating government. Each government shall appoint its director and alternate and any nominee or proxy in a manner to be determined by it. Such director shall serve for a period of two years, subject to the pleasure of his government. An alternate and a nominee or proxy shall serve for such period as shall be determined by his government. The Bank shall pay such reasonable expenses as are incurred by the directors and alternates and nominees or proxies in attending any meetings of the Board or any committee of the Bank. The voting power held by a participating government shall be exercised by the director and in his absence by the alternate and in the absence of both the director and alternate by the nominee or proxy of such government in such manner as the Board may provide by regulations. The alternate may otherwise participate in the activities of the Board.

B. Meetings of the Board of Directors shall be held not less than four times a year and may be held either at the principal or any branch office or at any other city in a participating country as the Board may determine. The president may call special or extraordinary meetings of the Board at any time. All meetings, regular, special or extraordinary, shall be held upon such reasonable notice as the Board may provide by regulations.

C. The Board of Directors shall select a president of the Bank who shall be the chief of the operating staff of the Bank and who also shall be ex-officio chairman of the Board, and one or more vice presidents, who shall be ex-officio vice chairman of the Board. The president and vice presidents of the Bank shall hold office for two years, shall be eligible for reelection and may be removed for cause at any time by the Board. The Board of Directors shall determine the order in which vice presidents shall serve as acting president and chairman in the absence of the president.

D. The departmental organization of the Bank shall be determined by the Board of Directors. The heads of departments and other similar officers shall be appointed by the Board on the recommendation of the president. The remainder of the staff shall be appointed by the president.

E. The Board of Directors may also appoint from among its members an executive committee. The Board may at any meeting, by a four-fifths majority vote, authorize the president or the executive committee or any other committee of the Bank to exercise any specified powers of the Board; provided, however, that such powers shall be exercised only until the next meeting of the Board and shall be exercised in a manner consistent with the general policies and practices of the Board. The Board may also, by a four-fifths majority vote, delegate to designated officers and committees of the Bank, for such periods as it may determine, power to make loans and extend credit in such small amounts as may be fixed by the Board.

F. The Board of Directors may appoint advisory committees chosen wholly or partially from persons not regularly employed by the Bank.

G. The Board of Directors, within a year after its first meeting, shall by regulations prescribe the reserves to be established and maintained against demand deposits and other obligations of the Bank and shall prescribe a limitation on the amount of intermediate and long-term assets in relation to capital and surplus; and such regulations shall not be amended, modified or revoked except by a four-fifths majority vote of the Board.

H. Before the Bank finally approves an intermediate or long-term loan or extension of credit, a full written report on the merits of the proposed transaction shall be prepared by a committee of experts which may include persons other than officers and employees of the Bank.

I. Except as herein otherwise provided, decisions of the Board of Directors shall be by simple majority of the votes cast. In the case of equality of votes, the chairman, or in his absence the vice chairman serving in his stead, shall have a deciding vote. When deemed by the president to be in the best interests of the Bank, decisions of the Board may be made, without a meeting, by polling the directors on specific questions submitted to them in such manner as the Board shall by regulations provide. The Board shall by regulations determine what constitutes a quorum for a meeting.

J. Authorization or approval by four-fifths majority vote of the Board of Directors shall be required for the making and granting of intermediate and long-term loans and credits, including the assumption of the obligation of a guarantor on intermediate and long-term loans and credits; the acquisition and sale of, and dealing in intermediate and long-term obligations and securities; the discounting and rediscounting of intermediate and long-term paper; engaging in bullion and foreign exchange transactions and guaranteeing the availability and the rates of exchange of the currencies of participating governments; the issuance of debentures and other securities and obligations of the Bank; the payment of interest on deposits of governments, fiscal agencies and political subdivisions thereof and central banks; the selection or removal of a president, the vice presidents, heads of departments and other similar officers of the Bank; the determination of the departmental organization of the Bank and of the functions and duties of the officers and principal employees of the Bank and the executive and other committees; the calling up of the balances due on stock; the establishment, creation, change or discontinuance of the principal office and branches and agencies of the Bank, and for amending the By-Laws, except that Article 5 A of these By-Laws may not be amended, and except that the provisions of these By-Laws relating to the manner and effect of the making of a timely objection by a participating government may not be amended except by a unanimous vote of the representatives of all the participating governments (and not merely unanimity of the votes cast).

K. Authorization or approval of specified series, classes, groups or other categories of transactions may be made in advance by the Board of Directors by the vote required in such cases by these By-Laws.

4. Accounts and Profits

A. The financial year of the Bank shall end on December 31.

B. The books and accounts of the Bank shall be expressed in terms of dollars.

C. The Bank shall publish an annual report and at least once a month a statement of account in such form as the Board of Directors may prescribe. The Board shall cause to be prepared a profit and loss account and a balance sheet for each financial year. All published documents shall be printed in the official languages of the participating governments. The Board shall designate a committee of Directors to arrange for examination, at least once a year, of the books and accounts of the Bank by competent experts to be selected by the committee.

D. The yearly net profits of the Bank shall be applied as follows:

1. Not less than 25 per cent of such net profits shall be paid into surplus until the surplus is equal in amount to the par value of the authorized capital stock of the Bank.

2. The remainder of such net profits shall be applied towards the payment of a dividend of not more than 3 per cent per annum on the paid up amount of the stock of the Bank; provided, however, that dividends shall be noncumulative and no dividends shall be paid so long as the capital of the Bank is impaired.

3. The balance of such profits shall be paid into surplus and be designated a dividend reserve.

E. The Board of Directors by a four-fifths majority vote may declare dividends out of the dividend reserve in surplus of the Bank, provided, however, that total dividends in any one year, including dividends paid pursuant to paragraph D2 above, shall not be more than 3 per cent of the paid-up amount of the stock.

F. The Bank may not be liquidated except by a four-fifths majority vote of the Board of Directors. Upon liquidation of the Bank and after discharge of all the liabilities of the Bank, the assets remaining shall be divided among the shareholders.

G. The shares shall carry equal rights to participate in the profits of the Bank and in any distributions of assets upon liquidation of the Bank.

5. Purposes and Powers

A. The Bank is created by the American Republics to carry out the following purposes:

(1) Facilitate the prudent investment of funds and stimulate the full productive use of capital and credit.

(2) Assist in stabilizing the currencies of American Republics; encourage general direct exchanges of the currencies of American Republics; encourage the maintenance of adequate monetary reserves; promote the use and distribution of gold and silver; and facilitate monetary equilibrium.

(3) Function as a clearing house for, and in other ways facilitate, the transfer of international payments.

(4) Increase international trade, travel and exchange of services in the Western Hemisphere.

(5) Promote the development of industry, public utilities, mining, agriculture, commerce and finance in the Western Hemisphere.

(6) Foster cooperation among the American Republics in the fields of agriculture, industry, public utilities, mining, marketing, commerce, transportation and related economic and financial matters.

(7) Encourage and promote research in the technology of agriculture, industry, public utilities, mining and commerce.

(8) Engage in research and contribute expert advice on problems of public finance, exchange, banking and money as they relate specifically to the problems of American Republics.

(9) Promote publication of data and information relating to the purposes of the Bank.

B. In order to carry out the foregoing purposes, the Bank shall have specific power to:

(1) Make and grant short-term intermediate and long-term loans and credits in any currency and in precious metals to participating governments and to fiscal agencies, central banks, political subdivisions and nationals thereof; provided that any such loan or credit having a maturity exceeding two years to any such fiscal agency, central bank, political subdivision or national shall be guaranteed by the government thereof, and provided further that any such loan or credit having a maturity not exceeding two years shall not be made or granted by the Bank to any such fiscal agency, central bank, political subdivision or national if the government thereof makes a timely objection.

(2) Buy, sell, hold and deal in the obligations and securities of any participating government and of fiscal agencies, central banks, political subdivisions

and nationals thereof, unless such government makes a timely objection to the purchase thereof; provided that such obligations and securities having maturities exceeding two years as are not the direct liability of such government are guaranteed by such government; and provided, further, that the Bank shall not buy obligations and securities that are in default in whole or in part as to principal or interest.

(3) Guarantee in whole or in part credits and loans made from any source to any participating government and to fiscal agencies, central banks, political subdivisions and nationals thereof, provided that such credits and loans having maturities exceeding two years as are not direct obligations of such government are guaranteed by such government, and provided further that such credits and loans having maturities not exceeding two years as are not direct obligations of such government shall not be guaranteed by the Bank if such government makes a timely objection.

(4) Act as a clearing house of funds, balances, checks, drafts and acceptances.

(5) Buy, sell, hold and deal in precious metals, currencies and foreign exchange for its own account and for the account of others; provided, however, that no such transaction shall be entered into with a fiscal agency, central bank, political subdivision, or national of a participating government, if such government makes a timely objection; and guarantee the availability and the rates of exchange of the currencies of participating governments.

(6) Issue or sell debentures and other securities and obligations of the Bank to obtain assets for the purposes of the Bank, provided that such debentures and other securities and obligations shall not be issued or sold by the Bank in the territory of any participating government which makes a timely objection. The Bank may also borrow in any other manner from participating governments, and from political subdivisions and banking institutions thereof unless the government of the lender makes a timely objection.

(7) Accept demand, time, and custody deposits and accounts from others, including participating governments and fiscal agencies, central banks, political subdivisions and nationals thereof unless the participating government makes a timely objection; provided that the Bank shall pay interest, if any, only on deposits of governments, fiscal agencies and political subdivisions thereof and central banks.

(8) Discount and rediscount bills, acceptances and other obligations and instruments of credit of participating governments and fiscal agencies, central banks, political subdivisions and nationals thereof, provided that such paper having maturity exceeding two years as is not the direct obligation of such government is guaranteed by the government, and provided further that

such paper having a maturity not exceeding two years as is not the direct obligation of such government shall not be discounted or rediscounted by the Bank if such government makes a timely objection.

(9) Rediscount with any government, fiscal agency or banking institution bills, acceptances and instruments of credit taken from the Bank's portfolio; provided, however, that the Bank may not rediscount with a fiscal agency or a banking institution in the territory of a participating government which makes a timely objection.

(10) Open and maintain demand, time, and custody deposits and accounts with governments and banking institutions and arrange with governments and banking institutions to act as agent or correspondent for the Bank, unless such banking institution is situated in the territory of a participating government and such government makes a timely objection.

(11) Act as agent or correspondent for any participating government and for fiscal agencies, central banks and political subdivisions thereof, unless the government makes a timely objection.

(12) Engage in financial and economic studies and publish reports thereof.

(13) Buy, sell and deal in cable transfers, accept bills and drafts drawn upon the Bank, and issue letters of credit; all subject to the limitations herein provided with respect to loans, extensions of credit, discounting and rediscounting of paper, and dealing in obligations and securities.

(14) Adopt, alter and use a corporate seal; acquire, own, hold, use or dispose of such real and personal property as may be necessary for the transaction of its business; and make contracts subject to the limitations herein provided.

(15) Exercise incidental powers necessary and proper to carry out the powers expressly authorized herein.

C. The Board of Directors shall determine the nature of the operations which may be undertaken by the Bank in the exercise of its powers and in order to effectuate its purposes. The operations of the Bank shall at all times be conducted in conformity with the laws of the territory where the Bank is acting and, so far as possible, be conducted in conformity with the policies of the participating government directly concerned.

6. Interpretations and Definitions

As used herein:

A. Four-fifths majority vote of the Board of Directors shall mean four-fifths of the votes cast.

B. "Short-term" shall mean a period less than one year; "intermediate" shall mean a period from one to five years; and "long-term" shall mean a period longer than five years; and the period applicable to any outstanding obligation shall be the period remaining to its maturity rather than the period from its issuance to maturity.

C. A government shall be deemed to make a timely objection only if such government, after its director is notified by the Bank of the Bank's proposed action or course of action, presents to the Bank within the reasonable period of time fixed by the Board, through such government's director, alternate, nominee or proxy its objection to such action or course of action. The Bank shall notify the directors representing the governments concerned when the Bank contemplates action or a course of action as to which provision for such timely objection is made in these By-Laws.

IDLE DREAM OR PRACTICAL VENTURE?

It is obvious that the powers entrusted to the Hemisphere Bank are far reaching. Indeed the inclusiveness of its purposes caused a critical banker to declare: "No institution directed by human beings could, under even the most auspicious circumstances, live up to its roseate expectations."

We cannot agree with the pessimism of this banker. When drafting the statutes or by-laws of any new world enterprise, there should be included as many powers as possible, even if it be not then intended to exercise them. This practice has always proved to be useful. In order to appreciate the underlying influences which motivate the provisions of such plans, an all-embracing analysis and examination of their universal implications and an international outlook and judgment is imperative. The proposals may be good for certain countries and have fatal consequences for others. Some proposals may be momentarily advantageous to the United States or other nations but may present a definite pitfall to a lasting world solution. Or, if the capitalists of a particular country should look upon the plan as an opportunity of advantage to themselves alone, both the advantage and the plan may prove short-lived and the ultimate objective of the plan will fail. The project of the Hemisphere Bank must be viewed in all its phases and implications with an eye to the future universal economic peace solution.

PLAN FOR PERMANENT PEACE

The plan for the Hemisphere Bank, under joint ownership and operation by the governments of the United States and Latin America,[3] had scarcely been published, when—just as in the case of the advent of the Bank for International Settlements—objections were raised. Some of these aimed at killing the plan, but others carried with them constructive suggestions.

In such proposals [writes the *New York Herald Tribune,* on March 16, 1940] and in the various suggestions that the Export-Import Bank advance credits to Latin-American governments, the danger exists that domestic as well as international politics will play too large a part. It is impossible to consider new credits to Latin-American governments without examining the fate of past credits. A number of nations, like Argentina, have honored their foreign obligations dollar for dollar. Others have defaulted. Some could not avoid default. Others did it out of expediency. Whatever the reason, the fact remains that today many loans to Latin-American countries made by private investors in the United States are not being paid. Why should new loans be made unless settlements of the outstanding debts are first concluded? Why, furthermore, should the American government make any advances to those Latin-American nations which, like Bolivia and Mexico, have taken the property of American citizens in disregard of accepted practices of international law and without paying for them?

Yet politics may well dictate making such loans without previous settlements of outstanding claims. Politics may also suggest the granting of fresh export credits without too great examination of the purchaser's credit status, solely because the sale of more American goods abroad stimulates business at home. The trouble lies in the fact that politics is not a good bedfellow for lenders or borrowers. If the purpose is to grant political subsidies, why not do this through normal channels, instead of creating an intergovernment bank?

---

[3] Canada has not as yet been invited to take part in the Hemisphere Bank, because it is a dependent and, at present, a belligerent country. In the spirit of our Monroe Doctrine, however, this dominion of the British Empire has always enjoyed the friendship and protection of the United States. The role that she might play after this war cannot yet be foreseen. It has always been an intermediate between England, France, and the United States, between Europe and our Western Hemisphere. As an Anglo-Saxon country, it will always feel that it is bound to England as much as to the United States. I believe, therefore, that a participation in the Bank on the part of Canada would create a stronger bridge between the Western Hemisphere and our friendly European neighbors and, at least economically, bind Canada more closely to the United States and Latin America.

THE INTER-AMERICAN BANK

Those bankers who do not reject the project entirely think that most of its purposes are laudable, but "that a 'B.I.S. of the Western Hemisphere' is not the most suitable for carrying them out." Edward H. Collins, Financial Editor of the *New York Herald Tribune*, states:

Their objections are summed up in a rhetorical question put forward by one of their members: "Why," asked this banker, "if we must have a bank, should we wrap it up in Pan-Americanism?"[4]

This does not mean [continues Mr. Collins] that the bankers, either as a group or as individuals, are opposed to the efforts of the Administration to bring about closer relations with Latin America. On the contrary, they have every reason for being sympathetic with the program. But they are vigorously opposed to mixing politics and business.

This, in my opinion, is no argument against the Bank in principle; it is merely a question of bank policy. The "mixture" can be avoided by strict separation of its functions, just as we have been able to accomplish this division of functions in the Federal Reserve System and in the Reconstruction Finance Corporation.

It is true, we are the creditors of Latin American countries; nearly all other countries are our debtors, and there may be conflicts with regard to the old obligations. However, as Warren L. Pierson, of the Export-Import Bank, speaking before the Academy of Political Science, said,

We should lend money to those countries which show a determination to meet their obligations; to those who do not, we should turn a deaf ear.

This is a sound general rule [responds Mr. Collins] but what is going to happen if you, as a representative of the chief stockholding nation of a bank such as is now proposed are asked to pass on a loan to a country whose representative sits at your left, but whose credit does not conform to the standards laid down by Mr. Pierson? It seems to me that only one of two things can result. Either you will veto the loan proposal, in which case you will almost certainly cause friction with your neighbor, and with his country; or you will approve the loan, in which case it will be a political loan pure and simple. And as a banker I regard a political loan as infinitely worse than no loan at all. It is simply a thinly veiled attempt to buy the good will of another nation, and as such is hardly more than a refined form of bribery.

[4] *Banking*, the Journal of the American Bankers Association, May, 1940.

No, if we are to set up an international bank in this hemisphere, let us set it up on a basis which will express realistically the underlying relationships of the countries of this area. Let us not tie the hands of this country in advance by making it a political institution. To do so would not merely impair its usefulness as a bank; it would, I unhesitatingly predict, render it a liability rather than an asset, in the prosecution of our highly desirable good neighbor policy.

These conflicts can and must be avoided. Those things which can best be done commercially, should be done by the Bank in a business-like manner, or left to private enterprise, and those which can and must be done for political, social, or security reasons should be done by the Bank as a political task and treated separately.

With regard to the issue of debentures and the long-term credit functions of the Hemisphere Bank, Herbert M. Bratter, Washington correspondent of the journal, *Banking,* writes:

Since the Inter-American Bank is primarily a device for syphoning capital from this country into Latin America, it is contemplated that the bank will *issue debentures.* From the American viewpoint some criticism has arisen. It is expected that the United States will seek to assure itself the *veto power* over the bank's activities. According to the original draft of the by-laws, this could be accomplished in so far as concerns medium-term and long-term loans, through the acquisition by the United States of more than *one-fifth ownership of the bank's stock.* If the United States acquires that much stock, it will be by far the largest shareholder in the bank.

While the proposed bank may *on occasion perform a useful service in ironing out non-chronic shortages of dollar exchange in different Latin-American countries, its most important function will be in the long-term development field. Intermediate credits* for Latin America are already being provided by the *Export-Import Bank.*

Holders of defaulted Latin American bonds also are interested in the Hemisphere Bank. According to the proposed by-laws, the bank may not buy securities which are in default; but it is proposed that the bank lend new money to defaulting governments or their agencies. If such loans are made, and if the borrowing country is thereby enabled to give better treatment to existing bondholders, the effect will be to benefit the former investors at the risk of the government which participated in the bank.

All these complications or obstacles are not of sufficient importance to warrant the defeat of the Hemisphere Bank.

How can the Inter-American Bank plan, carefully prepared by the Inter-American Economic and Financial Advisory Committee, fulfill its great task; how can it live up to the hopes and expectations of its advocates? We must clearly distinguish between public, i.e., governmental, activities for more or less political purposes and those tasks which have heretofore been considered as belonging to the sphere of private initiative. Even the most optimistic believer in the necessity, usefulness, and capacity of this institution for our Western Hemisphere must recognize that its success must depend upon the possibility of its becoming a commercially conducted international enterprise. If private banking, private industry—in short, private capital—in general is excluded from the Bank, its success cannot be assured.

Even those who are in favor of a radical change in our socio-economic structure, who believe in fundamental changes in our political and functional thinking and acting, cannot deny the necessity of having the bank guided by a commercial, rather than by a bureaucratic, organization. This proposition does not preclude public operation or government subsidy policies. But, whenever the Bank is obliged to carry out a subsidy measure merely for political reasons, the Bank must treat it as such. It need not fear to make a frank admission of those public subsidies which are for the benefit of inter-American policy or for national and inter-American social and political security. These transactions must be treated separately and distinctively from the Bank's normal business transactions.

If, on the other hand, the Bank endeavors to penetrate South American territories to engage in new fields of business commercially, it should follow a thoroughly commercial pattern of behavior. In order to compete with other nations successfully and permanently, it must adapt itself to the demands and requirements of Latin America.

In the past, foreign loans have been issued by private lenders. This field of activity presents some of the darkest chapters of our capitalist history. Ever so much has been said and written about it, but nobody has so comprehensively collected and realistically reported the arbitrary methods applied in the past in floating foreign bonds, especially Latin American loans, as Bernard C. Rice.[5]

In no single field of finance [states Mr. Rice] is the betrayal of the American investor more brilliantly demonstrated than in that of numerous issues of foreign bonds. $6,293,000,000 of bonds were sold to the public during the years 1923-1930. Of these practically $2,000,000,000 are now in default. These were sold by the high priests of American finance. . . .

The experiences gained from these foreign loan practices show us how cautiously we must proceed if we want to create a permanently sound commercial lending and issuing institution.

The bulk of these loans issued by the Hemisphere Bank in the form of debentures or bonds would of course be derived from United States capital funds, and their safe and productive investment is largely our own concern. If, and in so far, as private institutions cannot, or are unwilling to, fill the demand for these loans and the Hemisphere Bank undertakes the responsibility, there can be no excuse whatsoever for doing this lending in an unbusinesslike manner. For this kind of loan, commercial principles and rules must be strictly observed.

This type of loan has nothing in common with subsidy loans or supporting measures in various forms. If we are eager to sell more to Latin America and are forced to grant subsidy credits or other facilities and privileges (as the Export-Import Bank has done), or if political or national security considerations demand such tactics, these transactions must be charged to a different and separate account.

A planned program of constructive loans is essential for our Western Hemisphere and constitutes one of the principal tasks of the Hemisphere Bank. Those responsible for the Bank's commercial policy should make sure that the revenues from the projects to be constructed are ample to cover the loans and that no money be lent to enterprises which are not commercially justified.

We have in the United States outstanding banks—institutions such as the Guaranty Trust Company, the National City Bank, the Chase National Bank, the First National Bank of Boston—and other banks

[5] *False Security* (2nd ed.; New York: Dodge Publishing Company, 1938), chap. 5.

178

and bankers who have considerable experience with Latin American trade financing in all its complexities and methods of handling. A net of branch banks is spread over our hemisphere, and we can be sure that in our present emergency situation these banks will assume more aggressive business methods and adjust our short-term credit usages to Latin American requirements. If we do not grant the same credit facilities to Latin American customers as do European credit banks, e.g., in the case of the three-month bill of exchange, we shall not be able to compete permanently with those countries.

When the British withstood the Nazi assault in the fall of 1940 the imminent necessity for enactment of the convention of an Inter-American Bank by the United States Senate was somewhat abated. But by the time this book is published the issue will once again be to the fore and we can expect an assault upon it from commercial banking circles.

The *New York Herald Tribune* reported on February 7, 1941, that:

A group of three bankers—W. Randolph Burgess, Vice-chairman of National City Bank of New York; Robert F. Loree, Vice-President of Guaranty Trust Co. of New York, and Charles E. Spencer, Jr., President of First National Bank of Boston—is expected to hold further discussions with Administration officials with respect to the Inter-American Bank.

The bankers, it is understood, have been trying for nearly four weeks to convince Administration officials that the new $100,000,000 Hemisphere Bank should not be empowered to deal directly with commercial customers. The argument of the bankers is that the Federal Reserve Banks and the Export-Import Bank, as well as such international institutions as the Bank for International Settlements, are bankers' banks, that is, they can make loans only to governments, banks of issue or to commercial customers on the guarantee of an acceptable commercial bank.

The present charter for the Inter-American Bank would permit the new institution to deal directly with the public. In the view of the bankers, the new institution should be limited to the powers which have been vested in the Federal Reserve Banks and the Export-Import Bank. In this way, the new bank would not be permitted to compete directly with private commercial banks.

The agencies of the government directly concerned with the Inter-

American Bank are the State Department, Treasury Department, Federal Reserve Board, Federal Loan Administrator and the office of the coordinator of commercial and cultural relations between the American republics. It is understood that Nelson Rockefeller, the coordinator, has been more active than other government departments in preparing the Inter-American Bank resolution for the Senate.

We can fully understand the reaction of the big banks toward the plan for the Hemisphere Bank. As far as their demands are justified they can and should be fulfilled. But on the other hand we must equally well understand the attitude of the Administration. Is it necessary or desirable that the statutes of the Inter-American Bank be limited in this manner, so that the Bank becomes a sterile tool after the pattern of the Bank for International Settlements? Should we not draw the boundaries so that its functions may have a maximum flexibility? At the same time should we not give the Bank executives certain general directions and precise powers and entrust them only with those policies which they are able and suited to carry out successfully? How can we conciliate the two opposing viewpoints to the benefit of the country?

Before this question can be answered we must first understand the real issue with regard to the tasks and purposes of the Inter-American Bank. If we really want to help the Western Hemisphere financially and economically; if we want to help trade and commerce, construct new industries and utilities and create new capital wealth and purchasing power, short and long-term constructive credits must be granted unstintedly.

For the customary short-term bank credit transactions or for the issue of normal bond and share issues our private banking institutions and issuing houses—if they assume a more active policy in the future— may be best suited to continue in their realm of private banking and their powers might well be expanded to the extent of the powers held by the "Big Five" in London or the big banks on the European Continent. But that is not the whole picture. Three more and very vital tasks for our national and Hemisphere economy must be fulfilled.

(1) First of all, if we want to carry out a successful and constructive long-term credit policy in the Americas we must repair one of our most dangerous neglects during the last decades. We must first create

the specialized credit vehicles to carry those credits successfully and initiate the safeguarding institutions which must control, safeguard, amortize, and reproduce the long-term credits, vehicles which for over a hundred years have been a requisite of Germany, and later of 22 other nations in the world. Banking institutions in this country are not what they ought to be and what they are in the classical European banking countries, namely creators and constructors of these credit vehicles and institutions and creators and helpers of industry—so-called "consortial banks." The non-existence of consortial banks in this country may be one of the reasons why we have no mortgage banks for real estate, no ship mortgage banks, no specialized industrial credit institutions, no building societies, no underwriting trusts as the English have, etc., and no property-life insurance companies to safeguard, amortize and reproduce the long-term constructive credits.[5a] The creation of this credit and safeguarding apparatus in the United States and Latin America is clearly a task of private enterprise, and the government should do everything in its power not to hinder the creation of such a wide-spread specialized credit apparatus, but to give private banking, private lenders, and private capital all possible stimulus to bring those ventures to life as soon as possible.

Until now the banks, as well as the money lending institutions and private capital, have disregarded, neglected or even repulsed these ventures.

It may be that in the era of American prosperity these technically advanced credit instruments were not so badly needed, that in an epoch of steadily rising values very primitive mortgage bond schemes and mortgage lending practices were satisfactory. But sincere observers of our present economic situation have long since recognized that in the housing, shipping and industrial fields we are badly in need of the specialized and perfectly controllable classical mortgage bank and long-term credit apparatus. If we want to enter the long-term mortgage and credit fields in Latin America such controlling and specializing institutions are indispensable.

The inhibition of a relatively small group of our money lending

---

[5a] For further details on these credit improvements cf. Heymann, *Property-Life Insurance* (Harper & Brothers) and the author's next volume on our domestic problems.

institutions to help in building up this apparatus may have been influenced by ignorance of its merits and by shortsighted and unjustified fear of competition, which must be eliminated through intelligent information. The examination of these universally established and thoroughly proved creative and constructive investment institutions "has revealed the excellence of their work and the facility with which they meet the problems of long-term credit and mortgage financing." (New York Mortgage Commission.) For more than five years Governor Herbert H. Lehman and New York State Superintendent of Insurance Louis H. Pink have courageously fought for the initiation of these institutions. However, so long as the private banks and other private capital institutions and investors do not assume their responsibility and contribute their part in building up these specialized credit instruments—with all legislative and public support necessary—we cannot limit or reduce the statutes of the Hemisphere Bank, we ought rather expand them. If, for instance, private initiative does not live up to these vital duties, the Hemisphere Bank must be able to step in and itself create this apparatus for the control and safeguard of its long-term credits. But as stated before, this being the natural task of private capital, private enterprise should be given the chance to live up to its obligations in this respect.

(2) The second task, that of money and credit creation, i.e. the issue of money (e.g. an Inter-American currency) for short-term credits to trade, etc. and the issue of serial notes (promissory notes), for long-term credits to productive and income producing capital, can only be mentioned in this chapter, but a provision for these powers should be included in the statutes.

(3) For one reason, however—and above all other suggestions—the statutes of the Hemisphere Bank cannot and must not be restricted. National and especially Hemisphere defense imperatively demand an efficient public banking and lending apparatus with inclusive and comprehensive powers and great flexibility. This is the demand of the hour and the private banks and lenders must find a way to coordinate their tasks in this sphere with these most vital aims of the Hemisphere Bank, as they have done in the national defense program. First defense and then private interests.

IF THERE STILL BE DOUBTERS . . .

If there are still those who question the desirability or feasibility of the Bank, let us examine the alternative picture.

William L. Culbertson in his careful analysis of the "Economic Defense of the Americas" draws an impressive picture of what we may have to face:[6]

If Germany should succeed in creating a European economic system unified under her political power, she would be in a position to deal with individual Latin American countries on her own economic and political terms. If she should continue to use foreign trade as an instrument of her policy of crusade and conquest, her bargaining power, if unopposed, might be a menace to the security of the Western World and a challenge to the principles of the Monroe Doctrine and of the Declaration of Lima. An impoverished Europe would seek markets at any cost. Refugees and the demobilized millions would produce goods on the economic level of poverty and desperation, and Germany, if in control, would offer these goods in return for the food and raw materials of Latin America.

With these offerings our manufactured goods could not compete. Faced by such a comprehensive barter scheme, our investments in Latin America would be cramped and forced into retreat, for an attack on our trade front would be inevitably followed by an attack on our investment front. If the exportable surpluses of American-controlled industries in Latin America were to be drawn into the orbit of Nazi barter, dollar exchange would become less and less available to pay dividends and bond service in the United States. The tendency would be to render sterile our property holdings in Latin America. Moreover, Germany might take over the investments in Latin America of conquered European countries. The vast power in securities and in investments would add double strength to the economic penetration at first implemented by trade aggression. Finally, political and cultural ties would be loosened and the solidarity of the American states would be weakened if not destroyed.

If this be true, no half-way measures will suffice. The Americas may have no other choice but to create a geopolitic and economic area strong enough to outbalance the gigantic totalitarian group. In this area parts of the British Empire may have to be included.

[6] *Annals of the American Academy of Political and Social Science*, September, 1940, pp. 186-87.

PLAN FOR PERMANENT PEACE

In the summer of 1940, Secretaries Harry Hopkins and Adolf A. Berle, Jr., initiated a strong movement for the creation of an All-American economic union, an export cartel, to match the aggressive tactics of a threatened European bloc. The plan was to purchase and valorize the entire available surplus in raw materials produced in Latin America. Our economic weapons, consisting of our capital power and wealth, are still our strongest weapons. Intelligently organized, the capital strength of our continent cannot easily be beaten. Well-organized and social-minded capitalism is the strongest armor of our foreign policy.

President Roosevelt's original plan of a hemisphere surplus corporation, coordinated with the Inter-American Bank, called for an amount of two billion dollars to be appropriated by Congress and approved by American diplomats.[7] But how infinitesimal such and similar sacrifices appear in comparison to a possible loss of our independence and our very principles!

Every American should appreciate the spirit in which the idea of the surplus cartel was conceived. At the Havana Conference, Secretary of State Hull explained the gist of the project to the Ministers of Foreign Affairs of the American republics as follows:

. . . the American nations can build a system of economic defense that will enable each of them to safeguard itself from the dangers of economic subordination from abroad and of economic distress at home. It is no part of our thought to obstruct in any way logical and natural trade with Europe or any other portion of the world, but rather to promote such trade with nations willing to meet us, in good faith, in a spirit of friendly and peaceful purpose, and on a plane of frank and fair dealing. Against any other kind of dealing we naturally will protect ourselves.

[7] What would be the powers and purposes of this commodity clearing house or surplus agency? *Time* gives an example (June 24, 1940): "The Corporation would open up a $300,000,000 credit for Brazil. Brazil would have to use that credit for purchases in the United States or ask the Corporation to buy abroad for her. Then the Corporation would take over all Brazil's exportable surpluses: coffee, cotton, etc. The United States at its option would then barter, sell, give away, dump or destroy those goods. If the United States sold Brazilian coffee in Europe, it would reduce the $300,000,000 credit by the amount sold. Theoretically such transaction should be done at a profit—and profits were mentioned at the White House—but no profits can be foreseen. Actually, the program would probably show a dead loss of $300,000,000 to $500,000,000 annually. This cost, Mr. Roosevelt was advised, would be better defense than $500,000,000 in tanks."

These words are ample proof that Secretary Hull, who enjoys the full confidence of the Latin American nations, was not motivated by any imperialistic aims or selfish advantages for the United States. His entire attitude clearly shows his conviction as to the mutual advantage of a strategic and economic defense of all the nations of our hemisphere. He conceived of defense as a "common enterprise."[8] Aside from the military defense accord, by which twenty-one American republics pledge themselves to oppose transfer of the sovereignty of any territory in the Western Hemisphere from any non-American nation to another, however, the Havana Conference went no further than to advise the Inter-American Economic Conference:

(a) To cooperate with each country of this continent in the study of possible measures for the increase of the domestic consumption of its own exportable surpluses of those commodities which are of primary importance to the maintenance of the economic life of such countries;

(b) To propose to the American nations immediate measures and arrangements of mutual benefit tending to increase trade among them without injury to the interests of their respective producers, for the purpose of providing increased markets for such products and of expanding their consumption;

(c) To create instruments of inter-American cooperation for the temporary storing, financing and handling of any such commodities and for their orderly and systematic marketing, having in mind the normal conditions of production and distribution thereof;

(d) To develop commodity arrangements with a view to assuring equitable terms of trade for both producers and consumers of the commodities concerned;

(e) To recommend methods for improving the standard of living of the peoples of the Americas, including public health and nutrition measures;

(f) To establish appropriate organizations for the distribution of a part of the surplus of any such commodity, as a humanitarian and social relief measure;

(g) To consider, while these plans and measures are being developed, the desirability of a broader system of inter-American cooperative organization in trade and industrial matters, and to propose credit measures and other

---

[8] Sumner Wells, Under-secretary of State, speaking before the Foreign Affairs Council of Cleveland on September 28, 1940, hinted at the possibility that "Pan-American defense policy, already aimed at the solution of certain problems presented by the war in Europe, would be extended in the direction of a common front by the Pan-American Republics in the defense of the Western Hemisphere."

measures of assistance which may be immediately necessary in the fields of economics, finance, money, and foreign exchange.

Culbertson, in the aforementioned article has discussed most of the consequences which may arise from the hemisphere surplus project

The proposal of the inter-American marketing organization has in its favor that it has dramatized the crisis which we *may* (and I emphasize the contingency) have to meet. But on second thought—on the morning after as it were—we have the disillusioning emotion that the solution is too simple; that a limited application of the idea here or there (for example, in the marketing of certain of the competing surpluses of the United States and Argentina) may be useful, but that only as a desperate measure of self-defense should we embark on a scheme to create a gigantic monopoly of the export trade of the Americas. . . . It is only as a temporary measure that anything can be said in support of the marketing cartel. Like warships and bombers, it may become an undesirable necessity. It may be an instrumentality of economic defense and warfare which we shall have to adopt just as we mine the Panama Canal and build airfields at strategic points. If the masters of a unified Europe should undertake to buy the surpluses of the Americas on their own terms, offering goods in barter, defense would demand unified bargaining in this hemisphere (and probably something more), for dependency of Latin American countries upon a Nazi-dominated Latin America. To such a problem a joint marketing agency would not be a complete answer—but it might be one of the answers, and distasteful as it might be, we might have to accept it as the least of several evils.

Culbertson's major concern lies elsewhere; he believes

that the tragedy of a proposal such as the inter-American marketing organization is that it plays into the hands of those reformers who oppose the system of private enterprise and who favor government control and operation.

He believes further that

their [the reformers'] objective is to extend the New Deal technique to foreign economic relations [and he demands that] the vigorous expressions of private enterprise, represented by the principles and methods of the trade treaties of Mr. Hull, still should remain the norm from which departures like the marketing cartel, if adopted in any form, should be considered only as a temporary concession to collectivism.

He points to the sound approach to economic aggression proposed by the Colombian delegation of the Lima Conference in its draft of a convention:

(1) a reaffirmation of the system of liberal commerical policy, including the unconditional most-favored-nation principle; and

(2) a condemnation of economic aggression and an agreement "to adopt a uniform and joint commercial policy with respect to those states which have or hereafter may establish restrictive systems of international commerce contrary to the principles inspired by this treaty.

He finally agrees, however, that

if a European system under dictatorial power should attempt economic aggression in the New World a joint marketing agency would be justified as a means of defense . . . as a political instrument, just as are tanks and airplanes. But just as with the passing of the emergency military disarmament becomes desirable, economic disarmament becomes equally desirable. In the setting up of any marketing cartel it should be affirmatively asserted as a part of the scheme that when the reason for its existence—economic aggression—disappears, the cartel shall be dissolved and private enterprise shall resume its sway . . . what I am trying to say is that the postwar world cannot be rebuilt by marketing cartels, state loans, subventions, and relief. By these and other governmental means we could patch up a sort of existence, but an impoverished world will ask for something more. It will ask for an economic system which will release the creative powers of man and which will provide economic stability and a degree of prosperity necessary for peace and for free democratic institutions.

Meanwhile Mr. Jesse Jones, head of the Federal Loan Agency, and Secretary of Commerce, has suggested some practical measures: the expansion of the lending authority of the Export-Import Bank, and the making available of funds for the organization of the Rubber Reserve and Metal Reserve Companies to build up reserves of raw materials needed for our national defense. President Roosevelt asked Congress for legislation making an additional five hundred million dollars available for the Export-Import Bank, in addition to the

two hundred million dollars already appropriated, to enable the Ba
to make loans to governments and governmental agencies of oth
Western Hemisphere countries. Among other purposes, the Preside
asked in his message that the appropriations be used for "handling a
marketing of some part of their surpluses."[9]

This problem should be viewed in all its phases before we deci
upon it, but, in order to keep all possibilities open, the charter of t
Hemisphere Bank should allow for the introduction of an inte
American currency. Our problem is not an easy one, for the Lat
American countries cannot boast sound currencies and never enjoy
a classical education in currency problems. On the other hand, the ti
for cooperative action has never been more opportune. Any potent

[9] The bill (H. R. 10361) as amended was passed as follows: AN ACT To provide
increasing the lending authority of the Export-Import Bank of Washington, and for ot
purposes.

*Be it enacted by the Senate and House of Representatives of the United States of Amer
in Congress assembled,* That the fourth paragraph of section 5d of the Reconstruction Fina
Corporation Act, as amended, is hereby amended by renumbering subsections "(1)" and "(:
thereof "(2)" and "(3)", respectively, and inserting therein the following new subsection:

"(1) To assist in the development of the resources, the stabilization of the economies, and
orderly marketing of the products of the countries of the Western Hemisphere by supply
funds, not to exceed $500,000,000 outstanding at any one time, to the Export-Import Bank
Washington, through loans to, or by subscriptions to preferred stock of, such bank, to ena
such bank to make loans to any governments, their central banks, or any other accepta
banking institutions and, when guaranteed by any such government, a central bank, or
other acceptable banking institution, to a political subdivision, agency, or national of
such government, notwithstanding any other provisions of law insofar as they may rest
or prohibit loans or other extensions of credit to, or other transactions with, the governme
of the countries of the Western Hemisphere or their agencies or nationals: *Provided,* That
such loans shall be made in violation of international law as interpreted by the Department
State, or of the Act of April 13, 1934 (48 Stat. 574), or of the Neutrality Act of 1939. U
the written request of the Federal Loan Administrator, with the approval of the Preside
the bank is authorized, subject to such conditions and limitations as may be set forth in su
request or approval, to exercise the powers and perform the functions herein set forth. S
loans may be made and administered in such manner and upon such terms and conditions
the bank may determine."

Sec. 2. Section 5d of the Reconstruction Finance Corporation Act, as amended, is her
amended by adding at the end thereof the following new paragraph:

"The amount of notes, bands, debentures, and other such obligations which the Reconstruct
Finance Corporation is authorized to issue and have outstanding at any one time under existi
law is hereby increased by $1,500,000,000."

Sec. 3. That section 9 of the Act approved January 31, 1935 (49 Stat. 4), as amended,
hereby amended by (a) striking out "June 30, 1941" and inserting in lieu thereof "January
1947"; (b) deleting from the first proviso thereof the figure $200,000,000" and inserting
lieu thereof the figure "$700,000,000"; and (c) striking out the second proviso thereof.

Approved, September 26, 1940.

pposition of Latin American nations would be entirely superseded by
heir feeling, which they do not hesitate to voice, that their economic
nd political security depends upon the closest possible collaboration
vith our country.

But of what possible use is a surplus cartel or agency in this hemi-
phere, without a banking apparatus capable of creating international
noney and credit, i.e., in this case an inter-American medium of
xchange and long-term promissory notes? Is this cartel to be no more
han a method of price-pegging, valorization, or organized scarcity, or
hall we, at least, have the courage to take the bull by the horns and
ermit our instrument to create *purchasing power* at home and abroad?

In the creation of a hemisphere bank, a trade cartel, or a customs
inion, it is imperative that we present a plan for an international credit
nd currency mechanism in a form appealing to the majority of the
rospective participants. I note with satisfaction that the ground is
eing broken for an answer to Schacht's Europa Bloc and other cur-
ency areas. But I am fearful that we are too slow to act and may be
utsmarted and outdistanced as a result of our indecision and our
lmost willful refusal to observe the danger signals. Let us hope that,
vith regard to the Hemisphere Bank (and the surplus problem), the
nd of the war will not find us unprepared, but ready to act with the
itmost determination.

Although the Hemisphere Bank, as its name indicates, is considered
rimarily as an auxiliary instrument for our Western Hemisphere, a
world-wide economic system is only a matter of time. If a universally
organized capital economy were a psychological possibility at the end
of this war, we would hardly need a Europa Bank or a Hemisphere
Bank for the duration of the transition period of geopolitical group or
Dominion economies. A complete universal solution, right at the start,
would undoubtedly be preferable to this part solution, even if our
economic system were forced to undergo a more radical change. But
the establishment of the Hemisphere Bank and the transformation of
the Bank for International Settlements into a Europa Bank do by no
means preclude or hamper an eventual comprehensive solution by way
of the Bank of Nations and affiliated functional organizations if we

keep in mind that these regional systems are the first step in th
creation of an all-inclusive world system.

In the meantime we must direct our policies toward the creation o
increased purchasing power in the Americas so that we may be able t
absorb more of the raw materials produced. This can be done throug
a prudent credit and investment policy, greater industrialization, bette
communications, development of new products less competitive wit
United States products, expansion of imports from Latin America, nov
supplied by other continents, and concessions for more imports from
South America in general because our economic unity and politica
harmony largely depend upon the generous application of the principl
of live and let live.[10]

Obstacles on our continent have always been overcome by th
pioneers. But more and more the European situation may force us t
devote all our energies to that sphere. One need not be an isolationis
in order to become a friend of the Bank and to wish for an economi
integration of our hemisphere. Circumstances and world development
may be more serious than we have anticipated and impose much grave
decisions upon us than we have ever thought of making. We may hav
to change the entire economic structure of our country and the Amer

[10] During the discussion before the United States Senate, led by Senators Danaher, Taf
Vandenberg, and Wagner, concerning the policy to be pursued by the Export-Import Bank
Mr. Taft has mentioned a few of the normal methods we may apply:

"It seems to me that if we go ahead and promote our trade in South America by norma
methods, if we pursue a 'good neighbor' policy, if we keep on a friendly basis, there will b
some opportunity for us to make constant headway in the esteem of our South America
neighbors.

"There are many things we can do. Our main purpose should be to do in detail every littl
thing we can to help our exporters to South America to be really friendly to South America
We can buy more coffee, for instance, from Brazil and sell it through the food-stamp plan.
can be done. We can insure short-term credits, as Germany does and as England does, in Sout
America. We can reduce steamship rates, which the South Americans think are much too high
for products transported between the United States and South America. We can even perhap
reduce taxes on the profits from export trade. We can develop strategic materials in accordanc
with the terms of my amendment. I may say that we have already authorized the Departmen
of Agriculture to spend a large amount of money in developing the production of rubber i
Brazil, a specific project. I am willing, under this measure, to give general power to th
Export-Import Bank to lend money to Brazil or concerns in Brazil to develop rubber plantations
I am willing to lend money to Bolivia to develop tin that we may need. Those are purpose
which in the long run will benefit us, because increasing the exports from South America t
this country is the only means of increasing in the long run the exports from this country t
South America; so in that we have a particular purpose which will improve South America
relations."

:as. We may have to include other countries or even continents in our
emisphere realm, and what was supposed to be a transition period
nay become an epoch and the ideal world solution may be postponed
ndefinitely. The scientific reformer can, however, design that ideal
olution and in so doing he may help in improving and forging our
conomic world structure.

The promotion of liberal economic policies has been and will continue to
e a vital part and a dominant purpose of the foreign policy of the United
tates [President Roosevelt stated when opening the Foreign Trade Week
n Washington].

The administration's policy of reciprocal trade pacts would be the one
ontribution which America might make to world reconstruction following
he war in Europe. . . . The tragic events taking place in Europe bear
loquent testimony to the fundamental need for liberal economic policies in
nternational relations, if, in the future, frictions, conflicts, and wars are to
e avoided. . . . They serve also to emphasize the inescapable fact that our
.ation cannot enjoy sustained and satisfactory prosperity unless adequate
oreign markets exist for our exportable surpluses and unless our necessary
mports are unhampered by adverse developments at home and abroad.

These words propound eternal truth. The prosperity of a harmonious
raternal unity of our hemisphere in the final analysis depends upon
iberal and free trade policies, which the United States must not only
iropound, but actively help to construct with the finest technique in
which the Americas have proven to be the masters of the world—I
nean the capitalist technique thoroughly reformed and improved in
he spirit of social economic welfare for all peoples.[11]

Unity makes for strength. This is an eternal truth fully valid for our
Americas. We shall soon discover that intermediate loans made by the
Export-Import Bank will not suffice; that an increased standard of
iving in the Americas and collective American unity call for an instrument of organization, a powerful and creative socio-economic mechanism, which I visualize in a world banking apparatus such as the

[11] The reader is recommended the excellent book *Isolated America* by Raymond Leslie Buell
(New York: Alfred A. Knopf, 1940).
   See also the analysis of Mordecai Ezekiel, "Economic Relations between the Americas," *Inter-
national Conciliation,* Feb. 1941. (Included is an address by Henry Wallace on "Pan American
Defense," Oct. 11, 1940.)

PLAN FOR PERMANENT PEACE

Hemisphere Bank, or its logical expansion into an Intercontinenta
Bank or Bank of Nations.

Our problem is not one of production for American use alone, bu
production for world use and distribution, organized and facilitate
by a system of planned and creative trade and investment credit. W
cannot maintain or raise our standard of living in the United State
or in the Americas, for any length of time, if likewise, after this wa
we do not cooperate in raising the living standard of other peoples b
a new creative international economic system.[12]

[12] See hearings on *Inter-American Bank* (May 5 and 6, 1941) before a subcommitte
of the Committee on Foreign Relations, United States Senate, especially testimony c
Hon. A. A. Berle, Jr., Assistant Secretary of State, in which he acknowledges con
tribution of author to this subject (p. 22).

CHAPTER VII

AN ORIENTAL BANK

SOCIAL CAPITALISM can make peace. If this theme of the second part of
this book be recognized as fact, if it be true that economics must be the
basis for a lasting peace, then the fact is certainly of peculiar significance
in the Far East.

For centuries the world's eastern Asiatic economic policies have been
concentrated on China. This oldest of cultural centers, this dreamland
and "other Eden" of our earth, has been the aim and object of capitalist "colonization" and "exploitation." Too long isolated by the
"Wall of China," too long conservative in the sense of upholding
tradition, it has not been able to keep step with advancing industrial
"civilization."

The twentieth century finds the "good earth" of China, once one of
the mightiest and most dignified empires of our planet, delivered up
to exploitation. Tragic is the fate of the 450 million Chinese souls.
Hungry and poor because of their virtues, they have fallen prey to the
insatiable greed of other nations for the treasures of this country of
450 million "consumers." China has been unjustly punished for her
virtues, traditions, pious conservatism, diligence, thrift, and peaceful-
ness. But virtues cannot be suppressed indefinitely. Lands may be conquered by "colonization," by narcotics, alcohol, capitalism, armies,
and nationalist ambitions—but not virtues. A nation born and raised
on its soil cannot be pulverized even by the most efficient methods
of war.

I cannot help but admire and pity this brave and unfortunate country
with its "Open Door" for all imaginable "endowments of civilization"
in the worst and most cynical sense of the phrase. I admire its tenacity
and energy in a fight against a whole world of aggression in every

disguise, even that of "help" and "assistance." I admire her virtues, now concentrated on preserving her soil, her national integrity, and her independence. If China's misery is to be ended, an entirely different spirit of international relations and cooperation with the Orient must be bred among the people of the West. *Solidarity of interests* is the new magic stroke by which a veritable castle of enchantment may be opened to the world. Credits—creative and cooperative credits—are the magic instruments by which happiness may be restored to the Chinese people and a just return made to those who are willing to collaborate in the development and reconstruction of "colossal China."

The United States of America is a nonbelligerent, powerful nation with a highly developed moral constitution and a strong sense of justice. It is, obviously, the only nation which could actively assist in saving eastern Asia from a situation of turmoil and chaos. Here evidently lies one of her first tasks of active foreign policy. If we succeed in solving the knot of these troubles in such a way as to guarantee a reasonably prosperous future to China and all her neighbors, customers, colonizers, and concessionaires, our efforts will not go unrewarded. With such a settlement accomplished, we shall logically be considered as peace arbiters for the other parts of the world.

It is the main task of this book to emphasize the vital need for an active, neocapitalist foreign policy on the part of the United States. For the student of economics it is sometimes very depressing to witness the pessimistic and sometimes smug attitude of the Anglo-Saxon peoples.

A European observer cannot but receive the impression that a large sector of this most successful race of mankind has already given up hope for an evolutionary and constructive solution of the present world dilemma. He cannot understand our silent, complacent attitude toward the revolutionary processes which, for so many years, have been consummated in Moscow, Berlin, and Rome. I do not suggest that we should adopt European-made "isms" or programs borrowed from the other side. I merely doubt the wisdom of the apathy and blindness toward world tendencies and changes in which we are so thoughtlessly indulging. I deplore our reluctance to use our own creative intelligence. America does not need to break with the past. It does not need to yield up its ideals by giving in to a revolution on the European model. We need revolutionary changes only in our national capitalist attitude, changes which lead us toward national and international social capitalism, toward a socio-capitalistic cooperation with all the nations of the world.

What has really been done on our side? Have we instituted great enlightening social reforms? Have we made any constructive proposals to the troubled peoples of the world as to how their desperate situation might be mitigated without completely overthrowing the present order? Where is our plan for construction, reconstruction, lasting peace, and a new peaceful world order? Where are the great ideals of our time to awaken the enthusiasm of the people? With phrases and expressions of good will we cannot organize a new world. How much wealth, how many great achievements, how much of our unique efficiency are wasted because we shut our eyes to the real goal of our time and do not cooperate constructively! With inactivity or even passive resistance we are impeding the wheels of progress, reform, and betterment.

The disentangling, arranging, and organizing hand of a country which enjoys the confidence of the world may work miracles. This work must begin in the Far East and will succeed if undertaken with the necessary fervor and fairness to the interests of all nations concerned. By fairness is meant a just consideration of the socio-economic needs of the nations in question.

Let us frankly admit that such a peace settlement in the Pacific is also a prerequisite for our own national security and the security of our Western Hemisphere. More than that, it will move the center of gravity toward the Western world. It will free our hands for a strong and decisive policy in the European struggle and peace.

Nobody believes that the settlement in eastern Asia is mere child's play. It is, in fact, a most complicated and intricate task. It seems quite hopeless to attempt to reduce the antagonistic interests to a common denominator; only a mechanism so overpowering in its simplicity and so convincing to the conflicting individual interests can win the public support necessary for this enormous task.

Before we study this instrument of socio-economic peace let us view the present problems of eastern Asia as objectively and correctly as possible.

CHINA AND JAPAN

In the relations between Japan and China we must distinguish between the justified needs of Japan for the satisfaction of the wants of its impoverished population and, on the other hand, its imperialist dream of Pan-Japanism, its dream of embracing the whole of Asia in order to carry out its divine mission of "Pan-Asianism." In the (Tanaka) memorandum of Count Tanaka, a plan for the achievement of Japan's aims was proposed, and the war against China was considered by Japanese militarists as a suitable method of obtaining their aims.

From the Chinese point of view, Madame Chiang Kai-shek writes:[1]

The Japanese have always hoped that they would be able to achieve a position of dominance on the continent which would enable them to monopolize the exploitation of the natural resources and labor of the country without any difficulty. Eventual control, they considered, would then be easy, and a Japanese continental empire could certainly be established. Their dreams have not been confined solely to China.

Is it really possible [asks Freda Utley[2]] that our industrialists and bankers think that if Japan is given a free hand "on the mainland of Asia" she will forever cease from troubling and leave South China, Australia, and the Dutch East Indies alone, although it is only in these countries and in India that Japan can "fulfill her destiny," by obtaining the raw materials that are essential to her? . . . The rulers of Japan are out for colonies and empire . . . if Japan is allowed to entrench herself in Manchuria and China and subsequently to develop her strength unmolested, her next step must inevitably be to turn on Singapore and the Dutch East Indies and finally on India, Australia, and Australasia.

In order to justify their tactics on the continent and especially in China, the Japanese have first argued that they are in need of "living space"—colonies with space for their increasing population and land

---

[1] *This Is Our China* (New York: Harper & Brothers), p. 285.
[2] *Japan's Feet of Clay* (New York: W. W. Norton & Co.).

to supply the missing raw materials. To sanction their attack on China they have

endeavored to convince the world that China was chaotic, incompetent, and incorrigible and badly in need of a stern, disciplinary hand. Probably it was not realized by foreigners abroad that Japanese agents were behind much of the rebellion and internecine warfare, just as they are busy trying to create puppet states now. Then, too, there was the attitude of many foreigners in China who had no patience with the growing pains of the country during its transition from the ancient monarchical autocracy of the Manchus to a modern republican form of government. . . ."[3]

What will happen if Japan is victorious? Madame Chiang Kai-shek summarizes:

Japan will have under her control the vast resources of China to build up her fighting forces, and with these she will set about the fulfilment of her ambitions to bring all Oriental peoples under her sway in pursuance of her Pan-Asiatic policy. India will be sure to fall because of the very incongruous texture of its peoples. And the rounding off of Japan's continental empire will involve the acquisition not only of China and Siberia east of longitude 110°, but also of all the land east of that longitude from latitude 20° north to 50° south, which means of course the Philippines, East Indies, the Pacific Islands, and Australia . . .

In spite of the possibility that a victorious Japan might dominate the yellow race and the whole of Asia, Australia, and Australasia, or establish a self-sufficient commonwealth of nations, England, who would be the main loser by such far-reaching ambitions, has, until today, supported Japan, and the United States has acted similarly. Japan occupies a dual position; on the one hand it constitutes an imperialist danger, on the other it is the fortunate holder of the balance of power in the Far East. The Japanese position serves to keep potential Russian aggression in check.

Since the world balance of power has been disrupted and shattered by Germany, another important factor has been added to Japan's decisive position as a balancing instrument for the world powers. The United States must create a military machine great enough to offset

[3] Madame Chiang Kai-shek, *op. cit.*

the weakened military machines of the Allies. The fact that the United States must keep part of her fleet in the Pacific has become a serious obstacle to the achievement of a balance of world power, for which the United States must strive for the sake of her national security and that of our Western Hemisphere. It is for this reason that we have decided to build a two-ocean navy. These are factors with which we must reckon in our foreign economic policy. But a peace in the Far East which would be no more than a truce, and would enable us to remove our fleet, now shackled to the Pacific, is not a sufficient guarantee of security. In the face of the awful experience this world has had with the truce of Versailles, we know all too well that a peace settlement in the Far East must be a functional one. In other words, it must fulfill the vital needs of all partners in that peace.

To find a basis for an Oriental peace we must first of all establish well-functioning economic fundamentals. What is "economics"? We have been taught that economics is the study of the satisfaction of human needs and wants. If we could find a way to satisfy the human needs and wants of China as well as those of Japan and the other powers interested in a Far Eastern settlement, the peace would become a real and lasting one.

If we want to procure a sound and fair solution for these two countries and all others, we must assure and satisfy their governments of our respect for their economic and social welfare.

As long as the foreign trade policy of nations is prevalently neo-mercantilist, as long as the conflict between domestic need and foreign need is mostly decided in favor of domestic need, there will always be created dissatisfaction, distrust and an explosive situation. Unless countries like China and Japan are assured a functional economic and social peace in their trade relations with other nations, and in the development of their resources, commerce and industry, we cannot hope for a permanent solution.

If in addition to the economic basis for peace, a political supernational new order could be found by which all nations "save face," the hatchet can be buried and everybody will have won.

JAPAN, CHINA, AND THE SOVIET UNION

One of the leading principles of the peace in East Asia must be understanding and adjustment between China and Japan and the Soviet Union.

In the 1940 publication of the Japanese Press Club, *Japan Surveys the European War*, the main current of public opinion in Japan is expressed in the following terms:

Japan should not consider readjusting her relations with any particular nation at the present moment, but should rather practice a form of independent and autonomous diplomacy based on free and unbiased moral principles with the disposal of the China affair as her final objective. This opinion has been expressed by almost all the critics and publicists in this country. . . .

In this respect it should be recalled that in the Konoye statement of November 3, 1938, Japan's fundamental policy for disposal of the China affair was declared to be the establishment of a new order in East Asia, or the creation of a co-operative unit in this part of the world by co-ordinating relations among Japan, Manchukuo, and China, while at the same time respecting their respective independence to the fullest possible extent. It is indeed the immutable policy of this country, just as it is the ultimate objective of our diplomacy, to establish an East Asiatic new order, no matter what cabinet may be brought into being and no matter how radically the international situation may change in the future. This is why the Abe Cabinet immediately after its formation declared, with the unanimous support of public opinion, its policy of concentrating its energies on the settlement of the present China affair.

With regard to a Japanese-Soviet rapprochement, Japan considers herself in a very different light from that of Germany in respect to relations with the Soviet Union. While the close mutual relationship between Germany and Soviet Russia in the fields of trade and economics is recognized,

a good many issues between Japan and the Soviet Union still remain unsettled, as for example the fishery question, the oil and coal concessions in North Saghalien, the border troubles meanwhile settled, and the Soviet assistance to the Chiang Kai-shek regime. Unless these pending issues are settled satisfactorily, the proposed non-aggression pact between Japan and the Soviet Union would be devoid of any significance. . . .

Occupying thus a bargaining position in international politics [the report continues] Japan . . . may maintain her amity with Italy, without repudiating the anti-Comintern pact, even though the spirit of the pact has been infringed upon by Germany, and thereby may considerably restrain the activities of Great Britain in the Far East. On the other hand, however, by adjusting relations with Great Britain with regard to the China affair, Japan may impose restraint on the Far Eastern policy of the Soviet Union. Moreover, the adjustment of Japanese-American relations in addition to the alleviation of Soviet-Japanese friction, thus effected, will enable Japan to assert herself more strongly than ever as a stabilizing influence in her part of the world.

Without being discouraged in the least by the unexpected conclusion of the German-Soviet non-aggression pact, on the one hand, while stressing, on the other, the advantageous bargaining position in which Japan now finds herself, public opinion in this country advocates enforcement of an independent and autonomous diplomacy based on morality. And it concludes that the success or failure of the stupendous task of establishing a new order in East Asia depends to a large extent on whether or not Japan is clever enough to make the best of the present world situation, which is undoubtedly favorable for exercise of this independent and autonomous diplomacy.

Since this was published, early in 1940, the situation has changed substantially. By reason of the European war, Japan's sources of raw materials and her markets have gradually narrowed. This has greatly affected her bargaining and staying power. For her imports and exports, Japan has become more and more dependent upon the United States. If the American market were made inaccessible to Japan, this would have a great influence on Japanese foreign policy. It would render Japan's position in China almost untenable.

When on January 26, 1940, the United States called off the 1911 commercial treaty with Japan, this action raised a storm of protest, although no act of discrimination was intended at the outset. On the other hand, the incident made us fully aware of the decisive influence our foreign trade policy can exercise upon Japan in its present emergency situation. Although Japan is being gradually relieved of English and French pressure, the still unweakened power of the Soviet Union will undoubtedly change Japan's policy.

Will Japan fulfil China's minimum conditions stipulated by Madame Chiang in 1939: "Peace with honor, which must include the territorial integrity of China, administrative sovereignty and 'equal treatment' "? Can these countries return to the old order? John Gunther writes:[4]

[4] *Inside Asia* (New York: Harper & Brothers), p. 249.

The Japanese may choose instead to let the fighting fray out, hold what they have, and attempt to proceed with economic exploitation without calling off the war. But they must face the united and regenerated force of the Chinese nation. They are fighting a people that have never before been permanently beaten.

Such "undeclared peace" does not seem to be the solution. In my belief, the key to the solution rests in the hands of Soviet Russia and finally in the hands of the United States.

Josef Stalin, born in Siberia, is Asiatic in outlook and his ultimate aim is the advancement of Siberia. All his actions on behalf of Siberia show clearly that he is favoring and developing the hardly exploited treasures of this vast territory. He has made the arctic Siberian regions accessible, he has created new cities and brought culture to Siberia, granted concessions for gold production near the Ural and in southern Siberia, built railroads and air lines, and by means of political influence "acquired" three extremely wealthy provinces in southeastern Siberia. His aspirations are directed toward Siberia and the Far East. His dream is a direct railroad connection from Vladivostok to Narvik in Norway, from the Pacific to the North Sea, and a net of railroads and airlines spread over Siberia. After having achieved most of his aspirations in the West, he would perhaps make sacrifices and peace concessions in Europe if his dreams could be realized. One of the most promising and most dynamic projects of the twentieth century is the opening up of the vast resources of the Soviet Union for the whole world. In February, 1940, during the Russo-Finnish war, Stalin closed a trade pact with Hitler which included German help in organizing Soviet industries. A similar treaty is pending in the East. Available to mankind here in Siberia and China are constructive projects which would not only satisfy the nations of eastern Asia but enrich the population of the world and create ample universal living standards and abundance. But in order that these projects may succeed we need productive credit, created by all the nations and peoples of our earth. We need the money and credit of the world. We need economic solidarity.

Now the question arises: Is it possible for Japan to make an adjustment with Soviet Russia and to divide the spoils of the China incident between Russia and Japan?

Apart from the difficulties of a Russo-Japanese rapprochement covering the unsettled differences between these two countries, and the Japanese aspirations for the Maritime Province, the strength of China—incredible as it is—would scarcely permit such a partition. China is a colossal country; its manpower is inexhaustible. Its resistance has constantly stiffened and even been hardened by new attacks. The strong influence that Soviet Russia exerted in Manchuria and the Sin Kiang and Outer Mongolia provinces was successful so long as such influence and support was directed against Japan. Even the Chinese Communists would not aid in the division of China. They are primarily Chinese nationals.

The chief resistance to such a partition of China would come from China herself, led by Chiang Kai-shek. The Sino-Japanese war has awakened the country. China has organized an armament industry of her own, producing mostly weapons for guerrilla warfare. Japan has not succeeded in isolating China, which has maintained supply connections with the outer world and with Soviet Russia. Even if these supplies were completely cut off China could probably not be forced to an unfavorable peace. Japan is fully aware of this situation. It has seen before its eyes, before the eyes of its army of occupation, how Chiang Kai-shek succeeded in reorganizing China, its army and socio-economic institutions. In other words, if Japan were able to withdraw from China under face-saving peace conditions, she would probably make substantial concessions to China.

China's latest military offensive to free Hongkong and the decimation of a Japanese army near Canton, have made the situation for Japan, with part of her army still spread over northern China, very awkward indeed.

Chiang Kai-shek has refused alluring peace offers on the part of Japan. The United States has granted several credits to China, the last amounting to $500 millions, of which part will be used for the reorganization of the Chinese currency. The Western powers are doing what they can to stiffen Chinese resistance against Japanese aggression and threat against South China and India.

THE UNITED STATES AND EASTERN ASIA

Since the breakdown of France and the preliminary victory of totalitarian powers in Europe, Japan has exerted a more imperialist and ambitious nationalist policy. It has propounded an Eastern-Asiatic Monroe

Doctrine without taking into account the difference in the motives and aims of the United States Monroe Doctrine. It has declared French Indo-China and the Dutch East Indies as its sphere of interest and has demanded respect for "the stabilizing force in East Asia." Germany and Italy, however, by refusing to allot to Japan a share in the peace benefits as a result of the conquest of France, drove Japan increasingly into the Axis orbit. Finally, Japan has joined the Axis in a tripartite antiaggression pact clearly directed against the United States, and has been accorded privileges in Indo-China by the Vichy government in France. Japanese forces have overstepped these concessions and penetrated Indo-China, Burma Road and Singapore, i.e. the eastern Asiatic strategic key position. This represented the first grave political blow against Great Britain and the United States, designed to upset the status of the East.

Japan's provocative declaration, through Prince Konoye, that it intended to create a "new order in Asia," based on Eastern-Asiatic Monroe Doctrine and Japan's reliance on armed force, did not yet entirely destroy the principal viewpoint of our foreign policy. Our stand was clearly expressed by Sumner Welles, Under-Secretary of State, on September 28, 1940:

No problem is presented in the Far East that could not be solved pacifically if all powers concerned were willing to enter into sincere negotiations. But while the United States Government had repeatedly pointed to the possibility of settling international grievances at the conference table, it had been vigilant in preparing its national defense against any possible threats to our security and it was now preparing for all eventualities.

With these words Mr. Welles had again pointed out the willingness of the United States to negotiate on Far-Eastern problems as a fundamental basis for our Far-Eastern policy.

But Japanese policy (he declared) had been to build a "new order" by the use of force and to determine the limits of United States' rights and American interests by unilateral decision on its own part.

He repeated the primary requirements of the United States in the Far East as follows:

Complete respect by all powers for the legitimate rights of the United States and of its nationals as stipulated by existing treaties or as provided by the generally accepted tenets of international law.

Equality of opportunity for the trade of all nations.

And finally, respect for those international agreements of treaties concerning the Far East to which the United States is a party, although with the express

understanding that the United States is always willing to consider the peacef
negotiation of such modifications or changes in these agreements or treaties
may in the judgment of the signatories be considered necessary in the ligl
of changed conditions.

However, the Government of Japan, in its endeavor to create a "new ord
in Asia" has relied upon the instrumentality of armed force and it has made
very clear that it intends that it alone shall decide to what extent the histori
interests of the United States and the treaty rights of American citizens in th
Far East are to be observed. . . .

After this statement by Mr. Welles, and during most of the year c
1941, the situation remained the same in kind, but different in intensity
In the Spring of 1941 Russia negotiated a friendship pact with Japa
(which was never ratified by Japan), intended by the Axis to relieve th
latter from the ever constant pressure from the Russian giant to enabl
her to continue her aggression in the Far East. It enabled the Japanese t
move an expeditionary force into Indo-China, under quasi-consent c
the hard pressed Vichy government.

The German invasion of Russia has, however, intensified the situatior
In Russia's fight for her life lies the key to Japanese action. In the mean
time Roosevelt and Churchill, at their historical meeting in the Atlanti
decided that once and for all that "Japan must be stopped." The poolin
of the United States and British navies to protect the lend-lease gooc
released large English fighting units from the British Isles to other par
of the world and negotiations with Japan were started with seemingl
greater weight on the part of the Western powers. The assumptio
prevailed, that as long as the Russo-German war does not come to
decision or a stalemate, Japan would use a wait-and-see method an
neither make peace nor war. Negotiations were waged fiercely i
Washington and Tokio. The United States used an elastic economi
pressure in order to force Japan to come back to reason; but not to
hard as yet to drive her to desperation—to a war with the West.

It appeared, however, extremely difficult to build a bridge betwee
Japan's ambitions and Western interests. It was thought that the onl
way by which Japan might be induced to give up her ambitions withou
losing face and the logical means by which a solution may be brough
about was: *economic* reasoning. Instead of dreaming of vast Japanes
empire building in the Pacific, Japan may listen to *economic* proposal
for a "greater East-Asia co-prosperity area."

But the failure of the German conquest of Moscow and Leningrad the turning of the tide on the Russo-German front to Russia's favor and the unexpectedly successful winter attack of the Russian army, forced Hitler to bring pressure to bear on Japan, and events developed with amazing rapidity.

Let us retrace the kaleidoskopic sequence of events of the memorable week from December 1, to December 7, 1941:

On December 1, in the speech at the anniversary of Japan–Manchukuo–Nanking Government cooperation, Tojo rejected the principles underlying U.S. proposals for the settlement of the crisis as fantastic and restated Japan's insistence on the New Order in East Asia. General Ando cited the aims of the new order and underlined the obstruction of Great Britain and the United States. He predicted the collapse of Netherland Indies and Chunking Governments "after the elimination of the obstacles presented by the U.S." Tokio Authorities stated that they wanted to continue the talks with Washington for at least 2 weeks. Domei declared that Tojo demanded "purge of the exploitation of Asiatics rather than that of the exploiting powers." Officials in Washington reported that the allied powers, especially Great Britain, United States, China and the Netherlands collaborated on the preparation for any action of Japan that might occur.

But peace hopes faded. On December 1, Roosevelt had to rush back to Washington to confer with Foreign Secretary Hull, Admiral Stark, Henry Hopkins, and Sumner Welles. The Pacific fleet was believed ready for action.

But Germany pressed Japan to fight. It is now generally assumed in Washington diplomatic circles, that Wiedemann, the former General Consul in San Francisco, after having been sent back to Germany, brought Hitler's final directions for the Japanese attack with him on his trip via South America to the Far East. Since his arrival in East Asia, he and other German diplomats in the Far East were the guiding spirits of the Japanese war preparations and actions and of German participation and aid in the event of war.

Meanwhile, Mr. Hull and Mr. Welles conferred with Nomura and Kurusu in Washington. Nomura cited "wise statesmanship" and Kurusu commented peacefully. But Washington saw little hope for peace and believed the United States could defeat Japan quickly and easily. This false hope became fatal to the United States and the United Nations. Although the responsible statesmen and War Cabinets of the nations involved in the Far Eastern emergency situation hastened preparations for all eventualities, whatsoever was done, was too little and too late.

On December 2, in Tokio, Yomiuri stated that Hawaii was "the key to peace between the U.S. and Japan," and, by comparing Japan's aims to those of the American Revolution, he turned the tables on us and declared that "the U.S. desired to destroy Japan and to control Asia." On December Nakano urged: "immediate Japanese action to gain the strategic mastery i the Pacific. Japan needs raw materials. The United States must recogniz Tojo's peace program."

Meanwhile Great Britain, shunning the role of peacemaker and backed b the Netherlands Government in exile, advised the United States, "she woul fight if Japan invaded Thailand." The United States was constantly warne by Great Britain of the immediate danger of the outbreak of hostilities. Th situation became more critical every hour. Cordell Hull clearly recognized tha "force was the chief issue," but Nomura and Kurusu and Washington's Japanes Embassy assuaged and indicated that "talks will continue." Singapore source predicted the Japanese move against Thailand and warned that "the Britis stand in event of such incursion would be uncertain."

For a certain time, the popular idea prevailed that Japan acted independentl of Germany. But neither Washington nor London took this notion seriously On the report of new Japanese troop movements in Indo-China, Presiden Roosevelt appealed to Japan, to Hirohito, while Lt. General Suzaki warne the United States that "Japan's patience nears its end." On December 7 th American press discussed Manila's vulnerability to incendiary attack, an Manila's civilians were urged to leave the city to free facilities for compulsor evacuation, if needed.

In spite of this general awareness of the fact that any minute open hostilities could break out, Japan's attack on Pearl Harbor found the American fighting forces in complete and tragic slumber.

Nothing, however, could have awakened the American Nation to greater willingness to fight back, than the treacherous and catastrophic attack on Pearl Harbor. This and the following Japanese blitz-conquest of the most valuable strategic Pacific positions has brought home to the American people the direct life danger in which the nation finds herself. The second World War is no longer a question of American and Hemisphere isolation or intervention, but a life and death struggle for political, economic and intellectual independence. It is the question, of whether the world shall live in liberty or slavery; under the command of the Nazi pyramid of power or under a democratic control of world affairs. There can be no doubt but that at the end of the war the strongest moral and social order will have won the final victory. We are striding from static nationalism towards a super-ordinated dynamic and universal order of society.

Public opinion in the United States recognizes more and more, that

Japan, with a population of about 75,000,000 will—under a normal birth rate—have increased to about 90,000,000 by 1960. This expanding people occupies an area smaller than California or 1/20 the size of Australia with a population of only 7,000,000. Although considerably self-sufficient in food and coal, it is lacking in most natural resources. It must import its entire supply of cotton, nickel, mercury, 90 per cent of its oil, 70 per cent of its iron and steel, and must import much of its copper, zinc, aluminum and lead.

One might argue that Japan can buy most of these materials and that lack of supplies does not justify its offensive policy. But, we know only too well that the United Nations were in a position to cut off Japan's supply lines at a moment's notice and could have used rationing and embargo measures as political pressure. We know equally well that Japan does not have the cash to buy the raw materials. It cannot import enough nor pay with adequate exports.

We know that the Japanese are an industrious people, with mystical, but proud and war-like traditions and exaggerated Spartanic virtues. They have accumulated a gigantic national debt, their situation is aggravated from day to day, inflation is progressing, prices are rising accordingly, their trade balance has become more and more unfavorable. The Chinese campaign has caused fearful loss of human life and war material and the people were constantly forced to make sacrifices. The control of all political, economic and social life was centralized in the hands of a small group of ambitious and totalitarian-minded militarists. Small wonder that these leaders could easily convince the nation that they must have and will "fight for the same advantages that Western powers enjoy."

The result was the attack on Pearl Harbor and the rapid conquest of East Asiatic co-prosperity targets. Japan has become an object of "Axis grand strategy," forming the left wing of a giant pincers movement to join with the Nazis somewhere in the Indian Ocean. Japan is endeavoring to break her own blockade and dependency upon other nations and is thereby helping the Nazis in their aim to break the European blockade and sea control.

The growing universal recognition that the future order of the world must furnish a comprehensive economic control of the world's resources and raw materials will undoubtedly lead to a wiser universal policy which may internationalize sea-ways, colonies, gold production, etc. It will lead to a wiser respect of the economic positions of all nations, including Japan. Every nation wants to plan its economy, to expand it trade and commerce. Its spheres of interest are becoming unlimited a to space and time. But all these spheres of interest must be integrated and organized in a world-wide super-structure, which will make war more and more improbable and unnecessary. With the increasing wa power and war production of the United Nations and with the ove expansion of Japanese war potentialities, Japan may soon realize tha trade and investment concessions on a large scale from the United Nations concessions in the fields of money, credit, immigration, shipping, aviation fisheries, etc., are more important than the occupation of vast terri-tories with a hostile population. Japan's gold production amounts to only about $62,000,000 a year. Her present gold reserves are placed at abou $100,000,000. Although the country has made feverish efforts to increase gold production, especially on the island of Formosa and in occupied China, its ability to obtain gold is decreasing rather than increasing.

A constructive policy of industrial development in China with the help and backing of the United States and the leading European powers. on the basis of economic solidarity, is more important than all the sinister political and militaristic measures, from war and policing to puppet regimes. A free China, protected against floods and famine, guaranteed by all nations, primarily recognizing the vital needs of the Japanese people; a Soviet Russia developing the earth's great treasures in Siberia; England, France, Germany and Holland—or a Federated Europe—and the United States, as well as all the other nations of the world, trading and investing in eastern Asia on a mutual, safe, and efficient basis—is this pure utopia?

It is a disgrace to our generation that an order that could have been so easily established, a mechanism so simply organized, and a victory so easily won have been ignored.

A powerful Oriental Bank should be formed as the backbone of a new order in eastern Asia and as a forerunner of the Bank of Nations, with powers similar to those of the Hemisphere Bank, its share capital might be a hundred or two hundred million dollars, and its initial credit volume two billion dollars, of which 1 billion would be needed as first credit for reconstruction in China and additional amounts for Japan and other nations. Its location might be in San Francisco or on the Philippine Islands, with branches in all nations bordering on the Pacific.

Japan cannot establish a self-sufficient economic eastern-Asia bloc.

China, badly in need of almost everything, is entirely unable to make even a Japan–China–Manchuria group autarchic. Scrap iron, oil, wool, and innumerable other commodities must be bought from the outside as before. For this purpose Japan needs gold or foreign currency. On the other hand, favorable trade treaties and import quotas granted by the nations of the world collectively, razing of the tariff walls created by the Ottawa System and Smoot-Hawley tariff and similar agreements with China and the Philippines, a customs union or agreement among nations and other trade and commercial facilities must round out the entire program of the proposed Oriental Bank.

The main difference between the Japanese Greater East Asia Co-prosperity Area and the Bank of Nations—respectively Oriental Bank ideas, is this:

The Japanese dream of a New Order in the Far East, is to bring the nine hundred millions East-Asiatic peoples under the political and military control of Japan, closing the Open Door to China for the other nations and giving Japan the privilege for the East-Asiatic political economy. This block of yellow nations would then be organized and prepared for the future world struggle of the yellow race against the whites.

The Bank of Nations and Oriental Bank ideas, on the other hand, provide for a general settlement, an economic world peace of equal partners for all nations alike. The Oriental Bank would first of all help China to become a strong and independent member of the family of nations. Secondly, it would help Japan and all other nations of the world interested in a human and functional peace in the Pacific and everywhere. Even if Japan insists upon pursuing a policy which aims at the conquest of Asia and succeeds partly or totally, it will never be able to consolidate its position without international credits and an Oriental banking system.

China and Japan, provided with an international medium of exchange issued by the Oriental Bank or the Bank of Nations, with short and long-term credits and export facilities, will see a renaissance such as they have never seen before. There can be no new order in eastern Asia and the Pacific at large without an economic mechanism which, with its dynamic functions, guarantees that order. The Oriental Bank, as part of the new economic and political world organization coordinated into the Bank of Nations, Federal World authority, and international Labor Organization, will form the best attainable guarantee for a true and lasting peace in the Pacific.

CHAPTER VIII

THE INTERNATIONAL LABOR ORGANIZATION— ITS POTENTIALITIES

A STRONG hope of mankind for a functional, nonpolitical organization of the wealth and manpower of the world and for the successful establishment of international understanding on a thoroughly practical basis rests in the International Labor Organization.

It has been the principal task of the I.L.O. to lessen the danger of wars through the establishment of rules, regulations, and universal standards of social and economic justice. And since the outbreak of this new war the I.L.O. has remained the last international body which continues to work for international understanding, for the welfare of labor, and for the common good of nations both neutral and at war. One cannot write the economic history of the last twenty years without taking into consideration the great achievements of the immortal "chevaliers de la paix et de la justice sociale," who fought for half a century to build this fraternity of human labor and who made it an institution for eternal international cooperation.

Ethel M. Johnson, head of the Washington Branch of the I.L.O., correctly states in her pamphlet, *The United States in the International Labor Organization,* that the title, "International Labor Organization," has given rise to misconception as to the nature and activities of the body. The I.L.O. is not a trade union or a federation of trade unions. It is not a superstate or superlegislative body. Rather, it is an agency for international cooperation in the advancement of social and economic standards. The conventions of treaties which are prepared by the official delegates of the member countries acting at the International Labor Conference are proposals, to be submitted to the different countries, upon which each country decides for itself what action it will take. "The I.L.O. is a world association of nations working for improved labor standards and closer harmony in labor relations in the various countries of the world."

There is no other path toward the abandonment of war and the victory of peace than the difficult but sacred one taken by the pioneers of the I.L.O., in carrying the cross of humanity and preparing for the resurrection of mankind and civilization.

On February 14, 1918, during the period of hostilities in the World War, the Interallied Labour and Socialist Conference in London adopted a resolution that an international conference be called to

endeavor by mutual agreement to arrange a program of action for a speedy and democratic peace. [The Conference was of the opinion] that the working classes, having made such sacrifices during the war, are entitled to take part in securing a democratic world peace, and that M. Albert Thomas (France), M. Emile Vandervelde (Belgium), and Mr. Arthur Henderson (Great Britain) be appointed as a Commission to secure from all the governments a promise that at least one representative of Labor and Socialism will be included in the official representation at any Government Conference.

The conference regretted the absence of the United States, and a deputation headed by Camille Huysmans was delegated to confer with representatives of the American democracy on the whole war situation. After innumerable negotiations and conferences, in which Albert Thomas and Samuel Gompers (then president of the American Federation of Labor) were the leading lights, in 1919, the I.L.O. became a reality. Unfortunately, the United States only joined the I.L.O. in 1934. Today, however, it is one of its most active members.

However, long before the peace was concluded, the United States had paralleled the efforts of the allied and associated powers by proposing considerations for the improvement of the lot of the working class, which had suffered most by the war. At the end of the World War, therefore, an "Organizing Committee" was constituted to draft the labor provisions for the peace treaties. Samuel Gompers was chairman of the committee, and its draft has frequently been called the "Magna Carta of Labor." The labor provisions of the Organizing Committee, drafted for the peace treaties, began with the following two principal statements:

1. Universal peace can be established only if it is based upon social justice.

2. The failure of any nation to adopt humane conditions of labor is an obstacle in the way of other nations which desire to improve conditions in their own countries.

It was the First International Labor Conference in Washington, D. C., in 1919, in the midst of the social disappointments and economic disturbances of the World War, which took the initiative in investigating the problem of reparations and to score its faults. Germany and Austria, prominent in labor reforms, were invited and became members of the movement, and an Italian labor delegate proposed "that there be created some system of distribution under international control for the fair allotment of the raw materials of the world."

As John G. Winant, when Director of the I.L.O., pointed out:[1]

Long before the World Economic Conference of 1927 was called, a workers' delegate proposed that *an international Conference be called which should comprise qualified representatives of all the important economic factors: commerce, industry, agriculture, labour and consumption. . . .*

In 1932, one year before Hitler's rise to power, when the world was in a state of confusion and anxiety, we had been warned by another Director's report that

There is such a state of general panic that a policy of economic armaments is being adopted on all sides, on top of the policy of military armaments.

Today we know [writes Winant in 1939] the extent to which it is true and how far this policy has drawn the world toward economic and political strife and the increasing dread of world war. . . . In approaching labour and social problems we are forced to face the economic consequence of war and peace. This holds whether it be in relation to trade conflict or war economy.

It was the I.L.O. which observed and exposed the influence of armaments on everyday life, the costs "added to each loaf of bread we buy,

[1] *The World of Industry and Labour,* report of the Director of the I.L.O. to the twenty-fifth session of the International Labor Conference, Geneva, June 1939.

every acre of land we cultivate, and to the length of day we labor to earn a living"; in short, it demonstrated how "the diversion of a substantial part of the total income of any nation from useful production and services to armament reduces our standards of living." It was the I.L.O. and its members who untiringly unmasked the serious consequences of "moral" and material armament: "War not only affords no solution to the human wants with which people are confronted, but it is the very negation of everything they seek."

Can we imagine a greater tragedy than that the same working class which fought for a democratic peace in 1918 must now again turn to the production of armaments and other instruments of destruction?— that either voluntarily or by force the same laboring class must again take part in the mechanization of war and in the perfection of the modern war machine—the same war machine which eventually will destroy those who manufactured it and their fellows in other lands who are members of the same labor organization that was created for the express purpose of avoiding war? When will the labor and production classes of the world wake up and recognize this illogical, vicious circle and do something about it?

Let it be stated, once and for all, that through international agreements among the working population of the world, in cooperation with governments and industries and by means of a functional world organization, this tragedy can be entirely avoided. A Bank of Nations is not an unrealistic ideology; it is a very realistic ideal that may be achieved, although only with great human effort. Is it nothing more than an idle fantasy that out of this war will arise the creation and organization of such a mechanism? I cannot believe it.

Unfortunately the I.L.O. was too loosely organized and too weakly welded together with the economic structure of the world to enable it to intervene in the menacing war situation. There was no powerful organism to back the I.L.O. in its effort to enforce a general international settlement at the right time. After this war, when starvation and pestilence, revolution and bankruptcy have disintegrated the peoples of the world and crushed their excesses, we may be wiser. A much more powerful body may be born, which by its own force and momentum can exercise a controlling influence on erroneous and excessively iso-lated acts of nations or groups to the detriment of the world population.

If a plan for permanent peace after the design here presented—an economic world organization, with all its agencies, subagencies, and affiliated departments, in collaboration with the I.L.O. and a Federal World Authority—could be brought to life, the situation would be different. If all nations, all economies, were so closely interlocked and coordinated, war excesses would not only be extremely difficult, waste-ful, and uneconomic, but would also completely lack the moral or nationalistic palliatives with which ambitious leaders are able to dis-guise their obscure activities. Where are, for instance, the "have-not" and "lebensraum" or "elbowroom" arguments in an organized world economy? Of how much value are boundaries in a customs union of nations? And of what importance are the problems of unemployment and bad crop situations causing scarcity in farm products, if a world reserve, insurance, and distribution system were to function well?

The next famine in Europe and Asia may be the worst in history. Our Western Hemisphere may be willing to do its best to help by offering our surplus to the hungry millions overseas. How much would that help be, compared to a raw material reserve built up during fat years and ready when needed in abundant measure? Moreover, it is extremely doubtful that famine disasters would develop to such dimen-sions, or would occur at all, if the motives for civil or political wars and revolutions were absent.

Harold Butler, the predecessor of J. G. Winant in Geneva, has uttered the memorable thought that

the chance of remaking peace may come like a thief in the night; but unless the implications of a real peace, and particularly its economic implications, have been thought out in advance, unless statesmen and peoples can see the issues with clear eyes, when the critical moment comes, the chance may again be lost, as it was lost in 1919.

Are we prepared for the coming peace? Is it imaginable that there is a soul under the sun who does not reflect upon this impending adventure? How much sincere thought and effort is now being devoted by scientists, businessmen, labor leaders, statesmen, and artists toward making this peace a festival of enlightenment?

INTERNATIONAL LABOR ORGANIZATION

The I.L.O. has given us an illustrious example of how moral and ethical thought can be transformed into practical organized deeds. Let us, briefly, view this organization, its reason for being, its objectives, how it operates, and its results (cf. the prospectus of the I.L.O.).

The International Labor Charter

I. Preamble

Whereas the League of Nations has for its object the establishment of universal peace, and such a peace can be established only if it is based upon social justice;

And whereas conditions of labour exist involving such injustice, hardship and privation to large numbers of people as to produce unrest so great that the peace and harmony of the world are imperilled; and an improvement of those conditions is urgently required: as, for example, by the regulation of the hours of work, including the establishment of a maximum working day and week, the regulation of the labour supply, the prevention of unemployment, the provision of an adequate living wage, the protection of the worker against sickness, disease and injury arising out of his employment, the protection of children, young persons and women, provision for old age and injury, protection of the interests of workers when employed in countries other than their own, recognition of the principle of freedom of association, the organisation of vocational and technical education and other measures;

Whereas also the failure of any nation to adopt humane conditions of labour is an obstacle in the way of other nations which desire to improve the conditions in their own countries;

The HIGH CONTRACTING PARTIES, moved by sentiments of justice and humanity as well as by the desire to secure the permanent peace of the world, agree to the following: [*here follow the detailed provisions for the establishment of the* I.L.O.].

II. General Principles

The following methods and principles for regulating labour conditions seem to the High Contracting Parties to be of special and urgent importance:

First.—The guiding principle that labour should not be regarded merely as a commodity or article of commerce.

Second.—The right of association for all lawful purposes by the employed as well as by the employers.

Third.—The payment to the employed of a wage adequate to maintain a reasonable standard of life as this is understood in their time and country.

Fourth.—The adoption of an eight-hour day or a forty-eight-hour week as the standard to be aimed at where it has not already been attained.

Fifth.—The adoption of a weekly rest of at least twenty-four hours, which should include Sunday wherever practicable.

Sixth.—The abolition of child labour and the imposition of such limitations on the labour of young persons as shall permit the continuation of their education and assure their proper physical development.

Seventh.—The principle that men and women should receive equal remuneration for work of equal value.

Eighth.—The standard set by law in each country with respect to the conditions of labour should have due regard to the equitable economic treatment of all workers lawfully resident therein.

Ninth.—Each State should make provision for a system of inspection, in which women should take part, in order to ensure the enforcement of the laws and regulations for the protection of the employed.

The I.L.O. functions through three agencies: (1) the International Labor Conference, (2) the Governing Body, and (3) the International Labor Office.

International Labor Conference[2]

The International Labor Conference is a parliament or assembly made up of delegates from the member countries. It meets at least once a year, usually in Geneva. Each country is entitled to send four delegates to the Conference—two representing the government and one each representing respectively the principal association of employers and the principal association of labor in that country. It is thus a tripartite body on which management and labor are equally represented, with the balance of power in the hands of the government delegates.

The Conference discusses proposals for labor treaties which, when adopted by the delegates, are called draft conventions. It also adopts recommendations as suggestions for national legislative action. Neither the convention nor the recommendations have binding effect until they are ratified or approved by the countries desiring to take such action. Each country is free to make its own decision in the matter. The only obligation imposed is that the conventions adopted at a given conference shall be submitted to the appropriate

[2] Ethel M. Johnson, *The United States in the International Labor Organization*, Washington Branch of I.L.O.

legislative authority of the member countries within one year after its adoption, with an outside limit of 18 months.

Matters which came before the Conference in 1939 include the following: Technical and vocational education and apprenticeship; recruiting, placing, and conditions of labor of migrant workers; regulation of contracts of employment of indigenous workers; regulation of hours of work and rest periods of professional motor transport drivers.

In view of the amount of preliminary work required, the Conference Agenda must be arranged well in advance of the meeting. The agenda for the 1940 conference has already been approved. It will contain the following questions: organization of labor inspection; weekly rest periods for commercial and office employees; safety provisions for underground work in coal mines; rights of performers in broadcasting.

Governing Body

The Governing Body is the executive board of the Organization. It elects the Director of the I.L.O., formulates general policies for the Office and prepares the agenda for the International Labor Conference. The Governing Body consists of 32 members, of whom sixteen represent governments, eight represent employers, and eight represent workers. Of the government representatives, eight are named by the countries of chief industrial importance. The countries with permanent seats include the United States, Canada, France, Great Britain, and India. The remaining eight government seats are filled by election in the Conference for a three-year term. The workers' representatives are elected by the workers' delegates at the Conference; and the employer representatives are similarly chosen by the employer delegates.

The Governing Body meets as a rule four times a year, usually in Geneva, Switzerland. Occasionally, however, the Governing Body by invitation meets in another country. The session in October, 1937, was held in Prague at the invitation of Czechoslovakia; the October, 1938, session met in London at the invitation of the British Government.

International Labor Office

The International Labor Office is the permanent secretariat of the Governing Body and of the International Labor Conference. Its seat is in Geneva, Switzerland, on the shores of Lake Geneva. The personnel, appointed by the Director, numbers around 400 and is drawn from the various countries in the world. Approximately 40 nationalities are represented on the staff.

French and English are the official languages at the Office and all of the official publications are issued in both languages.

The work of the Office includes preparation of material for the use of the Governing Body, its committees and the International Labor Conference, and the execution of decisions of these bodies. In addition to work of this nature, the International Labor Office conducts a number of important services which have won for it recognition throughout the world as a research center and technical agency in the field of labor standards.

It collects and disseminates on an international scale current information with regard to labor events and movements. It conducts research in the field of economic and industrial problems, studying such subjects as regulation of hours of employment, methods of wage payment, technological causes of unemployment, problems of migratory labor, industrial technology and industrial safety, social insurance systems, problems of agricultural labor, technological unemployment, and scientific management.

The office publishes several economic and technical periodicals such as the *International Labor Review, Industrial Safety Survey,* and the *Bibliography of Industrial Hygiene.* There are also several publications of an informational nature as the *Official Bulletin, Industrial and Labor Information,* and the *I.L.O. Month by Month.* It issues a *Legislative Series,* analyzing the principal labor laws enacted in the various countries, a *Yearbook of Labor Statistics,* and various monographs dealing with social and economic questions and the ways in which various countries throughout the world have attempted to solve them. *Technical Progress and Unemployment, Economical Administration of Health Insurance Benefits, Labor Problems in Indo-China, Industrial Labor in India, Safety in the Construction and Use of Lifts, Social Problems in Agriculture, The Minimum Wage—an International Survey,* and *The Workers' Standard of Living*—titles of some of the publications recently issued—illustrate the wide range of interests of the International Labor Office and the broad field covered by its studies.

I.L.O. Committees

Much of the important work of the International Labor Organization is carried on with the aid of committees. These include, in addition to the standing committees of the Governing Body, committees of outside experts and mixed committees made up of members of the Governing Body and representatives of other organizations. There are, for example, the correspondence committees, special technical committees of experts, and permanent technical committees established to deal with specific subjects.

The correspondence committees are advisory groups, the members of which do not as a rule meet but are consulted by the Office for information and advice on subjects in which they are specialists. Among the correspondence committees are those on Accident Prevention, Social Insurance, Industrial Hygiene, Migration, Unemployment Insurance and Placing, and Women's Work. Committees of experts are appointed from time to time for a particular purpose where immediate study of a technical problem is required and specialized knowledge is essential, particularly in preparation for the Conference.

It might be interesting at this point to explain the present procedure before a new subject is included on the Agenda of the annual International Labor Conference. For example, the Governing Body in the case of accidents in coal mines may approve a study which involves the calling of experts. The Office prepares a digest of the existing laws and practices on the subject in the countries of the world. This digest is then sent to the experts selected by the coal-producing countries. The experts meet in Geneva for discussion. These discussions are recorded and digested and the committee is reassembled to approve a draft. A tripartite committee representing the employers, workers, and governments is then asked to discuss the draft and to make recommendations to the annual I.L.O. Conference, to which all member governments send employer, government, and worker delegates, supported by experts.

Technical Committees

Sometimes following a meeting of the Conference, a permanent technical committee is set up to provide for continuing study of a given subject. Such is the International Tripartite Committee on the Textile Industry authorized by the Governing Body at its February, 1939, meeting to implement the resolution adopted by the Tripartite Technical Conference on the Textile Industry in Washington in 1937. It will be the function of this Permanent Committee to consider labor conditions in the textile industries throughout the world with special reference to those points which directly or indirectly may have a bearing on the improvement of working conditions. The Committee will be organized with panels representing various branches of the textile industry. It will conduct studies and will make recommendations to the Governing Body.

The Permanent Agricultural Committee, which was established in 1937 and which held its first session in February, 1938, is concerned with the social problems of agriculture. It is responsible for assisting the Governing Body and the Conference in their work with respect to agricultural labor. Members of the Governing Body representing the three constituent groups—governments, employers and workers—serve on this Committee. There are also representatives of agricultural employers and agricultural labor, agricultural experts and representatives of international bodies dealing with social problems in agriculture.

One of the most recently established of the permanent committees of the I.L.O. is the International Public Works Committee. This Committee is intended to provide an avenue for continuous exchange of information and experience between the countries of the world on advance planning of public works as a means of reducing economic depression and preventing unemployment. The first meeting was held in Geneva in June, 1938.

Preliminary Technical Conferences

Somewhat similar to the special committees of experts, although operating on a larger scale, are the tripartite technical conferences which are convened to advise the Governing Body with reference to matters coming before an I.L.O. Conference or to make preliminary scientific exploration of a problem under consideration for Conference action. These technical conferences usually include representatives of the government, employers, and workers. Among these conferences may be mentioned the Technical Tripartite Conference on the Coal Industry, that on the Chemical Industry, and that on the Printing Trades.

The most noteworthy of the technical conferences arranged by the International Labor Organization was the Preparatory Tripartite Technical Conference on the Textile Industry held in Washington in April, 1937. Its purpose was to explore all phases of the situation that directly or indirectly affect the social and economic conditions in that industry and to lay the foundation for future action. It considered the interrelation between the textile industry and other industries with special reference to the influence of agriculture. The work of these technical conferences illustrates the scientific approach which the International Labor Organization makes toward the solution of labor problems with which it is concerned.

I.L.O. Conventions

Few persons not in close touch with the work of the Organization appreciate the amount of careful and detailed study that goes into the preparation of a draft convention or labor treaty. Under the regular procedure it is customary to devote two sessions to a subject before the convention is adopted

This means at least two years of research, study, discussion, and conference action. Preliminary, however, to the first discussion of a given subject by the International Labor Conference, such for example as the minimum age for employment of children in industry, a report is prepared by the International Labor Office outlining the existing legislation and practices in the various countries with regard to the subject. This report is then made available to the members of the Conference before their initial meeting for consideration of the question.

At this first meeting, the subject is discussed, but no definite action with regard to a convention is taken. From the major points raised in the discussion at the Conference, the International Labor Office prepares a questionnaire which is sent to the governments of the member countries for their views with regard to the issues raised. The replies to this questionnaire are then compiled in another report which is submitted to the second Conference at which, after thorough discussion, final action may be taken with regard to the adoption of a convention. In some instances where the issues are not too involved, or where there has been a special preliminary technical conference to consider the subject, action in adopting a convention is taken at a single session. A two-thirds vote of the delegates is required for adoption. The convention is then submitted by the member countries to their legislative bodies for consideration. In case of ratification it is registered with the Secretariat of the League of Nations at Geneva.

To June, 1939, 67 conventions have been adopted by the International Labor Conference. Several of these, however, represent revision of previous conventions. In all, 59 different subjects are covered by the conventions which have been adopted. These deal with such matters as the minimum age for the employment of children, regulation of the hours of labor, night work in bakeries, weekly rest periods, employment on public works, unemployment, social insurance, workmen's compensation, industrial accidents, occupational disease, and safety provisions in the building trades.

One group of conventions is concerned with the protection of seamen. Six maritime conventions were adopted at the special Maritime Conference held in 1936. Five of these have been ratified by the United States.

In addition to conventions or proposed treaties, the Conference, by majority vote, adopts recommendations. These are suggested to the member countries with a view to the enactment of national legislation or regulations on a given subject. Some of the recommendations deal with matters which are not yet ripe for a convention. Sometimes they are concerned with details which can best be left to legislative action in the individual countries rather than attempting to cover them in a general treaty. Among recent recommendations are those calling for international cooperation in connection with public works, national planning of public works, minimum age for employment of children in family undertakings, cooperation in accident inspection, and provision for a model safety code for the building industry. Approximately 60 recommendations have been adopted.

Application of Conventions

Questions may be raised as to the significance of the conventions after their adoption. Until ratified, the proposed conventions have no binding effect. They are suggestions from the International Labor Organization to its members. Each country is free to decide for itself whether or not it wishes to ratify. The only obligation imposed is that each country shall within a specified time submit to its appropriate authority for decision the conventions and recommendations adopted after its adherence to the Organization.

In the case of the United States, the President submits the proposed conventions to Congress or to the Senate. Of the 23 conventions and 22 recommendations that have been adopted since the United States became a member of the International Labor Organization, all but those dealing with maritime affairs have been submitted to both branches of Congress. The six maritime conventions and the two maritime recommendations were submitted to the Senate only. This is consistent with the constitutional provisions that specify that the President and the Senate constitute the treaty-making authority.

When a country ratifies a convention, it is then under obligation to enact implementing legislation and to submit an annual report to the International Labor Office with regard to the measures taken to make the convention effective. Up to September, 1939, there were recorded 859 ratifications. Great Britain, France, Sweden, Belgium, Mexico, the Netherlands, Bulgaria, Uruguay, and Yugoslavia have each ratified more than 20 conventions. A few countries have not as yet ratified any. It is provided in the Constitution of the International Labor Organization that the government of a federal state with limited power to ratify conventions on labor matters may treat a draft convention to which such limitations apply as a recommendation only.

Ratification is given effect through the provision in the Constitution of the I.L.O. authorizing complaints by organizations of employers or by member states. There is also provision for investigation through a Commission of Inquiry composed of nominees of the member states, other than those directly concerned in the complaint; and there is further provision for the publication of the recommendations and findings of such a commission. In the last resort, a non-compliance may be brought before the Permanent Court of International Justice.

Other Activities and Services of the I.L.O.

Although the formulation of labor treaties and the research work preparatory to the adoption of such treaties represent a major part of the work of the International Labor Organization, it is by no means the only work. The International Labor Office has become the leading international research center on subjects dealing with labor and industrial relations. Requests for information on these subjects come to the Office from all parts of the world.

The Office maintains a special reference library on labor and industrial problems—a collection numbering more than 400,000 volumes, books and pamphlets. It is the most comprehensive collection of its kind in the world. More than 4,000 periodicals in 45 different languages are received currently. In its legislative section the Library collects the labor laws from all the nations in the world. The facilities of the library are open to students of all nationalities and countries. The special reports, studies, year books, and periodicals issued by the International Labor Office constitute an appreciable library in themselves. The average annual output of literature by the International Labor Office comprises something over 30,000 printed pages.

An important but little known service of the Organization is the technical assistance given to various countries in connection with their problems of labor legislation and labor law administration. When the Social Security Board in the United States was preparing to set up a system of unemployment compensation for this country, one of the officials from the International Labor Office who is an expert in this field was sent over to assist in formulation of the plans.

Assistance has been given by the Organization to South American states desiring to organize a labor department or develop a system of factory inspection, or a code of labor legislation. Officials from the Central Office were assigned to spend several months in the countries requesting this assistance, working directly with officials of the government in drafting legislation and formulating plans for administrative machinery.

As the work of the International Labor Organization has developed, attention is increasingly being given to the underlying causes of labor problems—the social-economic conditions that are at the foundation of current issues in the field of labor relations. Emphasis is being placed on raising the standards of living, on reaching the causes of unemployment, and on methods of providing social security.

Report of the Director

The enlargement of the original concept of the International Labor Organization is discussed in recent reports of the Director which stress the interrelation between social and economic forces as an explanation of the new emphasis of the Organization on economic progress. The Director's Report is not only a discussion of the activities of the International Labor Organization, but a survey of social and economic problems throughout the world.

Particular interest attaches to the Report for 1939 because of the critical period in world history with which it deals and because it represents the message of a citizen of the United States speaking from an international forum. Written in the crucial months preceding the outbreak of the European war, the Report discusses the problems of "near war" and of peace and the role of the International Labor Organization in contributing toward their solution. It calls attention to the fact that increasing armaments eventually mean lower standards of living and worsening conditions of labor and that international action is necessary to anticipate needs arising from the situation.

In the meantime, the grim realities of war increase the difficulties of the work of the I.L.O. and at the same time increase the need for that work. There is the matter of protecting the workers of civilian populations from exploitation; the safeguarding of labor standards, won after many years of struggle; the demonstration that humane conditions of employment are essential to effective production. Beyond these pressing problems of the moment is the vital question of ultimate peace. The obligations of peace are no less real than those of war. The essential thing, if real peace is to be secured, is that the statesmen and the peoples of the world think through in advance the economic implications upon which such a peace must be based. A contribution which the I.L.O. can make in this connection is to assist in the preparation of a practical social program which can assure to the working people throughout the world recognition of their ultimate needs.

. . . .

In reviewing the twenty years of intensive work for a new practical internationalism, we cannot but admire the achievements of the I.L.O. It has become a "living reality, instead of a mere abstraction in the minds of those whose problems it was created to solve." Winant is right in stating, in his 1939 report, that

an important aspect of the universality of the organization is its tripartite character. The representation of Governments, employers, and workers in an international body has given internationalism a new meaning. The fact that meetings held under the auspices of the Organization include non-Government representatives has always been one of its greatest sources of strength. In certain of its aspects the Organization reaches across frontiers instead of emphasizing them. Perhaps more than any other body it speaks for the peoples of the world. The fact that many hundreds of thousands of men and women in all the continents of the world regard it as "their" organization is the most precious asset that any international institution can possess.

During the twenty years of its development, the I.L.O. has created an International Labor Code in accordance with the fundamental principles of its constitution.

Gradually, however [as Winant states in his report], it has become clear that the real utility of such a code could be greatly enhanced if the Organization did not confine itself to setting up standards, but also did something to bring about the necessary *organization and coordination of social policy* on which the improvement of living and working conditions depends. A shifting of emphasis in this direction has taken place, especially in the last few years.

As examples of this development, we may mention preparatory conferences for the organization's program for reduction of hours of work. In the Coal Conference (1938) and in the Rail Transport Conference (1939), to some extent "the whole social and economic situation of these two key branches of production" was treated. In the textile industry "this process of enabling an industry to see itself as a whole has been carried a stage further" and a Permanent International Tripartite Committee on the Textile Industry has been set up "which would make it possible, for the first time, to review continuously the world textile industry, with a view to determining what can be done to improve the situation of the fourteen millions of men and women engaged in it."

Most gratifying is the fact that the Conference on Migration for

Settlement has proposed that a permanent International Committee on Migration for Settlement should be created. Another example is its project on public works:

Perhaps the most striking example of the changed emphasis of the outlook of the Organization is to be found [states Winant] in the work of the International Public Works Committee, which held its first meeting in July, 1938, and was attended by representatives from 25 countries. The origin of the Committee lay in the idea that advance planning of public works programmes is an important means of diminishing economic depressions and that national action needs to be supplemented by international exchange of information and perhaps by definite international action. The specific task of the meeting was to draw up a uniform plan on the basis of which Governments would be invited to furnish information concerning their public works policies and programmes. The success of this action already seems assured. Eleven Governments have notified the Office that they intend to give effect to the Public Works (International Cooperation) Recommendation, while four others have advised the competent authorities in their own countries in favor of adherence. Furthermore, seven other countries are known to be taking action with a view to approval. There is thus every probability that further meetings of the Committee will soon be convened, so that the Committee should be in a position to make an important contribution to the coordination of the policies of the Member nations in the common struggle against the causes of unemployment.

Besides these more or less unrelated movements, the International Labor Office has created what Winant calls an International Civil Service, an international clearing house of information on labor, economic, and social questions of all kinds. As we have seen, it has taken part in social legislation, industrial hygiene, social insurance, colonization, drafting of a labor code, research work, and comparative studies of all kinds. At the end of his review, Mr. Winant summarizes the work which, until now, the I.L.O. has done in this respect.

The work done on economic depression and unemployment is an instance of how, through research based on wide international experience and broad outlook, the organization has helped to guide world opinion towards more effective methods. Many years before it became a generally accepted standpoint, the International Labour Office was insisting that the means of dealing with industrial depression was not to bring about general wage reductions and to multiply tariff barriers, but to reinforce purchasing power through the long-range planning of public works, backed by appropriate monetary policy and made general by international co-operation. In this, perhaps the most important of all social-economic questions, whether seen from the standpoint of the workers, or of the employers, or of the Governments, the International Labour Organisation has been a pioneer. Mr. J. M. Keynes, in his *General Theory of Employment*, speaking of schemes of public investment as a means of maintaining the optimum level of employment and of improving the international economic situation, writes: "The consistent appreciation of this truth by the International Labour Office, first under Albert Thomas and subsequently under Mr. H. B. Butler, has stood out conspicuously among the pronouncements of the numerous post-war international bodies." From the small beginning in the Recommendation concerning unemployment, adopted by the International Labour Conference in 1919, urging States Members to "co-ordinate the execution of all work undertaken under public authority, with a view to reserving such work as far as possible to periods of unemployment," to the Public Works (International Co-operation) and Public Works (National Planning) Recommendations of 1937, the International Labour Organization has studied and progressively developed the technique for dealing with industrial depression some five or ten years in advance of public, or even expert, opinion. The detailed resolution submitted to the World Monetary and Economic Conference of 1933, presented jointly by the leaders of all three groups, and unanimously adopted by the International Labour Conference, set out certain of the essential means of meeting economic depression which only now are beginning to be applied.

Another example of the value of the research work of the Office—and only a few examples can be given—is to be found in its studies of silicosis. These studies were reinforced by the international Conferences on this subject held in Johannesburg in 1930 and in Geneva in 1938, which made experience concerning this occupational disease acquired in certain countries, especially in the Union of South Africa, available to other countries interested in the solution of the problem. With a similar object in view the Office endeavours to collect and disseminate data bearing on the subject.

The standardisation of labour statistics and improvement in their comparability brought about by the Office's research work, assisted by the Committee of Statistical Experts and the successive Conferences of Labour Statisticians, is more important than the general public may realise. The existence of adequate and internationally comparable statistics is essential for the close study of fact which should precede legislative measures, and therefore provides a firm basis on which international labour legislation can be built up.

Many other examples of the kind of work which the International Labour Office does might be given. But apart from these, there is something else which the Office represents. It is a fact of the utmost importance that, at a time when national rivalries made such an achievement more than usually difficult, it has been possible to build up the nucleus of an international civil service. Experience has proved conclusively that men and women of different nations, of widely different cultures and habits of thought, can work together in an objective spirit in the service of an ideal. Their national patriotism is not destroyed, but is enlarged into a world loyalty based on the idea of common humanity. This result has been possible only because the Organisation does serve an ideal, and because the individuals making up the Office believe in that ideal.

The value of an international civil service is manifold. The duties of the International Labour Office staff range from telephonic interpretation, making possible simultaneous rendering of speeches in several languages, to the habit of mind which sees social and economic questions from the point of view of the world as a whole. Such special aptitudes are not rapidly or easily acquired; but if the nations of the world are to find their way to a better understanding, no instrument is more necessary than a personnel which makes this understanding practically realisable. The fact that in the course of the last two decades the authority of the International Labour Organisation has steadily developed must be attributed in no small part to the fact that the international staff brought together in Geneva has made its cause their own.

These few examples may give some idea of the direct and indirect influence which the work of the Organisation in its various forms has exercised, viewed from a general international standpoint.

Both the I.L.O. and the League of Nations have done an immensely creative work in the broad field of international labor cooperation. It is only natural that these activities had to be spearheads directed toward the different branches of world economy. What is still missing is a coordinated system welded together into a mighty, well-functioning mechanism. The impulse for such concerted action can only come after a heavy world crisis of revolutionary proportions, such as we are witnessing now. Only a world catastrophe of the first rank can create the psychological and political conditions necessary to bring this change about.

In the second part of Chapter IV, we have shown how international labor and capital can be organized through the Bank of Nations in cooperation with the I.L.O. The first step must be the establishment of an International Planning Board, as the permanent central planning authority for the new labor and capital organization. This institution must coordinate the unrelated planning activities of all functional organizations of the I.L.O. and the Bank of Nations on a world-wide scale. With the help of the I.L.O. and the Bank of Nations, it must preplan and predetermine the socio-economic activities of the world and gradually bring order into our disturbed and impoverished generation, stop waste and scarcity measures, distribute and redistribute wealth, create new productive works of public benefit, new purchasing power and a higher standard of living for all the peoples.

This venture must, of course, be financed. But in a world which annually spends some thirty-five billion dollars on armaments, the amount necessary for the financing of this mechanism will be but a bagatelle. Each of the fifty-four member countries of the I.L.O. is assessed annually in proportion to its size and industrial importance. In 1940, the contribution of the United States amounts to less than two hundred and fifty thousand dollars. The capital invested in the famous Peace Palace of the League of Nations, the Agricultural Institute in Rome, the Permanent Court of International Justice at the Hague, and the International Labor Organization in Geneva amounts to less than the cost of a good battleship, which costs approximately seventy million dollars. The total budget of the International Labor Office for 1940 is only nine million, ninety thousand Swiss francs or about two million dollars. These are facts so startling that they might help to arouse our human intelligence. The Bank of Nations could certainly help in financing those institutions which are needed for human effort employed in the renaissance of the world.

On November 30, 1939, four months after the outbreak of the new European war, member states of the I.L.O. adopted the following

PLAN FOR PERMANENT PEACE

Declaration of Habana[3]

The representatives of the governments, employers, and work people of the American Continent, having met at Habana on November 21, 1939, in accordance with the generous invitation of the Cuban Government at the second labor conference of American states which are members of the International Labor Organization, adopts the following solemn declaration which may be cited as the Declaration of Habana, 1939:

Whereas, as is declared by the preamble to the constitution of the International Labor Organization, lasting peace can be established only if it is based on social justice; and

Whereas the existence of conditions of labor involving injustice, hardship, and privation to large numbers of people is calculated to produce unrest so great that the peace and harmony of the world are imperiled; and

Whereas the International Labor Organization has determined to continue the quest for social justice in peace and in war; and

Whereas these efforts of the International Labor Organization are completely compatible with the spirit of the Declaration of Lima of December 24, 1938, and the Declaration of Continental Solidarity adopted at Panama on October 3, 1939, and with the desire to set the world an example of a whole continent determined to resolve its differences without recourse to violence; and

Whereas in view of the constructive policy which it has adopted the International Labor Organization has an essential part to play in building up a stable international peace based upon cooperation in pursuit of social justice for all peoples everywhere: the representatives of the governments, employers, and work people of the American Continent,

Proclaim their unshaken faith in the promotion of international cooperation and in the imperative need for achieving international peace and security by the elimination of war as an instrument of national policy, by the prescription of open, just, and honorable relations between nations, by the firm establishment of the understandings of international law as the actual rule of conduct among governments, and by the maintenance of justice and the scrupulous respect for treaty obligations in the dealings of organized peoples with one another; and pledge the unwavering support of the governments

[3] Draft submitted by the resolutions committee on the proposal of Messrs. Marino López Blanco, government delegate, Cuba; Herminio Rodriguez, government adviser, Cuba; Antonio Villalobos and Enrique Jiménez, government delegates, Mexico; Francisco Posada, government delegate, Colombia; José Domenech, workers' delegate, Argentina; and José de Camacho, workers' delegate, Colombia.

INTERNATIONAL LABOR ORGANIZATION

and peoples of the American Continent for the continuance with unimpaired vigor of the efforts of the International Labor Organization to accomplish its high purpose of achieving social justice.

After reading this memorable labor declaration for peace in times of war, can there still be any doubt that right here in America is concentrated our faith and hope for international, political, and economic cooperation?

CHAPTER IX

WHAT KIND OF PEACE?

In conclusion, one basic question comes to our minds: Is there any possibility of obtaining an organized, cooperative, functional world peace in our time?

Political factions are likely to answer this question pessimistically. Many skeptical political scientists, pointing to past experience, will deny the possibility of establishing an international economic organization which would share authority with the individual nations.

As long as the political scene continues in its present sorry state, there is no way of convincing these skeptics of the feasibility of such a plan. From his own experience the author understands this attitude. Political realists will argue correctly that no peace can be concluded with nations whose leaders are responsible to no one and who are, therefore, totally unreliable in the execution of their promises. But is it not true that the very reason the world is at war is to abolish such irresponsibility? The aim of this book has been to search for the true causes of the war and obstacles in the way of peace, and, further, to outline an objective socio-economic plan, in an attempt to convince the peoples of the earth—totalitarian as well as democratic—that an organized peace such as is herein described holds greater promise of individual happiness for all the people than the narrow, egotistical, self-destructive ideals of totalitarianism and exaggerated nationalism.

Why entertain the hope that such a plan will be a stronger contribution to peace than skepticism, blind optimism, or apathy?

Many explanations are daily being offered by psychologists and philosophers for our human drives and impulses. The desire for economic and political security appears to occupy a powerful position.

232

WHAT KIND OF PEACE?

Among the countless factors that might be stressed, these incentives stand out as the paramount motivators of mankind.

One of our commonly accepted concepts is that economic activity is motivated by the drive to "satisfy human needs and wants." Schiller allots the greatest weight to hunger and love. "Der Hunger und die Liebe erhalten das Getriebe." This may be right so far as individuals are concerned. The economic drive and the *libido*, as Freud has termed it, hunger and love—especially love, consciously or unconsciously—certainly play a decisive part in individual human behavior. But in a group the economic drive, the desire for the satisfaction of human needs, appears stronger than any other impulse. The aggressive impulse in men, the *homo bellicosus*, is easily aroused by hunger (poor economic conditions), which hinders the satisfaction of other human wants (such as love and general well-being).

In times such as these the desire for economic security, which can only be achieved in conjunction with political security, is therefore our decisive human impetus. History has bequeathed us the task of finding a socio-economic conception based on a moral law—a new form of organization and civilization—that is stronger and better than the concept of power based on fear, or the exercise of lust and greed based on evil.

It is because of my faith in the strength of the creative human drives that I believe that, if an efficient organization adequate to our human wants can be visualized, our better impulses will assert themselves and strive for the attainment of such a superior organization. Humanity, recognizing the greater worth of this ideal, will turn its back upon aggression, oppression, and brutality, and will once more collectively strive toward a more worthy goal.

I do not sympathize or agree with maxims which proclaim the inevitability of constant wars and permanent revolution. I believe in continuous change and evolution and am convinced that civilization is based upon the idea of the power of organization as an instrument of progress. But the test of the efficiency of any form of organization is its ability to function justly and to react elastically to the changes of a changing world. It is, therefore, our faith and trust that the disillusioned and desperate people of a war-sick world will cry out for a sane and

233

intelligent organization, to be evolved from the two paramount principles of political economy and to combine the best elements of individualism and collectivism into one superior international form of social-capitalist political economy. Yet it is a sad but undeniable fact that an ordered peace at this time can arise only from the ruins and ashes of a world in chaos.

It has been the task of the first part of this book to show why so soon after the first World War the peoples of Europe resorted to another mortal struggle. Even though fifty years at least would have been required for recovery from a war of such dimensions, destruction, and indebtedness as the last one, now after some twenty years the world finds itself again in a most devastating war disaster. We cannot stress often enough the fact that the primary cause for the present war was that human wants were neglected and that, instead of actions in the spirit of international solidarity, shortsighted ambitions and excessive nationalist aspirations were allowed to reign supreme.

Hitler promised the distressed and desperate German people that he would tear up the Versailles Treaty, with all its economic injustices, would reinstate honor, provide bread, jobs, and colonies, and institute a world hegemony of the German master race—in short, a German world paradise—and found enthusiastic support. France and England staged no sweeping reform plan, no enchanting passion, no fascinating battle cry—only wilfully aimed at conserving the status quo and diverting the *furor teutonicus* toward the East. While Russia, Italy, and Germany prepared for moral and material armament and war, England and France prepared for doubtful national safety, false security, and business with profit.

The warnings of a few far-sighted men in England—men like Anthony Eden and Winston Churchill—for the nation to face the situation realistically remained unheard. The City of London believed more in the assurances of the juggler Schacht to Montagu Norman than in the warnings of those who saw the catastrophe coming with logical certainty and amazing rapidity—because it wanted to believe in them.

What was the result of Hitler's promises to the German people?

The "moral rearmament" which he conjured up before the people's eyes developed into total physical armament, the most cruel persecution, and the most destructive four-dimensional war—a war by land, sea, and air, and on the minds of men. The promised paradise was turned into a hell; in short, the German people were betrayed. What the German people now must suffer, and yet support with body and soul, not only is thoroughly disliked in Germany itself, but is perhaps the greatest disappointment of all times to all honest Germans. All their moral and spiritual values have been lost and trampled upon by nazi boots. Germany is forced to stick to brutality because it knows of no other alternative to the present tyranny and slavery.

I am sure that all German-Americans were deeply moved by the splendid message of Wendell L. Willkie broadcast to the German people:

My grandparents left Germany ninety years ago because they were protestants against autocracy and demanded the right to live as free men. I, too, claim that right.

I am proud of my German blood, but I hate aggression and tyranny.

Tell the German people that my convictions are shared to the full by the overwhelming majority of my fellow countrymen of German descent. They, too, believe in freedom and in human rights.

Tell the German people that free German-Americans reject and hate the aggression and lust for power of the present German government.

And, even if there may be many who adhere to dictatorial maxims or share in the corruption and profit from the present regime and enjoy giving full vent to their evil instincts, their days are numbered. The glorious nazi dream has already failed and sooner or later the nazi bubble of criminal megalomania will burst into nothingness. The subjugated nations of Europe and the Western democracies alike hate this medieval way of life; they shudder before the terror of this strange product of human misery and perversion. France had paid a heavy toll for her light dreams of safety behind an outmoded and incomplete Maginot line. And England is suffering more than a people can normally stand for her wishful thinking and unbelievable *laissez passer*.

Le monde ne va pas de lui-même. We must all actively contribute to its going. All nations must pull themselves together and rise to a more highly developed sense of moral and social integrity, to a superior organization—an organization that must stand firmly on the ideals of political economy as proclaimed in this social manifesto. Any plan for enduring peace must be of an actively cooperative construction. And, if we want to avoid a post-war chaos, we must now prepare for a well-functioning new order of peace.

And America?

In the midst of a world in ruins, America is still extremely fortunate to be able to embark on a constructive national program. England, finding herself in an emergency situation, is unable to carry out a complete program of social reconstruction. But a proclamation in favor of social capitalism is a most vital matter for England as well as for the United States. Both America and Great Britain must decide now to offer to their peoples a sweeping social reform if they hope for a victory of world democracy. Just as the United States must show the fettered people of Europe a sincere and enlightened plan of social reform, a way out of the darkness of brutal power politics, in the same vein England must give up some of the outmoded privileges of a conservative economic system.

Europe, Asia, Africa, Australia, and Latin America must all be convinced that the phrase "capitalist plutocracy" is today no more than a slogan of propaganda and that a new spirit of social behavior has penetrated the Western democracies. However, these social-capitalist reforms must take the form of action rather than words. If England cannot build up a complete social-capitalist structure now, while long range destruction is going on, it must, at least, enact the most urgent social reforms both at home and in her dominions. It must grant definite privileges to the laboring classes and be a splendid example of social consciousness to a world in which the fallacies and evil aspects of capitalism have led to disaster. Every move, every reform, in the direction of social capitalism not only will be favorably echoed by England's friends on this side of the Atlantic, but may well assure her of a victory over the pernicious elements of totalitarian philosophy. Indeed, is this not the answer to the "reforms" of the dictator nations?

The discouraged peoples of the European continent are not expecting an attitude of smugness or complacency from us. They are hopefully awaiting the coming of a just social system. Every man involved in the present struggle must know for what he is fighting and, *what kind of peace* he may expect if democracy is to make it.

WHAT KIND OF PEACE?

Is there no hope for such an enlightening national and international social reform? Are these high hopes mere rhetoric, or can they be attained in fact? The answer to these questions lies in the hands of the contending parties. If the nazis win, the answer is clear. If at the end of the war there is no victor but exhaustion, America will still be able to exert a strong influence on the peace terms in the spirit of practical democracy.

If the United Nations are victorious? This depends upon British and American leadership. British leadership, taught by proud empire history, and more than ever dependent upon the British Labor party. American leadership, founded in the democratic constitution and the Bill of Rights and permeated with increasing social consciousness. The importance of this dual dependency is admirably recognized in the appointment of John G. Winant as Ambassador to Great Britain. Winant, formerly director of the I.L.O. and Chairman of the Social Security Board, represents the United States on the one hand, and is, on the other, admired by Ernest Bevin and other leaders of the British Labor Party. Furthermore, he has won the friendship of other British leaders, such as Anthony Eden, now Foreign Minister.

Prime Minister Winston Churchill and President Roosevelt have as yet given us but the skeleton of the ultimate peace aims they may have in mind in their Atlantic Charter of August 14, 1941. (See the author's comment, "Epilogue to the 'Atlantic Charter,'" at the end of this volume.)

We may be certain that these two statesmen will ultimately go further towards a peace that can endure than Chamberlain would have— and we know what Chamberlain said about these matters. Would Churchill go as far as the British Labor Party and its stated aims? The least we know is that it would be somewhere between the two—and from present indications nearer to the Labor Party stand. What are these stated positions?

Prime Minister Neville Chamberlain stated:[1]

When we come to peace aims, we are dealing with something to be achieved in conditions we cannot at present forsee. Our definition of them

[1] *New York Times*, Nov. 27, 1939.

can therefore only be in the most general terms but there can be no harm in declaring the broad principles on which we should desire to found them

Our desire, then, when we have achieved our war aims, would be to establish a new Europe, not new in the sense of tearing up all the old frontier posts and redrawing the map according to the ideas of the victors, but a Europe with a new spirit in which the nations which inhabit it will approach their difficulties with good will and mutual tolerance.

In such a Europe, fears of aggression will have ceased to exist, and such adjustments of boundaries as would be necessary would be threshed out between neighbors sitting on equal terms around a table, with the help of disinterested third parties if it were so desired.

In such a Europe it would be recognized that there can be no lasting peace unless there is a full and constant flow of trade between the nations concerned, for only by increased interchange of goods and services can the standard of living be improved.

In such a Europe each country would have the unfettered right to choose its own form of internal government so long as that government did not pursue an external policy injurious to its neighbors.

Lastly, in such a Europe armaments would gradually be dropped as a useless expense, except in so far as they were needed for the preservation of internal law and order.

It is obvious that the establishment of this Utopian Europe which I have briefly sketched out could not be the work of weeks or even months. It would be a continuous process, stretching over many years. Indeed, it would be impossible to set a time limit upon it, for conditions never cease to change, and corresponding adjustments would be required if friction was to be avoided.

Consequently, you would need some machinery capable of conducting and guiding the development of the new Europe in the right direction. I do not think it necessary, nor indeed is it possible, to specify at this stage the kind of machinery which should be established for this purpose. I merely express the opinion that something of the sort would have to be provided, and I would add my hope that a Germany animated by a new spirit might be among the nations which would take part in its operations.

On January 31, 1940, at Dorchester House, London, Chamberlain said:

International trade must be restored through the abandonment of the vicious policy of economic nationalism and autarkie.

WHAT KIND OF PEACE?

On February 24, 1940, at Birmingham, Chamberlain declared:[3]

We are fighting for the freedom of individual conscience. We are fighting for the freedom of religion. We are fighting against persecution, wherever it may be found. And lastly we are fighting for the abolition of the spirit of militarism and of that accumulation of armaments which is pauperising Europe and nazi Germany herself, for only by the abolition of that spirit and of those armaments can Europe be saved from bankruptcy and ruin.

Well then, how, in concrete terms, are these aims to be achieved? After all, the independence of the Poles and Czechs must be restored. And, secondly, we must have tangible evidence to satisfy us that pledges and assurances, when they are given, will be fulfilled. Under the present government of Germany there can be no security for the future. The elements in Germany which are ready to cooperate in building the new Europe are ruthlessly proscribed. The nation itself is isolated even from contact with neutral opinion and the rulers themselves have repeatedly shown that they cannot be trusted to keep their word to foreign governments or even to their own people.

Therefore, it is for Germany to take the next step and to show us conclusively that she has abandoned the thesis that might is right. Now let me say this. . . . Others must come in to help us and particularly must they come in to bring about that disarmament which is an absolutely essential feature for any lasting peace.

That problem of disarmament has hitherto baffled all attempts to solve it because no nation is willing to abandon its own powers of defense while it thinks that others who have not disarmed may take advantage of its helplessness. But if once we could exorcise this fear, why, then, disarmament would surely follow, as day follows night.

Although disarmament must be a gradual process, although it may and probably will take many years to complete, yet if only we could establish confidence between the nations in one another's good faith we could, at least, make a beginning, and every step that we took forward in armament would make easier the step that would follow.

Thus far did Chamberlain go. Churchill, as stated above, would probably go farther in his organization of a peace economy. It has frequently been stated that he would tend further in the direction of the peace aims propounded soon after the outbreak of this war by the English labor leader, C. R. Atlee. Atlee presented six principles:

[3] According to the *New York Times*, February 25, 1940.

PLAN FOR PERMANENT PEACE

The first principle is that there should be no dictated peace. We have no desire to humiliate, to crush, or to divide the German nation. There must be restitution made to the victims of aggression, but all ideas of revenge and punishment must be excluded. If peace is to be lasting it must result from the agreement of all, not from the dictation of a few nations. The failure of the treaties at the end of the last war to bring abiding peace was largely due to the neglect of this principle. But if we desire to build a new world its foundations must be laid not only by the large and strong, but by the small and less powerful. It is the function of law to prevent the strong abusing his strength at the expense of the weak. The smaller nations, just because they are not aggressive, bring to the councils of the nation a most valuable element.

The second principle necessarily follows. It is the recognition of the right of all nations, great or small, of whatever color or creed, to have the right to live and to develop their own characteristic civilisation, provided that they do not thereby infringe the rights of others. The German, relinquishing his conception of the primacy of the German race, must recognise that the Pole and the Czech and the Jew have as much right as he, no more and no less, to a place in the world and to a share in the bounty of nature. Equally, the Briton must recognise that the same is true of the African or any other inhabitant of the British Empire. The German must concede to the Austrian the right to decide his own future. The Briton must equally concede the same right to the Indian.

Thirdly, there must be a complete abandonment of aggression and of the use of armed force as an instrument of policy. War must be outlawed and the rule of law accepted. Where disputes cannot be amicably settled by negotiation, they must be submitted to the decision of disinterested arbitrators and their decision accepted.

Fourthly, there must be recognition of the rights of national, racial, and religious minorities. While as far as possible every State should be left free to manage its internal affairs, there is a common interest in the prevention of oppression, and in the recognition of the rights of individuals. It may well be that later the principle of the recognition of the rights of the individual might be given still wider extension, and be firmly established as part of the law of nations. Here it is sufficient to lay down as a principle that, where there are racial minorities in any State, there must be some effective authority by an international body over the sovereign rights of the individual State.

Fifthly, there must be acceptance of the principle that international anarchy is incompatible with peace, and that in the common interest there must be recognition of an international authority superior to the individual States and endowed not only with rights over them, but with power to make them effective, operating not only in the political, but in the economic sphere. Europe must federate or perish.

Sixthly, there must be abandonment of imperialism and acceptance of the principle that, in the government of colonies and dependencies where self-government cannot yet be conceded, the interests of the natives must be paramount, and that there must be equal access for all nations to markets and raw materials.[4] This can best be achieved by an extended and strengthened mandate system under international authority. We hold that the redistribution of colonial territories between rival imperialisms is no solution, for we do not admit that any nation has the right to hold others in subjection.

Atlee expanded upon the subject as follows (and I quote at such great length only because he so well expressed most of the fundamentals of a functional permanent peace):

What is required of a peace conference is nothing less than the establishment of a New World Order. Civilisation is threatened with destruction because men have so far been unable to control the results of their own inventions. There have been many peace conferences in the past which have resulted in peace for a few years, but in none of them has there been the acceptance of principles which would secure lasting peace: in none of them has there been fully appreciated the necessity, if war is to be abolished, of some surrender of individual sovereignty by all States. . . .

In setting down the principles which should, we believe, be accepted as the necessary basis for a New World Order we are trying to offer to the

---

[4] Inspired by the great Immanuel Kant, Woodrow Wilson conceived his immortal "Fourteen Points," and it is only today that we are able to understand the great power of his ideals and the tragedy of their fate in a bitter and vengeful world. Although these fourteen points must be judged in the light of the situation in which they were conceived, some of them still retain their validity. E.g., Point III reads: "The removal, as far as possible, of all economic barriers and the establishment of an equality of trade conditions of all nations consenting to the peace and associating themselves for its maintenance."

In his last speech, the late Marquess of Lothian, British Ambassador to the United States, visualized how Anglo-American collaboration could ensure peace: "If we are to set the world going again, not only must we have strength, but we must not adopt the fatal policies we all pursued after the last war, the establishment of prohibitive tariffs, and then hoping to dodge the inevitable consequences of these follies by a policy of reckless lending. Markets and employment for all should be the main purpose of post-war economic policy."

world something more than a Party programme, something more than proposals which would, we believe, be advantageous to our country alone. We are thinking in terms of humanity. We are thinking of the millions of men and women in all countries who only ask to be allowed to live their lives free from the menace of war. We believe that the adoption of these principles and their application will advantage the German as much as the Briton or the Frenchman, the Chinaman and Indian as much as the Italian or the Pole, the Dane and the Belgian as much as the citizen of the United States. . . .

It will be seen that the acceptance of the six principles will involve the creation of international machinery in order to make them effective. If aggression is to cease, there must be some force by which the aggressor can be compelled in the last resort to desist. *If there is to be a rule of law, there must be a means of enforcing that law.*

The experience of the last twenty years has shown that to entrust the duty of enforcing the rule of law to individual States, operating with their own armed forces, has in practice proved unworkable, because the supposed interests of a particular State tend to outweigh consideration of the common good. National armed forces mean the continuance of the conditions that make for war and of the means for waging it.

There must instead be an international force, possessed of such overwhelming strength that no would-be aggressor would dare to challenge it. For many reasons an international air force is the most appropriate instrument, while, in addition, the abolition of national air forces will remove the apprehension of aerial attack which is today driving mankind back to the practices of the cave dweller. *In addition, every State must accept the obligation of bringing against any disturber of the peace the power of economic sanctions.*

As a natural corollary of the establishment of an international force, there must be a drastic reduction of all national forces to the amount necessary for the preservation of internal order. The greater this reduction, the less will be the possibility of challenge to the international force. Such armed forces as remain in the hands of individual States must be subjected to international inspection. *Private manufacture and trade in armaments must be abolished.*

The existence of an international force necessarily implies an international authority to control it. It would be unwise to attempt to set out in detail the exact nature of such an authority or do more than specify the principles on which it should be established.

WHAT KIND OF PEACE?

There are broadly two ways in which such an authority might be constituted. It might be autocratic or democratic. In the former case, a small number of great Powers might dominate and enforce their will on the remainder. In the latter, all States would share in decisions. A world or a Europe under the orders of four or five big States would not be free. It might merely be an imperialism in commission. *We as believers in democracy hold that the small nations which have formerly contributed and still do today so much of value to the world, should take their full share in an international authority* . . .

It would be a mistake to try to redraw the map of Europe as part of the proposals for a peace settlement. It is right to affirm that Austrians, Czechs, Poles and Germans are nations with the right to room to live, but it would be premature to consider exact boundaries until principles have been accepted. Adjustments of boundaries, and even, where necessary and practicable, just and peaceful transfers of population, could be effected through the international authority. In some instances there might have to be provision for a measure of local autonomy. The Jewish problem, which concerns so many States, can only be settled by an international authority. In all cases, the inculcation by all governments of the duty of tolerance and its exercise by all citizens is the most effective means of overcoming animosities which arise mainly from past events and present prejudices.

It would be equally premature to lay down as part of the conditions of peace whether the new international authority should in the first place be confined to Europe or whether it should embrace other continents. That must depend on how widely these principles are accepted, though clearly it ought to be built on the widest foundations.

No less dangerous than the political is the economic anarchy of the world. When the war ends, there will be widespread economic dislocation and great poverty while the drastic reduction of armaments which we envisage will release an immense industrial capacity which will be wasted unless steps are taken to divert it into a channel where it will be of service to mankind.

Bold economic planning on a world scale will be an imperative necessity to meet the post-war situation, and to avoid in the future recurrent economic crises. Only in this way can full benefit be taken of the achievements of science. Only an international authority can grapple with this immense problem, which will, however, be eased by the very fact that the military considerations which were partly responsible for the cult of economic self-sufficiency will now be absent, while the abandonment of imperialism will lead to freer trade. International institutions for this purpose must be created.

It is of at least equal importance that the scope and authority of the International Labor Office should be enlarged. It should be given the task of preparing international minimum standards of wages, hours, and industrial conditions, in order that, by increased production, by a more just distribution, and by the wealth released from expenditure upon arms, the standard of living of the workers shall everywhere be raised. For peace depends on social justice within States, no less than on political justice between States.

It may be urged that the principles which I have laid down are too far-reaching and that the whole scheme is chimerical, idealistic, and beyond the bounds of practical politics. It may be urged that it will be difficult to gain acceptance for such a vast change and that it would be wiser to seek a more modest objective. The answer to this is that remedies are conditioned by the gravity of the diseases which they are designed to cure. The deep-seated evil from which the world is suffering today will not be cured by some cheap and easy remedy. It is useless to treat the symptoms of a disease while neglecting to deal with the real cause. The experience of the last twenty years has shown the danger of half measures. If we want a peaceful world we must be prepared to face the great changes which must be involved.

A more recent statement of the Labor Party point of view is Harold J. Laski's book, *Where Do We Go From Here?*[5] I was deeply moved by Mr. Laski's honest and clear answer to the question of peace and his challenge to British democracy:

I do not underestimate the importance of machinery; but machinery is far less important than the basis upon which it rests. I therefore emphasize again that there can be no peace without international organization which abrogates the sovereignty of individual states; no abrogation of sovereignty until we begin to destroy within each state the vested interests which require sovereignty. We cannot solve the problem of peaceful change until we have ended the paradox of poverty in the midst of potential plenty, and we cannot end that paradox until we have effected a massive redistribution of economic power. Peace between states depends upon peace within states; international justice without depends upon social justice within. Leave, as

[5] New York: The Viking Press, 1940.

we leave, the profit-making motive its present theatre of operations, and even victory means only the beginning of a new cycle destined to end in a new conflict. Permit the great vested interests—banking, coal, steel, transportation, electric power, to take examples only—to treat with the nation-state as independent empires, and they will annex it in the future as they have annexed it in the past. Nothing less than a revolution in the spirit of man is necessary if we are to enter the kingdom of peace as our rightful inheritance; and a revolution in the spirit of man, as all history goes to show, must follow, and cannot precede, a revolution in the relationships of that material world by the exploitation of which he must live. . . .

These, I suggest, are the principles with which the British government must approach the peoples whom it seeks to emancipate. With less than these principles any victory it offers them will be as illusory as the Peace of Versailles. For, without them, it may put the defeated in chains; it will yet at every moment fear his escape from those chains. And a generation which, like ours, has known the heavy price of fear cannot afford to make the same mistake a second time.

In the United States President Roosevelt has devoted much effort to the study of peace proposals, and his domestic and foreign policy is ultimately aimed at American cooperation in the future peace. There has been no occasion for him to discuss the mechanism of peace, but he has expressed himself to a limited degree on the fundamentals upon which that peace should be built. In his address[6] to the nation on December 29, 1940, he stated:

In view of the nature of this undeniable threat, it can be asserted properly and categorically that the United States has no right or reason to encourage talk of peace until the day shall come when there is a clear intention on the part of the aggressor nations to abandon all thought of dominating or conquering the world.

. . . Is it a negotiated peace if a gang of outlaws surrounds your community and on threat of extermination makes you pay tribute to save your own skins?

Such a dictated peace would be no peace at all. It would be only another armistice, leading to the most gigantic armament race and the most devastating trade wars in all history. And in these contests the Americas would offer the only real resistance to the Axis powers.

[6] Reprinted in full in the *New York Times,* December 30, 1940.

Eight days later, in his address[7] to Congress on "The State of the Union," he added:

In the future days which we seek to make secure, we look forward to a world founded upon four essential human freedoms.

The first is the freedom of speech and expression—everywhere in the world.

The second is freedom of every person to worship God in his own way—everywhere in the world.

The third is freedom from want, which, translated into world terms, means economic understandings which will secure to every nation a healthy peacetime life for its inhabitants—everywhere in the world.

The fourth is freedom from fear, which, translated into world terms, means a world-wide reduction of armaments to such a point and in such a thorough fashion that no nation will be in a position to commit an act of physical aggression against any neighbor—anywhere in the world.

That is no vision of a distant millennium. It is a definite basis for a kind of world attainable in our own time and generation. That kind of world is the very antithesis of the so-called "new order" of tyranny which the dictators seek to create with the crash of a bomb.

To that new order we oppose the greater conception—the moral order. A good society is able to face schemes of world domination and foreign revolutions alike without fear.

Since the beginning of our American history we have been engaged in change, in a perpetual, peaceful revolution, a revolution which goes on steadily, quietly, adjusting itself to changing conditions without the concentration camp or the quicklime in the ditch. The world order which we seek is the cooperation of free countries, working together in a friendly, civilized society.

An outline for a "peace offensive" worthy of serious attention is that submitted by Dorothy Thompson, in the New York *Herald Tribune*, January 31, 1941. In answer to the question "Why does not Britain state her peace aims? she answers:

The answer to that is very simple; Britain cannot state her peace aims. For peace aims mean a plan of reconstruction and Britain cannot make any kind of reconstruction apart from us.

The peace of the world for many centuries depends on the solution of two

[7] Reprinted in full in the *New York Times*, January 7, 1941.

questions: that of Britain versus the Continent of Europe; and that of Europe versus the Americas. The failure to solve either of these problems in 1918 is the basic reason why this war could occur.

The solution of the whole world problem depends upon the relations between continental Europe, the British Commonwealth and North America. . . .

A solution for the problem, compatible both with the historic desire of the European Continent to unite and with the freedom and equality of the peoples of Europe with each other, and with the peoples of the British Federation of Nations, and with the republics of America, North and South would seem to be:

1. A United States of the Continent of Europe, in all probability established by interlocking federations of northern and southern blocks, in which certain matters, notably defense, customs and currency, are no longer matters of individual national sovereignty.

That would give Germany more influence on the Continent than that possessed by any other single nation of people, but it would not give her more influence than all the others put together.

2. The guaranteeing of the freedom and independence of the British Isles, Commonwealth and any parts of the empire that freely wish to join this Commonwealth on equal terms.

The British Isles themselves to be mutually guaranteed both by the Americas and by the Continent of Europe.

This could best be accomplished, in my mind, by the union of the English speaking world—of Britain and the Commonwealth with the United States in a loose federation.

3. A peace ratified between this federation and the federation of the European Continent—or between the three federations, Continent, Britain, American—and a common program of both or all for the development by colonization of the unused areas of this earth, and for free and equal access to raw materials. . . .

Obviously these cannot be British aims, for the simple reason that Britain is not strong enough to secure or enforce such a program.

But they might very well be British, American and German aims, since they are obviously in the equal interests of everybody concerned if justice, equality and peace are what we are looking for. And if Britain and America decide together on such aims, and keep the Nazis from winning the war, Hitler is defeated. . . .

I, therefore, am for a peace offensive from this country and from Britain, but not a peace offensive for a negotiated peace between two incompatible concepts, but a peace offensive for a real New Order between Europe, Britain and America, an order that makes as much sense for Germany as for any one.

It is ridiculous to think that there is nobody in Germany who would be open to such ideas. You cannot destroy the brains of a country in seven years. Our object should not be to destroy Germany, but to destroy Hitlerism in order that Germany and the rest of us can live.

Our defeatism consists in timidity before concepts that are as large as Hitler's but much more sensible.

Our problem is to turn Hitler's destruction into an eventual blessing to mankind instead of a curse.

When Europe and we find the framework in which we can collaborate, and be certain of peace with each other, this world is in for the greatest period of prosperity, development and liberation that it has ever known in human history.

The first organized effort, in the United States, in search of a peace plan is that undertaken by the Commission to Study the Organization of Peace, headed by Dr. James T. Shotwell, Chairman; William Allan Neilson, Chairman of the Executive Committee; Clyde Eagleton, Chairman of the Studies Committee; Clark M. Eichelberger, Director; and seventy additional signers. The Commission aims to

do its utmost to lead the American people to see more clearly than they did twenty years ago that, for selfish and unselfish reasons alike, all their efforts must have as their ultimate goal the creation of a better world in which to live—a world in which international cooperation will be able to use human intelligence and natural resources for the economic security and free development of all men.

In a preliminary report[8] the Commission states:

Peace under modern conditions cannot be a static condition of life achieved by the renunciation of war, nor a mere pious desire to live at peace. Peace must be a dynamic and continuous process for the achievement of freedom, justice, progress, and security on a world-wide scale. . . .

The organization of peace must have back of it the force of a unifying ideal. The sovereignty of the nation-state is no longer adequate. The alter-

[8] Commission to Study the Organization of Peace, *Preliminary Report*, *November, 1940* (New York).

natives are world empire, achieved by conquest, or some form of association, such as a world federation, achieved by consent. . . .

The report goes so far as to acknowledge that certain attributes of national sovereignty must be limited:

(a) Nations must renounce the claim to be the final judge in their controversies with other nations and must submit to the jurisdiction of international tribunals. The basis of peace is justice; and justice is not the asserted claim of any one party, but must be determined by the judgment of the community.

(b) Nations must renounce the use of force for their own purposes in relations with other nations, except in self-defense. The justification for self-defense must always be subject to review by an international court or other competent body.

(c) The right of nations to maintain aggressive armaments must be sacrificed in consideration for an assurance of the security of all, through regional and world-wide forces subject to international law and adequate to prevent illegal resorts to international violence.

(d) Nations must accept certain human and cultural rights in their constitutions and in international covenants. The destruction of civil liberties anywhere creates danger of war. The peace is not secure if any large and efficient population is permanently subject to a control which can create a fanatical national sentiment impervious to external opinion.

(e) *Nations must recognize that their right to regulate economic activities is not unlimited. The world has become an economic unit; all nations must have access to its raw materials and its manufactured articles. The effort to divide the resources of the world into sixty economic compartments is one of the causes of war. The economic problem arising from this effort has increased in gravity with the scientific and industrial progress of the modern world.* [Italics mine.]

Such renunciations of sovereignty for the common good will necessitate new institutions, world-wide and regional, to perform the services which can no longer be left to each state acting separately. The diplomatic system, international administrative unions, are steps toward a federal organization of the world, but they are not enough. International organizations must be created or developed on the bases of past experience. The following are essential:

(a) An international court with jurisdiction adequate to deal with all international disputes on the basis of law.

(b) International legislative bodies to remedy abuses in existing law and to make new law whenever technical progress requires the adjustment of international practice.

(c) Adequate police forces, world-wide or regional, and world-wide economic sanctions, to prevent aggression and to support international covenants.

(d) International machinery with authority to regulate international communication and transportation and to deal with such problems as international commerce, finance, health, nutrition, and labor standards—with regard to all of which the successful working of the constitution of the International Labor Organization offers valuable lessons.

(e) *Appropriate authorities to administer backward areas ceded to the world federation. Such administration should give precedence to the inhabitants of the area, looking to their eventual self-government; should assure all nations equal economic opportunity within the area; and should facilitate colonization and economic development of areas suitable for that purpose without injury to the native inhabitants. International corporations might well be encouraged to enlist world-wide support for the constructive task of developing such areas under supervision of such authorities.* [Italics mine.]

In addition to Great Britain and the United States—their governments and peoples—there is yet one other power which can and probably will greatly influence the organization of a peace, namely, the church.

It has always been the author's belief that one day the leaders of church organizations would more actively contribute to a functional socio-economic peace construction. He has always felt that for the churches it is not sufficient to speak against the communist, nazi, and socialist excesses, or to preach the immorality of war and the morality of the Ten Commandments, or to hail the Psalms, the beautiful Sermon on the Mount, and other highlights of the Old and New Testaments, and to praise the splendid philosophies contained in Buddhism, Confucianism, and all the other religious directions or sectarian ideologies. The momentous moral and spiritual influence of the churches must be more constructively utilized, for great socio-economic as much as for political reforms, in order to make them integral parts of the coming peace.

Certainly, we cannot expect the churches to draft the technical bases of a social, financial, and economic apparatus. This can be left to students and experts in those fields. But, once the responsible leaders of church organizations have recognized the importance of such reforms for the well-being and satisfaction of mankind, they should and will more actively cooperate in finding, establishing, and preserving the best attainable material order—an order which conciliates the opposing camps and parallels the strong and ethical influence that spiritual institutions are able to exercise on the brotherhood of men. The ministers and priests of the churches will soon recognize that a conciliation of struggling groups and the establishment of a sane, just, and enduring order of peace can best be based on the stable but elastic equilibrium of social capitalism. The concern of the churches with these seemingly materialistic problems is not incompatible with their great mission to create love among men and peace among nations; on the contrary, it is a prerequisite for the attainment of these ideals.

As early as 1896 Richard T. Ely proclaimed *social solidarity* as a universal ideal for our "human brotherhood" in the United States and the world in general. In his *Social Law of Service*[9] he states:

To upbuild human character in men you must establish for them right social relations. On the other hand, we fulfill our own mission and develop our own true individuality, not in isolation, but in society, and by bringing ourselves in body and mind into harmony with the laws of social solidarity. . . . Social solidarity means the oneness of human interests; it signifies the dependence of man upon man, both in good things and in evil things. Social solidarity means that our true welfare is not an individual matter purely, but likewise a social affair; our weal is common weal; we thrive only in a common wealth; our exaltation is the exaltation of our fellows, their elevation is our enlargement. Social solidarity implies not only fellowship in interest and responsibilities, but that unity in nature which is brought before us by the expression, "human brotherhood." Social solidarity signifies not only that man needs association with his fellowmen, but that he shares with them their sins and their sufferings. Our sin is sin for others; their sin is our sin. There is no such thing, either as purely individual sin, or a purely individual righteousness.

[9] Richard T. Ely, in "Social Law of Service," New York, 1896, pp. 127-128.

PLAN FOR PERMANENT PEACE

In a true establishment of social capitalism a universal socio-economi mechanism such as the Bank of Nations, with its coordinated functiona subsidiaries, must first be constructed, before the spiritual man can b reborn and all the great spiritual values brought again to life and t the light of the sun.

Similar tasks are awaiting educational and political leaders, institu tions of learning, schools, and parliaments. They must not hesitat to proclaim a new spirit of socially conscious international solidarity of a practical Christianity and mutualism. The word "peace" must b restored from a static to a dynamic, creative, and humanistic meaning

In 1939, in a Christmas Eve Message to the Sacred College of Car dinals,[10] *Pope Pius XII* wrote a new chapter in the history of inter national human relations. He expounded five principles:

[First:] The fundamental condition of a just and honorable peace is to as sure the right to life and independence of all nations, large, small, strong or weak. One nation's will to live must never be tantamount to a deatl sentence for another. When this equality of rights has been destroyed injured, or imperiled, juridical order requires reparation whose measure and extent is not determined by the sword of selfish arbitrary judgment, bu by the standards of justice and reciprocal equity.

[Second:] That order re-established in such a manner may be tranquil and durable—the cardinal principles of true peace—nations must be liberatec from the heavy slavery of armaments and the danger that material force in stead of serving to protect rights become the tyrannical violator of them. Con clusions of peace that did not attribute fundamental importance to disarma ment mutually accepted, organic and progressive both in letter and spirit and did not take care to carry it out loyally would sooner or later reveal their inconsistency and lack of vitality.

[Third:] In any reorganization of international neighborliness it could conform with the maximum of human wisdom for all parties concerned to deduct the consequences of past gaps or deficiencies, and in creating or reconstructing international institutions that have a mission so high but at the same time difficult and full of serious responsibilities, account should be taken of experiences that arose from the inefficacy or defective function ing of similar previous initiatives.

And, since it is so difficult, one would be tempted to say almost impos-

[10] *New York Times*, December 25, 1939.

sible, for human weakness to foresee everything and assure everything at the time of peace treaties, when it becomes difficult to be free from passions and bitterness, constitution of juridical institutions, which would serve to guarantee loyal and faithful carrying out of terms and, in case of recognized need, revising and correcting them, is of decisive importance for honorable acceptance of a peace treaty and to avoid arbitrary unilateral breakings and interpretations of treaty terms.

[Fourth:] A point that should attract particular attention, if a better arrangement of Europe is wanted, concerns the real needs and just demands of nations and peoples as well as of ethnical minorities; demands, which if not always enough to form a strict right when there are recognized or confirmed treaties or other juridical documents that oppose them, deserve anyway benevolent examination to meet them in a peaceful way and even where it appears necessary by means of an equitable, wise, and unanimous revision of treaties. Once real equilibrium among nations is thus brought back and the basis of mutual trust is re-established, many incentives to resort to violence would be removed.

[Fifth:] But even better and more complete settlements will be imperfect and condemned to final failure if those who guide the fates of peoples and the peoples themselves do not let themselves be penetrated ever more by that spirit that alone can give live authority and obligation to the dead letter of articles in international arrangements; by that sense, namely, of intimate, acute responsibility that measures and weighs human statutes according to the holy unshakable rules of divine law; by that hunger and thirst for justice that is proclaimed in the beatitudes in the Sermon on the Mount and which has as a natural presupposition moral justice; by that universal love that is the Christian ideal and therefore throws the bridge also toward those who do not have the benefit of participating in our own faith.

A year later, Pope Pius added:

Indispensable prerequisites for the search for a new order are:
One, triumph over hate, which is today a cause of division among peoples; renunciation, therefore, of the systems and practices from which hate constantly receives added nourishment.

Two, triumph over mistrust, which bears down as a depressing weight on international law and renders impossible the realization of any sincere agreement.

Three, triumph over the distressing principle that utility is a basis of law

and right and that might makes right, a principle which makes all inter
national relations liable [liable to fall].

Four, triumph over those germs of conflict which consist in two-sided dif
ferences in the field of world economy; hence progressive action, balanced
by correspondent degrees to arrive at arrangements which would give to
every state the medium necessary for insuring the proper standard of living
for its own citizens of every rank.

Five, triumph over the spirit of cold egoism which, fearless in its might
easily leads to violation not only of the honor and sovereignty of states but
of the righteous, wholesome, and disciplined liberty of citizens as well.

It must be supplanted by sincere juridical and economic solidarity, faterna
collaboration in accordance with the precepts of divine law among people
assured of their autonomy and independence.

As long as the rumble of armaments continues in the stark reality of this
war it is scarcely possible to expect any definite acts in the direction of the
restoration of morally, juridically inprescriptible rights.

But it would be well to wish that henceforth a declaration of principle in
favor of their recognition may be given to calm the agitation and bitterness
of so many who feel that they are menaced or injured in their very existence
or in the free development of their activity.

We express our heartfelt wish that humanity and those who will show
it the way along which it is to move forward will be sufficiently matured
intellectually and capable in action to prepare the ground of the future for
the new order that will be solid, true, and just.

We pray God that it may so happen.[11]

Leaders of the Protestant and Catholic Churches in Britain have
recently proclaimed joint proposals for statesmen's policies after
this war:

They joined their own five proposals, aimed at social and economic
equality and justice, with the five that Pope Pius offered last Christmas Eve,
suggesting that together they would provide the basis of lasting peace. The
association of the churches, including the established Church of England,
of which King George is supreme head, was believed to be without prece-
dent in a gesture of this sort. The Archbishops of Canterbury and York,
primates of England as spiritual leaders of the Church of England; Arthur,
Cardinal Hinsley, Roman Catholic Archbishop of Westminster and head
of the Catholic Church in Britain, and Walter H. Armstrong, moderator

[11] *New York Herald Tribune,* December 25, 1940.

of the Free Church Federal Council, propounded in a letter to the *London Times* "Five Standards" to guide statesmen in solving post-war economic and social questions.

The five standards are:

1—Extreme inequality of wealth should be abolished.

2—Every child, regardless of race or class, should have equal opportunities for education suitable to its peculiar capacities.

3—The family as a social unit must be safeguarded.

4—The sense of a divine vocation must be restored to man's daily work.

5—*Resources of the earth should be used as God's gifts to the whole human race and used with due consideration for the needs of present and future generations.* [Italics mine.]

The churchmen expressed confidence that the British Empire would accept these principles, and *The Times* intimated in an editorial that they should be taken into consideration in drafting Britain's war aims.[12]

Another statement that is worthy of attention is the findings of the Malvern Conference of leading figures of the Church of England, recently held under the chairmanship of Archbishop Temple of York. "In my humble judgment," stated Congressman Voorhis, "this conference may one day be marked as a turning point in British history."[13]

The sweeping character of its proposals includes:

1. The unification of Europe as a cooperative commonwealth.

2. A genuine interchange in international trade of materially needed commodities.

3. The satisfaction of human needs as the only true end of production.

4. Recognition of the rights of labor as in principle equal to those of capital in the control of industry.

5. Removal of the stumbling block of private ownership of the great resources of the community.

The Conference stated:

The war is not to be regarded as an isolated evil detached from the general condition of western civilization during the last period. It is one symptom of widespread disease and maladjustment, resulting from loss of conviction concerning the reality and character of God. The church has the duty and

12 According to the United Press, London, December 21, 1940.
13 *Congressional Record*, February 5, 1941, p. A446.

right to speak, not only to its own members but to the world, concerning the true principles of human life. The church, as we know it, does not manifest this life of the true community. We, therefore, urge that enterprises be initiated whereby that life can be made manifest.

The economic activity of man, which is entirely concerned with means, has become predominant, as though to produce material wealth were man's true end. Christian doctrine must insist that production exists for consumption. The industrial world, as we know it, offends against these principles. To a large extent, production is carried on, not to supply the consumer with goods but to bring profits to the producer. This method, which tends to treat human work and human satisfaction alike as a means to a false end—namely, monetary gain—becomes the source of unemployment at home and of dangerous competition for markets abroad. This system also tends to recklessness and sacrilege in the treatment of natural sources. It has led to the impoverishment of the agricultural community. The monetary system must be so administered that what the community can produce is made available to the members of the community, the satisfaction of human needs being accepted as the only true end of production.

The true status of man independent of economic progress must find expression in the managerial framework of industry; the rights of labor must be recognized as in principle equal to those of capital in control of industry, whatever the means by which this transformation is effected. In international trade a genuine interchange of materially needed commodities must take the place of a struggle for a so-called favorable balance. We must recover reverence for the earth and its resources, treating it no longer as a reservoir of potential wealth to be exploited, but as a storehouse of divine bounty on which we utterly depend.

After the war our aim must be the unification of Europe as a cooperative commonwealth.

Worship must be so directed and conducted that its relevance to life and to man's actual needs is evident. Our traditional form of matins and evensong, presupposing as they do acceptance of the tradition of the church and unfailing regularity of use, are largely unsuitable. They must in most places be supplemented by services of another type, whether liturgical or not, designed to bring before uninstructed people the truth concerning God.

We believe that the church should declare that maintenance of that part of the structure of our society by which the ownership of great resources of our community can be vested in the hands of private individuals is a stumbling block. The time has come, therefore, for Christians to proclaim the eed for seeking some form of society in which this stumbling block will be emoved. Christians, clergy, and laity alike cannot take part in this work unless they are prepared to advocate complete reorganization of the financial ife of the church.

These utterances must be of considerable hopeful significance to all who are concerned with peace. In the United States, the National Con- erence of Christians and Jews, the Federal Council of Churches, he new peace principles issued by the Quakers, and many other religious groups too numerous to mention, have embraced similar standards of world justice. A highly inspiring and ethical mani- festo of faith and hope in world democracy is *The City of Man*, a decla- tion by seventeen outstanding Americans.[14]

The remarkable and encouraging fact about all these public state- ments and numerous writings all over the world is that for the first time in history the center of gravity has been shifted so as to place the greatest emphasis on *social and economic justice on earth*. It has always been my deepest hope that, eventually, this great renaissance of human society would find its complete fulfillment. I, for one, firmly believe that our efforts in that direction will meet with success. This war cannot be won by ruthless and brutal warfare and power politics. This war will finally be won by the most just universal social order. I have faith that we will create that order.

[14] *The City of Man*, (New York: Viking, 1940).
The reader desiring a fuller list of the various plans for the creation of a new world order is referred to the bibliography "The New World Order," (Select Bibliographies No. 10, Dec. 12, 1940), published by the Carnegie Endowment for International Peace, Washington, D. C.

See also, *Foreign Policy Reports*, May 15, 1941, "Toward a New World Order," by Vera Micheles Dean.

CHAPTER X

DESIGN FOR INTERNATIONAL PLANNING
(THE UNITED STATES OF THE WORLD)

A GREAT social idea, a powerful moral impulse, must be the guiding spirit of the American program of action in a successful fight against the forces of totalitarian world domination. This program of action must be so dynamic, so self-evident, and so ethical that the evil spirits of the world will have to succumb to its greater power and justice.

The present apparent victory of the dictator nations does not demonstrate that the regimentation of men and things by brute force, military drill, and human indignity is a moral concept which will dominate our world. Their momentary success is more properly due to our neglect to watch and value our ideals of liberty and democracy. It is due also to the fact that we did not devote sufficient effort to finding the method by which our cherished ideals might overcome the evil and destructive forces of the world.

Although I have never liked the phrase, "God is with the strongest battalions," there is today more than a grain of truth in this Prussian slogan. Without devoting all our efforts toward moral and material armament, without striving for the highest development of our economic system and of our way of life, in short, without taking fearless, united action, God will not be with us in this greatest struggle in our history.

There can be no spiritual rebirth in our society without a realistic, well-ordered, economic, and material basis; without an all-embracing functional mechanism of production, distribution, and consumption. If America would take up the fight against imperialist dictatorial brutality, it must be in full possession and control of a convincing and forceful plan of action forming an unbreakable backbone of a possible total war.

It is hardly necessary to point out that such an inspiring idea did not exist in our capitalist setup. I believe that it is the absence of such a program which has caused despair and dissatisfaction within the nation. The lack of social conscience, which is a necessary part of this idea, has made us exponents of greed and plutocratic selfishness and has caused democratic traditions of liberty, equality, and justice to deteriorate into unvalued phrases. This unflattering but undeniable weakness has been successfully exploited in antidemocratic propaganda by the dictators. We have failed to realize what our destiny is; we have failed to find a system of social economy which is in harmony with our education and our character.

I have called this new concept Social Capitalism, because it expresses the logical evolution of all that is dear to us. Inspired with a truly social conscience, we must set in motion a national and international program of economic and social action.

Our now isolated capitalist system must assume the form of social, collective and democratic capitalism if we hope to achieve the voluntary unanimous collaboration of the peoples of the world.

The aim, which should be the basis of national unity and international victory, is that we should make democracy and liberty, equality and justice, work at home and abroad. We are able to make it work, because the technique of this system is considered everywhere as the most efficient and rational in the world. Only the excesses and short-comings of our system have discredited our institutions and our great reputation for being a free country. A program of national and international social capitalism, of national and world-wide free collective planning, of organized capital economy, will eventually triumph over regimented, dictatorial totalitarianism. It is certainly not sufficient to boast that we are a wealthy and mighty nation, which will now with a magic stroke create the strongest army, navy, and air force of the world. Behind our national armament, which was forced upon us by aggressor nations, must stand a national and international moral program of great intensity, so stirring in its concepts that it convinces the people of the world.

PLAN FOR PERMANENT PEACE

Only a small part of the program for national and international social capitalism has been sketched in this book; much more must be done to make it complete. But the idea of a liberal world program based on a voluntary practical technique rather than on force, dictation, and regimentation has inherent might in our fight against force. A thoroughly practical system for the creation of a new, wealthy, and productive world, for the achievement of a high degree of equality and liberty and of a fair standard of living for all human beings—anchored in a solid banking and credit apparatus, while at the same time retaining a capitalist basis—certainly seems worthier of human effort than the horrifying aspect of nazi world dictatorship and morality.

It seems inevitable that soon we shall envision the world, not as composed of many disjointed parts, but as a harmonious whole, and the human family as one large unit. This new sense of unity will make us visualize the world as one great organism, but in order to make this "vast creature" functional and alive, healthy and permanent, we must use our best efforts; we must organize the world.

Unfortunately the considerations of how it shall best be organized are still greatly influenced by power politics. In times of wars and revolutions, however, the most vigorous and progressive ideas of the people are conceived and, in all political, social, and economic fields, the strongest spirits come to the forefront. The average man is necessarily preoccupied with self-advancement and the struggle for existence. He has no time to study even the fundamentals of international politics and economics, quite apart from not having the necessary training. Consequently he is only too pleased to relegate that work to trained men in whom he has confidence. The average man is willing to accept an organization for the purpose so long as he feels that he has had some part in building it and still has a part in maintaining it.

In other words, any thinking man or woman resents and will never accept any imposed authority other than that sanctioned by men with the same wide international, interracial, and universal understanding in the spirit of mutual assistance and benefit. In each and every nation, and scattered through all social strata, there are men and women with this wide human understanding who would have or would easily attract the confidence of the masses and would arouse the necessary enthusiasm and support for constructive effort along these lines. I strongly feel

THE BANK OF NATIONS and COORDINATED INSTITUTIONS

DR. HANS HEYMANN
ALL RIGHTS RESERVED

RESEARCH PROFESSOR OF ECONOMICS
RUTGERS UNIVERSITY
1941

JUNE HILTS MEALD

FEDERAL WORLD AUTHORITY

Under Joint Guaranty of All Nations
THE BANK OF NATIONS
HEMISPHERE BANK · EUROPA BANK · ORIENTAL BANK

Court of Wisdom 20 Members

Department of Intellectual Cooperation
- World Court of Justice
- World Peace Department (Planning and Preservation)

World Economic Council

World Parliament (Council / Assembly)

World Army, Navy and Airforce

World Disarmament Office

International Red Cross

International Arbitration Board for Trade Differences

International Chamber of Commerce

World Economic Planning Board

International Cinematograph Institute

Bank for International Settlements (World Money Clearing Dept.)

International Institute of Agriculture

World Power Board

RAW MATERIAL RESERVES

World Raw Material Clearing House
- World Index Office
- International Crop Insurance Department

World Building and Colonization Department
- World Migration Department (Financing of Immigration)

Universal Postal Union

International Labor Office and Affiliated Departments
- World Labor Migration Department
- World Relief and Reparation Department
- World Unemployment Insurance Department
- World Social Insurance Department

Fort Knox of the World

NATIONAL BRANCH BANK of BANK of NATIONS (Credit / Issue)

Branch Bank of Bank of Nations

BRIDGE

INVESTMENT · CREDIT · TRADE

Department of Insurance

State Supervision

Department of Banking

National Construction Bank (National Trust Bank)

(Private or Semi-Public) Decentralized

National Credit and Investment Corporation

Capital Finance Corporation (for Large-Size Industry)

Industrial Credit Institute (for Medium-Size Industry)

Building Societies

Public Utility Construction Corporation

Real Estate Mortgage Banks

The Property Life Insurance Company

The Ship Life Insurance Company

Ship Mortgage Banks

Factory Machinery Depreciation Insurance Group

Small Business Credit Corporation

Underwriting Trusts

UNITED STATES FEDERAL GOVERNMENT

GOVERNMENT and PRIVATE CAPITAL

DEPARTMENT of STATE
- Export-Import Control Board

UNITED STATES TREASURY
- Export-Import Bank of Washington

INSURANCE
- Federal Housing Administration
- Federal Crop Insurance Corporation
- F.C.A. GROUP
  - Farm Credit Administration
  - Federal Savings and Loan Insurance Corporation
  - Federal Deposit Insurance Corporation
  - Regional Agricultural Credit Corporation
  - Federal Farm Mortgage Corporation
  - Federal Intermediate Credit Banks
  - Banks for Cooperatives
  - Federal Land Banks

LENDING and DISCOUNTING
- Proposed Plans for Small Business and Intermediate Credit (Bank Capital Credit Bank)
- Federal Reserve Board of Governors
  - 12 Federal Reserve Banks
  - 6,336 Member Banks
- Miscellaneous Lending Agencies
- World Insurance Lending Agencies
- R.F.C. GROUP
  - Reconstruction Finance Corporation
  - Commodity Credit Corporation
  - Home Owners Loan Corporation
  - Electric Home and Farm Authority
  - Rural Electrification Administration
  - Farm Security Administration
  - U.S. Maritime Commission
  - U.S. Housing Authority
  - Public Works Administration
  - Works Projects Administration
  - Federal Loan Bank Board
  - Federal National Mortgage Association
  - Federal Mortgage Company

REGULATION
- Federal Trade Commission
- Commodity Exchange Administration
- Comptroller of the Currency
- Securities and Exchange Commission
- Temporary National Economic Committee
- Board of Governors of the Federal Reserve System
- Anti-Trust Division (Dept. of Justice)
- National Defense Council
- Planning Group (Under the President)
- National Resources Planning Board

Division of Peace (Planning, Preservation)

that, in our future world, power will be integrated from within and not imposed from without. The common will of the people will be accepted as the supreme authority, represented by the constitution of the democratic world state, originated and controlled by the freely elected representatives of the people. Leadership will be offered, selected, and not imposed.

The greatest opportunity for a truly democratic world state evidently rests on the importance of having relatively equal partners rather than unequal powers form a constitution. In other words, if at the end of this war no power predominates, if there be no vindicated, have-not, or disinterested groups, we shall have an excellent opportunity for the creation of a just and lasting peace. The same opportunity will probably appear if only two hemisphere groups with more or less equal opportunities arise out of the present struggle. The nations of the world seem to nourish the belief that such relatively equal groups could more easily create a living peace than the more than sixty unequal nations which existed after the first world war.

But, if there are to be seven, six, or even only two large groups, why not integrate all the world into a whole—the United States of the World? based upon a universal Bill of Rights and Constitution. This may be more readily attainable if we agree to a system which appeals to the vast majority of mankind. What is this system to be? Socialism, with its various modifications; or capitalism, in private or state form?

The free countries of the West will hardly cherish any system of leveling mania or coercion from without, and the people of the East will probably be opposed to reckless or unrestricted capitalism. To the majority of mankind these extremes seem to appear unsocial and unethical. Can there be a bridge between these extremes? Can we combine the good features of both systems and eliminate the bad ones? Can individuality be combined with collectivity? Can private ownership be adjusted to public responsibility, free competition to planning, and laissez faire to organization? Can enlightened self-interest, free enterprise, and the venture spirit be maintained in a socially conscious world? Can these strongest incentives of mankind be led into the socially most advantageous channels?

This book represents an attempt to offer the bellicose and hostile world a plan and a technique for social capitalism; a plan which is dependent upon a nonexistent peace but is perhaps able to show a way to its construction. Although it is not the task of this book to show a political picture of the future commonwealth of nations, we have presented a few significant thoughts and included a few institutions of a supplementary international political and constitutional order in our plans and charts.

Never before have I felt so strongly the necessity of American initiative in the future world organization as I have since the conquest of the European continent by Hitler. But I know equally well that first an entirely new spirit of international responsibility and collaboration must be created in the United States, and that this spirit must be supported by an emotional belief in the efficiency, power, and moral strength of social capitalism. If the United States is brought to the point of suggesting the surrender of certain traditional ideals of isolation and indifference in world affairs, in favor of a more integrated world authority, it must be sure of the correct functioning of its own national system as well as of the international organization of the future.

The Bank of Nations idea, embracing the Hemisphere Bank, the Europa Bank, the Oriental Bank, the British Commonwealth, the Soviet Organization, and whatever other economic associations might develop out of the present struggle, might well appeal to American leaders because it represents the culmination and logical evolution of their existing institutions, such as the Federal Reserve System, the Hemisphere Bank, the Export-Import Bank, the Reconstruction Finance Corporation, and other government and private or semipublic institutions. The Bank for International Settlements, after all, was nothing but a creation of J. P. Morgan & Company, the First National Bank of New York, and the First National Bank of Chicago. But we must follow through to the end all the aims of these new economic and banking creations, and if we do we cannot but arrive at the conclusions of this book.

A recent Gallup poll (New York *Times*, March 5, 1941), indicated that about 8,000,000 American voters lean toward a reconstructed League of Nations and other political world associations. Lately, ideologies such as Union Now, Union with Britain Now, Union of the

English Speaking World, the United States of Europe, and the Commonwealth of Nations have grown in influence and following. The conviction prevails that these or more functional prospects of world organization must be studied and prepared, and that American rather than totalitarian initiative should guide these movements. It appears more and more imperative to coordinate a reformed and more perfect International Labor Organization and a regional and centralized economic banking and credit organization with a Federal World Authority and all its affiliated departments.

Sincere study of all the forces influencing world developments make us realize that only a universal socio-political organization can solve our problems, and that a way must be found by which at least the leading powers and groups can be united under a common Federal World Authority, a super League of Nations; that only if a common political formula can be accepted by all nations, the spirit of nationalist isolation and self containment can be overcome.

If we succeed in creating an organized world, not only economically, but also politically, our continent and the world at large will witness the greatest golden era of civilization and welfare the world has ever seen. With this thought in mind, it might perhaps be easier to sacrifice certain traditions and to unite our efforts with those of the world citizens of all nations. Only when a constructive universal peace organization which respects national traditions and institutions has been built, are the excesses and extravagances, the evil spirits and ideologies, of national revolution—and the Napoleonic ambitions of conquerors—doomed to die. A functional peace, based on international social capitalism and a socio-political new order, will revitalize and perpetuate our democracy.

The first world association, the League of Nations, created with such great hopes and expectations, lacked the authority, popularity, and representation of all the economic, social, spiritual, and political forces of the world. It was a representative body of politicians and diplomats which acted on behalf of unequal imperialistic and nationalistic groups. The United States, unfortunately, was not an active member. This situation caused the League to fall into disrepute until one nation after another resigned. Neither the economic, social, or political security of nations was sufficiently assured by the League. The International Labor

Office also lacked the authority, strength, and coordination to fulfill its hopeful activities and functions. An International Planning Board to preplan and coordinate its manifold tasks with the Bank of Nations would give the I.L.O. the necessary powers and sovereignties in world affairs. The future League, in turn, must be combined with the economic and labor organizations of the Bank of Nations and the I.L.O. into one unified functional organization for the United States of the World. It must organize a reliable World Army, Navy, and Air Force with sufficient guarantees and the cooperation of all nations so that war can really be outlawed. This international police force as well as the World Disarmament Office must be financed by the Bank of Nations, that is, by the joint contributions of all nations.

We have explained in former chapters what a disarmament of national armies means, and that we are faced here with a gigantic and very costly task. We must transform the armament industry into a productive peace industry for peace-time domestic and world production. All nations, and last but not least the United States, have invested and are continuing to invest large portions of the national income in armaments. This, we hope, will one day end all over the world and the reduction and final abolishment of armament capitalism will be followed by an era of peaceful social capitalism. The costliness of this enterprise will be immense and only by the combined efforts of all nations, with the help of the Bank of Nations, can such a venture succeed.

There is, furthermore, the International Chamber of Commerce to be enlarged by the addition of an International Arbitration Board to settle trade differences among nations; the Department of Intellectual Cooperation, to coordinate cultural and research achievements; the "Fort Knox" of the World wherein we may pool and bury the gold of the world; and the World Power Board, a most important instrument of peace. There is the Universal Postal Union, the International Red Cross, The International Institute of Agriculture, and the International Cinematographic Institute, and others which have already paved the way for closer international cooperation. The World Court of Justice must be revitalized and organized as an efficient instrument of international law and order and as an organ of the Federal World Authority; and, last but not least, a World Parliament, consisting of a World Council and Assembly, must be created as a permanent international constitutional organism of the highest integrity.

All these political world organizations can merely be mentioned in this book, because their organization clearly requires long, careful work, worthy of the collaboration of the best exponents of national foreign policies and of the best citizens of the world.

One institution, however, appears as timely as it is imperative, and no time should be lost in creating it. It is an Office of Planning, Establishing, and Preserving Peace. President Roosevelt has more than once given America and the world an example of his sincere desire for an organized and cooperative peace. Whether America is able to remain at peace or is forced to enter the war, the establishment of an American branch of the future World Department for Peace would make his peace work eternal.

This Peace Office might be initiated as a division of our State Department and should be composed of economists as well as political experts and representatives of labor and capital. Or, it might be organized in conjunction with Senator Robert F. Wagner's proposal for the planning for post-war reconstruction. At its head should be a sociopolitical economist who thoroughly understands international economic relations, money, banking, credit, trade, and capital and is experienced in government and international political service.

Albert Einstein recently recommended a Court of Twenty of the greatest minds of our world, an intellectual body of the leading spirits of all nations, which, I believe, could become an organization of the greatest influence in grave world decisions. This Court of Wisdom, this World Brain Trust, would probably enjoy greater popular support than any human aristocracy ever dreamed of. We can hardly hope that this organization will be completed during our lifetime, but I am thoroughly convinced that the present horrible world disaster will result in a strong incentive toward the introduction of such a functional peace organization.

Our children and children's children may be happier than we, and the vision of hope and peace so beautifully expressed by the German poet Richard Dehmel may one day come true:

> Unsere Kinder werden einst
> Auf dem Regenbogen spielen

—"our children may some day play on the rainbow" of peace, and not in the camps of war.

THE 1922 CONCEPTION OF THE BANK OF NATIONS

DIE VOELKERBANK (THE BANK OF NATIONS)*

By Hans Heymann, Ph.D.

AUTHOR'S NOTE

In 1922, when Walther Rathenau worked for an organized peace to rebuild the devastated areas of France and Belgium and to develop the vast resources of Russia for economic planning on a national and world-wide scale, he needed a mechanism capable of promoting "not the abolition of national industry, free trade, or tariff agreements, but the distribution and common administration of international raw materials, of international finance." He fought for world solidarity under which a syndicalized Germany could work hand in hand with the Western powers for a better world order. If nationalistic selfishness and competition could not be transformed into friendly peace agreements, he predicted: "Leagues of Nations and arbitration courts will merely lead to judicial extermination of the weaker [nations] by the recognized instrument of competition." He expressed these convictions in 1922, in his books, *Of Days to Come,* and *The New Economy.*

The allusions to an international bank contained in my book, *World Credit and Finance Reform,* impressed Rathenau so much that he urged me to prepare a memorandum which he could use at the Conference of Genoa. Upon the completion of this memorandum and after several discussions in Wilhelmstrasse, it became evident that this plan coincided with Rathenau's ideas and that it would be advisable to attempt a more detailed study. Consequently, I drafted a text which almost appears to be more appropriate today than it was some twenty years ago. In view of this fact, I should like to present this text in the original form without any alterations. I have included it for the reader who wants, in somewhat greater detail, a discussion of the technical instruments treated in the text of the volume. It should be kept in mind that this tract was written a year and a half before the breakdown of the German currency. Without this realization, part of the text may be confusing. I am confident that the reader will appreciate how different future history books would have appeared if a plan of this type had been introduced in preference to the much regretted megalomania of reparations.

* First published, Berlin: Ernst Rowohlt, 1922; translated from the original German, by Hans Heymann, Jr., 1940.

The secret of success is constancy of purpose.

—Disraeli

PREFACE

THIS book is an extended version of a comparatively short memorandum which I prepared for the Conference of Genoa and submitted to the German delegation as basic material for the negotiations of the Credit Commission. In view of the permanent significance of the great economic peace work that could be accomplished by the establishment of a "Bank of Nations," I have decided to submit a detailed description of the plan to the public.

Small matter whether this work will appear at a time prior to the closing of the discussions in Genoa or whether it will herald the approach of a world conference of central banks. Its theme (which has avoided a blind allegiance to the restoration of the gold currency) will stand or fall with the birth or death of the program of economic solidarity which is, at this moment, being slowly and painfully brought into the world.

That this program has long since seriously concerned me was proved to my friends in 1921, when my book, *The World Credit and Finance Reform, A Call to Solidarism,* was published. In this work I attempted to propound scientifically a method by which a uniform world economy was to be planned and constructed on the basis of the relation between human and material energies.

I attempted therein to design the foundation of a universal solidary credit system, on the basis of the common maintenance of property values, and I have been frequently reproached that this credit system bears too close a resemblance to socialism; but what I wrote at the end of the book, with regard to the "party of the party-less," i.e., the party of the courageous pioneers of a true economic League of Nations, might, in the light of present unhappy events, be called optimistic reveries. Nevertheless, I cannot retract any part of my philosophy. In this book I have had to be brief; for, in our days of excitement and turmoil but few have sufficient time and leisure to devote more than a short hour to the reading of literature, especially if it

PREFACE

smacks of an expert opinion, originating in the remote study of some learned scholar, secluded from the world. To this latter title, certainly, I may not lay claim; for my system, if one wants to use the term, has evolved from years of practical commercial experience. On the contrary, the central idea of facilitating the reconstruction of Europe by the establishment of a Bank of Nations will appear somewhat daring.

The question of whether it will be this, or a related institution, which will help the idea of solidarity credit on to victory, whether it will be accomplished completely or in part, at the start, is as immaterial *sub specie aeternitatis* as the question of whether the cooperative organization of productive forces became first apparent in a number of small villages or in one large town. In the final analysis, all the civilized peoples of the world have espoused a certain concept of organization, which has given meaning to the vital motives of mutual help in overcoming the difficulties and in facing the dangers apparent in the economic struggle of existence. I believe that the immense fields of modern credit, as applied to trade, commerce, transportation, construction of buildings and factories, and to the utilization of natural resources in economically undeveloped countries, should also be developed in the spirit of solidarity.

If we succeed in translating this idea into reality on a large scale, we shall have succeeded in our first step in the reconstruction of Europe and the resuscitation of our world economy.

Wiesbaden, Easter 1922

HANS HEYMANN, PH.D.

CONTENTS

INTRODUCTION

Les produits s'échangent
Contre les produits.
—P. J. Proudhon

THE year 1922 will constitute a turning point in the history of world economy. In all countries men have appeared with the courage to enter the lists in behalf of practical solidarity for the civilized world. Due to the indefatigable efforts of Lloyd George it was possible to assemble the peoples of Europe around a table. Their work cannot be in vain.

The tasks which the leading spirits of the different nations set before themselves as ideals—removal of all world trade barriers and combination of the productive forces of the nations for cooperation—were to become realities through the practical efforts of the delegates and experts at the conference.

However, in looking over the positive measures so far proposed, the serious observer cannot fail to notice one common quality in all the suggested plans; the belief appears to dominate that the broken-down machinery of world trade and world production can be repaired and restored to good working order by means of the most superficial, perfunctory methods and unscientific treatment. A few drops of oil are believed to suffice to overcome the dead point. In the hope of making the solution of the problem as easy for ourselves as possible, we instinctively avoid all thoroughgoing and serious effort and hope for some divine impetus, some *deus ex machina* to conjure up the incentive to mutual support.

Have the people already forgotten how thoroughly the subtle apparatus of economic collaboration in our world economy and its division of labor has been destroyed during and after the World War with its continued system of distrust, suspicion, and even animosity? Do we not all realize how frightful this world catastrophe actually is today, and what terrible consequences it may cause in the future if we do not immediately put to work the common will to help each other in common action? The program of the conference was wisely designed to create first a political basis for peaceful collaboration,

273

by means of contractual guarantees. May the great statesmen who represent these ideas achieve the success they deserve.

Now, however, it is a question of developing and putting to work the new program of practical economic solidarity. In this respect it is not yet sufficiently realized that this goal can never be achieved with the old methods of deliberate egotistical struggle for the greatest possible *national* gain. Of an entirely different nature is the new economic system, the construction or establishment of which was hoped for and expected from the Genoa Conference. An organization must be called into existence which will enable all those to collaborate who desire to fight on behalf of justice and sanity in world trade. We must have a mighty mechanism to carry out the *international* system of political economy.

Lloyd George aimed for the establishment of an international corporation for the reconstruction of Europe, and he appears to be the only statesman with the will, courage, and power to help this idea to victory. But he requires the help of experienced experts to show him what steps to take in order to make this corporation financially, technically, and economically capable of living.

It is my firm conviction that these steps must inevitably lead to the establishment of a Bank of Nations. But, if this international credit institution is to function properly, we must first make an exhaustive study of the applicable methods of granting short- and long-term credits. We must lay the foundation of a uniform international money economy, and this presupposes a uniform system of currency and payments between nations. This is the first difficulty in the way of reconstruction. For every nation must work seriously on the establishment of an equilibrium between its fiscal policies and its national economy, in order to utilize the newly created media of exchange with continued success. We must be absolutely clear on this account, and put an end to the aimless "scraps-of-paper economy" designed for the benefit of extenuated national finances; and anyone who argues for a continuation of the wartime paper economy automatically excludes himself from the community of nations desirous of deriving benefit from the Bank of Nations.

I will now venture to indicate a practical method of granting credits by means of the Bank of Nations, based on radically new, but unshakably secure, principles.

In my estimation this method is to be found in an international system of credit amortization. It must be left to the reader to decide how far we may go on that basis. If the creditors of productive capital are granted long-term credits, it will be necessary to require not only a joint solidary guarantee by all debtors engaged in similar activities within certain territorial limits, but also a mutual guarantee of the maintenance of the properties forming the collateral for the loan.

I should like to point out that the correct method of conserving the value of objects is entirely independent of all differences of individual or national concepts. All objects definitely require some system of renewal which would represent, so to speak, its financial minimum of existence. Only the complete adjustment of every human working method to this rational energy-saving device for property values can form the basis for the solidary credits, for which, in the last analysis, the people must vouch. In short, every piece of productively employed capital, every house, ship, machine, vehicle, power-house, etc., must be assured of its regeneration and reproduction within its useful life span, by means of the appropriate economic measures.

At this point mutuality and solidarity must step in, so that the entrepreneur in the free competitive market will not be, as heretofore, individually exposed to the cruel fluctuations of business cycles, but supported by the combined capital forces of his fellow entrepreneurs. It will probably seem shocking to the conservative adherents of *laissez faire* theories to expect the independent heads of commercial enterprises to bear part of other men's burdens; and yet, under pressure of distress, hundreds of entrepreneurs in Germany have already joined forces in a similar manner, in order to provide their invested capital with a planned system of maintenance and reproduction (building and machine life insurance). Now, however, it is a question of making available such collaboration to those who wish to take advantage of the credit facilities of the Bank of Nations. For this purpose we shall, of course, need a complicated system of safety measures, which might, at first sight, appear unwieldy. But no such credit instrument will ever see the light of day if its foundation is undermined by inadequate personal and material guarantees.

If we expect the Bank of Nations to operate successfully in developing world trade, we must not shirk the task of finding a plan for the re-creation of capital. We must indicate a way of restoring the inhibited and disrupted energies of production to good working order. The only obvious solution is international solidary credit on a technically and financially sound basis.

The Bank of Nations—whatever its tasks may be—will be the home of relentless systematic work. If the system of world credit supply is controlled from this central position, it will stimulate the circulation of the life-stream of productive energies which has now been interrupted. In this way the road would be cleared for the resumption of free exchange; products will be exchanged against other products by means of a uniform medium of exchange, in the spirit of Proudhon's *Banque du Peuple* of Paris. The reform of both credit and currency will blaze a trail for the creative efforts of entrepreneurs. Only in this manner can we live up to the precepts of practical solidarity.

Bear ye one another's burdens.
—The Epistle of Paul the Apostle to the Galatians, VI, 2.

THE ESTABLISHMENT OF THE BANK OF NATIONS AS THE ONLY WAY OF OVERCOMING THE WORLD CRISIS

IT SHOULD be apparent to every impartial observer that the tremendous pressure of the world crisis today weighs as heavily on countries with strong currencies as on those with weak currencies, who still appear to enjoy some vestige of prosperity but in actual fact find themselves on the brink of the abyss. If the reduction of exports, the unprofitableness of the best enterprises, and the unemployment problems continue in the countries which still boast of a comparatively well-ordered currency, their gradual impoverishment will be unavoidable.

In view of these facts, it is foolish to speak of some voluntary "relief action" on the part of these stronger nations for the benefit of the "economically weak nations"; what is really needed is an active will on the part of all nations to cooperate in preserving their economic existence. It is nothing less than the recognition of this mutual interdependence of all nations which has brought them together in Genoa. In this long awaited recognition lies the unshakable (so we hope) motive of all plans leading to a uniform international organization for the rebirth of Europe.

Of course, it was general distress, not unselfish brotherly love, which drove the stubborn statesmen to the "Council" of Genoa. In the year 1922 A.D. it does not appear entirely superfluous to remark upon this fact. Great progress in the field of political and economic organization has always been stimulated and inspired by periods of depression and distress. Today the threat of chaos may lead to the creation of a comprehensive system of solidarity, with the establishment of a sane world economy as its goal.

The earnest desire for the realization of this idea must be preceded by a carefully worked out plan. For the moment, the conference appears to consider nothing more substantial than the establishment of certain universal principles of currency and credit reform, which are to serve as a basis for further work. This attitude cannot continue for long! In order to go straight to the root of the matter, I wish to undertake to suggest the following points:

Twelve Functions of the Bank of Nations

1. First step in the reconstruction must be the introduction of an international auxiliary medium of exchange.
2. Introduction of such a medium of exchange would necessitate the establishment of a superordinated bank with the power to issue bank notes, in accordance with the highest money-creation principles.
3. The principal task of the Bank of Nations is the granting of short- and long-term credits on the basis of sound collateral.
4. The establishment of branch banks in every member nation, consisting of issuing and credit departments.
5. The establishment of subordinated national trust banks to finance new productive enterprises—factories, soil reclamation, public utilities, etc.—and to maintain and enlarge existing business and trade. Because of their productive character, these banks shall be called Construction Banks.
6. The Bank of Nations is to grant long-term bank note credits to the Construction Banks. These credits shall be amortized by a new method, according to the depreciation of the objects on which the credits are granted.
7. Aside from soliciting capital, the aim of the Construction Banks is to extract capital gradually from the market through bond issues. The payment of interest on these bonds may be dispensed with until the bonds are issued. This free-of-interest period may last from three to ten years. This is for the benefit of weak debtors.
8. When issued, bonds may yield the customary rate of interest as first-class securities and may be provided with a flexible share in the profits derived from the objects it has financed.
9. Until the end of the free-of-interest period, the bonds are to be held by the Bank of Nations or its branches as securities. At the end of the free period they should be issued in series in accordance with the ability of this market to absorb them. Payment by subscribers shall be made in Bank of Nations bank notes, which are to be destroyed when returned to the Bank of Nations.
10. Aside from amortizing their capital, the debtors must pay the following additions: (1) a fee to cover the operating expenses of the Constructive Bank from the end of the free-of-interest period; (2) the

interest on the bonds; (3) a share in the profits derived from the productive enterprises created by the loan. The loans are to be guaranteed jointly by all debtors and also by the Construction Banks, whose obligations thus become gilt-edged securities.

11. In order to be assured of their value, the objects serving as collateral for the loans shall be insured by a maintenance insurance which covers against premature decay of the property and provides funds for its upkeep and vital repairs. This will assure the maintenance of their value during the useful life of the objects.

12. The amortization of the loans by the debtors should proceed steadily until the debt of the Construction Bank has been completely repaid. The amortization is to be carried out according to statutory regulations in Bank of Nations Construction-Bank notes, which are to be destroyed when returned to the Bank of Nations. Thus the Bank of Nations is completely covered (even during the time when the bonds yield no interest). The joint guarantee of debtors can also serve as security for short-term trade credits. These credits must be examined individually and approved by the central bank in series.

The Currency Problem

THE tremendous difficulties which have arisen in the different countries and which stand in the way of a sensible solution of the currency problem have been clearly recognized by the committees of experts in Genoa. The general opinion appears to tend toward a return to gold currency as the only solution. For nations with a slightly devalued currency this is to be done by means of a return to the pre-war parity; for others, by stabilizing the rates of exchange or prices at a low level, corresponding to their advanced currency depreciation.

I, personally, consider this forced lowering of prices in England, America, Holland, Switzerland, Sweden, etc., by means of so-called deflation as a wrong move. This currency policy would only serve to make the crisis permanent and to lead it from bad to worse. A gradual reduction of all prices to 50 per cent or less of their original value, which would be necessary for this purpose, would soon make every enterprise unprofitable. On the other hand, if the currency reform in weak-currency countries is to effect a return to gold valuation, even in diluted form, it will have to be carried out by means of international gold loans, which today can hardly be procured. Even so, it would have to be considered a luxury for these countries to set aside a gold reserve merely for the rehabilitation of their paper moneys.

What is absolutely necessary, as I have already stated in the Preface, is the legalized absorption of the unproductive credits by the state, in the form of note issue against treasury bonds. Naturally it would be of little value to make especially strict demands against Germany in this respect, without limiting reparation claims to a reasonable amount. In this case, as in all cases, the prerequisite for the use of inflationary credits is a correspondingly increased tax burden and the application of internal and external credits for the purpose of incurring short-term debts (transformation of treasury notes into loans).

It would be possible to simplify such reforms if the issuing banks of different countries cooperated constantly in procuring for one another certain sums in gold or currency. One may well understand the opinion of Keynes, and others, that a currency agreement should be made at a later conference with the cooperation of America, the aim of which would be the acceptance of a uniform gold standard. But the struggle for gold, which would then begin once again with unprecedented fervor, would never permit the establishment of a stable world market price for gold. At every upward swing of business, drastic measures would have to be taken (such as a raising of the rediscount rate and considerable price changes) so as to avoid a loss of gold. I consider it quite senseless to attempt to restore the general dependence upon gold, which has become quite inadequate. But it appears to be an incurable superstition that the stabilization of currency can be achieved only by association with the fictitious material value of gold. It is quite understandable that the abuse of currency rights for the benefit of nations whose other sources of income do not suffice has given rise to a fierce dislike of a paper economy of that sort. Nevertheless there is no reason why we should throw out the child with the bath and reject en bloc all sensible paper currency arrangements.

Only after long years of bitter experience will humanity realize that a general return to gold is either quite impossible, or else can be achieved only at great sacrifice. We have probably forgotten that Wilson once suggested that the gold content of the dollar be increased with rising prices, and decreased with falling prices. He realized that its material value plays an inferior part in the dynamic functioning of legal tender, because the necessary scarcity can be achieved by other methods (by restriction of circulation, for instance).

It seems to me that, for the moment, some form of international emergency action in the field of currency policy is quite unavoidable, regardless of whether we are forced to choose temporary or intermediate measures, or whether we are compelled to the somewhat drastic solution of transferring, by loans, excessive accumulations of gold in order to avoid clashes between the strong and weak currency nations in their international trade transactions. These measures might be taken in Genoa, and, if properly executed, would be nothing less than utopian.

The Establishment of the Bank of Nations—Creation of Fictitious Gold Values

I should like to suggest that, for the establishment of the Bank of Nations and its branches, a share capital of one hundred million currency units (gold francs, gold dollars, gold gilders, or the like) be secured. As the bank is to be a credit institution for mutual benefits, it will be satisfied with limited dividends. For evident reasons this institution should be a semipublic enterprise, in which both public and private interests may participate as shareholders. It would seem appropriate to choose neutral territory for the headquarters of the Bank of Nations—possibly Berne or The Hague, where international institutions have previously been created.

The further question arises whether it would be wise to grant this bank the right to issue a new uniform medium of exchange, and upon what unit of value it should be based.

Many suggestions have been made to the effect that a gold fund be set up and bank notes three to five times the amount of the gold be issued. In accordance with this prevalent opinion, I myself suggested the possible creation of a gold reserve fund through the issuance of bonds by this international reconstruction institution; but at this time I consider this as an entirely unnecessary encumbrance upon the Bank of Nations. Under the joint guarantee of all nations, it will be possible to create fictitious gold values by connecting this medium of exchange to some existing currency unit, such as the gold franc or the gold dollar. In world trade it is customary to convert the quantity of any national unit of value to the purchasing power of that monetary unit whose value bears the closest resemblance to that national unit. The Bank of Nations could at this time change nothing in this respect; it would have to calculate with world market prices and pay the debtor in bank notes of his own currency to the extent required by the currency of the paying country. This would exert a balancing influence upon international exchange rates. The importer would no longer be forced to buy foreign money or currency with a fluctuating quantity of domestic currency, but would immediately receive the necessary quantity of international money, by way of credit. What security he must give for this credit, I shall discuss at a later time.

But what is implied, if the Bank of Nations issues a new paper money which by agreement is based upon fictitious gold values?

Until recently it was firmly believed that the value of bank notes, under normal currency conditions, is entirely dependent upon its redeemability in gold. This, however, was a grave error. When the German Reichsbank discounted a bill of exchange and paid the amount in bank notes, the coverage of these bank notes did not depend upon their redeemability in gold, but exclusively upon the amount paid for merchandise the salability of which was considered likely by the issuer of the bill of exchange. This really means an actual creation of money on the basis of an increase in the volume of products, and does not mean putting into circulation deposits or other savings which previously existed.

Anyone who accepted the bank notes as legal tender, it was believed, granted the Reichsbank a credit without interest, while the bank secured interest by discounting its loan to the drawer of the bill of exchange. I myself held to the opinion that the bank notes represented a real evidence of debt; however, this is a misconception, created by the wording of the notes. Under conditions of free exchange the bank note was simply fictitious gold money; i.e., the goldmark, because of confidence in its buying power, was considered the unit of calculation. A similar situation existed with the 5-franc silver coin, which functioned as a uniform interstate medium of exchange among the member states of the Latin Coin Union. After the depreciation of silver, 5-franc coins were generally called "credit money," which was kept in circulation merely because of its assumed relation in value to gold. This also was a misconception, for no one would care about the value of the silver metal and its relation to gold so long as it was kept in circulation by general confidence. I consider it foolish to speak of the "value" of any medium of exchange, in the sense of a material mass. It is absolutely nonsensical to set up such concepts of value. The early pioneers of gold currency have made themselves a laughingstock by propounding this notion. Everyone knew, after all, that gold money (and substitutes therefor, which constituted a valid means of payment) did not contain an immutable value, but possessed a certain purchasing power which differed vastly from country to country and from continent to continent. Even the term "purchasing power" is not entirely faultless; for the price relations existing at any period of economic development are not so designed that the quantity of products which the owner of money can procure in exchange for that money will invariably be forced upon him in that fixed volume. On the contrary, much depends upon what value the buyer may place upon the product, and how great he may deem the sacrifice which would be entailed by the reduced ability to satisfy the demand resulting from the expenditure.

The complete level of "market prices" results from the total amount of all such individual considerations of cost and utility, i.e., the so-called purchasing power of the money in that particular economic territory. Outside of this territory the money becomes what is commonly termed "merchandise." This applies only if the money has a material value, i.e., if, divested of its monetary functions, it is evaluated purely as to its metallic worth. If, on the other hand, a foreigner conserves currency or paper money of a foreign country, in order therewith to make payments in this country, the (relative) purchasing power of that monetary unit is decisive for its so-called external or internal value. It depends upon what quantity of social products may be purchased for the monetary unit in the country of issue, and upon the relation of the price level prevailing in this country to that prevailing in others. The so-called external value is always strongly affected by the confidence in the constancy of these price-level relations.

Upon close observation we find that price relations are never quite constant. The purchasing power of a monetary unit, regulated according to supply and demand, fluctuates with changing conditions of import and export and other exchange relations and obligations. These relations between purchasing powers are expressed by the international exchange rates, and only in gold-currency countries does a so-called parity exist between the currencies concerned, which parity must be maintained artificially in so far as this is at all possible.

I merely wish to state here that, even before the introduction of paper money economy in all countries having a developed system of issuing banks, millions or even billions of monetary units of all sorts circulated, the purchasing power of which was fictitiously placed on the same level with gold, through the solidary guarantee of the currency communities involved. Who would ever think of exchanging bank balances for cash at the Reichsbank? All transactions are made with an ideal quantity of value, without any transfer of actual hard money.

A large part of these so-called liquid capital funds was in the form of balances loaned on the open market, in the form of gold credits. However, we must not over-estimate the power of the aforementioned confidence. This confidence applies in the case of "money without material value" only if it is immediately used for government credit. This almost invariably implies an abuse.[1] Actually all currency should be protected by legislation against such arbitrary encroachment by the government. An international money could never be introduced without an internationally binding contract, regardless of whether such a money is to circulate temporarily or permanently and regardless of whether it is to have a gold coverage or not.

According to old ideas a uniform paper money circulating in several countries would take the form of a loan without interest granted to the several governments or central banks. How unscientific this idea is, is demonstrated by the fact that it considers national bank notes, still in circulation,

---

[1] Exception: Short-term government credits in return for treasury notes, to cover temporary differences between income and outgo during a certain fiscal period but not in excess of that period.

FUNDAMENTAL PROBLEMS

as nothing more than the debt taken over by the country, left over from long dead individual central banks. A circulating money can never be a debt of the community to its members or even to foreigners into whose possession such moneys may get.

Money can be exchanged only with merchandise, never with gold or other precious metals. If anyone needs gold as merchandise he may melt his gold coins or, in countries with a gold standard, he may demand gold from the bank in return for its bank notes. In the latter case he does not need the gold in the form of money but in the form of merchandise, to be used for coinage of other gold currency. The purchase of gold bars by means of any salable product would serve the same purpose.

I merely wish to prove that, in the introduction of a uniform international medium of exchange, money in the form of metal plays no part at all and that its relation to an existing unit of value is nothing more than an imagined attachment to some known yardstick of the pre-war or post-war period.

However, at this point one might object that the accepted nominal unit of value would have a different purchasing power in different countries and that then the 5-franc note would not, no more than at present, have the same valuation in France, Belgium, and Switzerland. This objection, on the other hand, overlooks the fact that the validity of Bank of Nations money would be universally recognized in all European countries, i.e., in all countries which are voluntary members of this monetary understanding. This avoids all annoying currency barriers; nowhere will the stream of payments between nations be interrupted by distrust, so long as the necessary control is exercised over the observance of sensible principles of money issuing.

How did newly coined or printed money get into circulation in the past? It is a sad fact that until now so few people have seriously thought about this. It is because of this lack of interest that the term "inflation" has been so much misused.

How do we differentiate between a money issue which exceeds the required amount and one which is in accordance with the required amount? If, in times of rising prices, new bank notes were issued in the amount of the increased production, was that inflation or was it a theoretically correct creation of money?

It is a well-known fact that, at certain times, all issuing banks attempted to put a halt to the continued increase of credit, namely, when they could no longer secure the required gold coverage. We clearly recall the catastrophes caused in 1847, 1857, and 1867 in England by the cessation of the discounting of bills of exchange, and whenever Peel's Acts were suspended many millions of new bank notes were again issued without in the slightest degree disturbing the market, thus disproving the misconception that redeemability in gold is absolutely necessary.

But it was not merely the system of strict limitation which caused such threats to the normal exchange of goods; even in countries with a more mobile currency such money crises arose (e.g., in 1907 in the U.S.). The prescribed gold coverage of the Federal Reserve note may, in times of crisis, be suspended. If, however, at a time when this redeemability may actually become desirable, it is suspended and becomes an illusion, why go to all the trouble of insisting on it in normal times, when no one except a violent gold-standard adherent is in the slightest interested in it?

The true security of the claims of an issuing bank lies in the redeemability of its credits. By this I do not mean the possible salability of securities put up by the creditor himself or by his debtors, but I mean simply the vendability of the products created by means of the credit, or the means of production built by the credit, the returns from which are obviously also salable. That which is unproductive or unmarketable hinders the repayments of all credits, whether they were granted in gold or in bank notes.

The first principle of intelligent money creation must be the stabilization of an average price level on the basis of exact index numbers. This merely means giving up any forced changes in the relation between money values in different countries. But it does not preclude aiming for the goal of helping back to normal the price level of countries whose products were unnaturally devaluated by the paper money economy. This may be done by allowing the strong blood of a uniform currency to flow into the weak body of the economy to the extent of the money demand, thereby making superfluous a corresponding volume of the weaker money.

The law of Gresham that "good money cannot chase out bad money" does not apply here, for there would be no advantage in hoarding this better money, since there is no expectation that its purchasing power may rise in the near future. Why should we fear a general rise in the price level, if the unnecessary consideration of gold hoardings and reserves forces us to an unnatural limitation of the creation of new money? In what direction could this international money flow, if it is as valid outside of the international border as within?

The more the value of the Bank of Nations currency fluctuated within the country, the more this would disturb the export of its national products. On the other hand, a fixed relation between the values of the national and the international moneys would then be more easily established than at present, where all exchange is disrupted by the currency contradictions. This, of course, does not justify the unrestricted granting of credit in bank notes by the Bank of Nations to all countries. On the contrary, in order to safeguard the credit, we must observe a strict production-for-use economy.

But what does such a production-for-use control consist of?

The Limits of Bank of Nations Credit

The financial experts of the Genoa Conference, in their suggestion for an International Convention on Exchange Rates, mention a Stabilization of Credit. These experts consider it possible that through this medium the parity between the different currency units can be maintained and that abnormal fluctuations in the purchasing power of money can be avoided. These arrangements, without impairing the initiative of central banks, are intended to set up international concepts to be observed by all issuing banks. This is evidently a *contradictio in adjecto*! It is quite possible to set up such concepts by means of a Bank of Nations with its branches, but not by means of a voluntary association of national issuing banks with vastly differing interests.

The stabilization of prices within a country by means of a certain money or credit policy is a task which an independent national issuing bank could well accomplish; but the stabilization of its rate of exchange and its value abroad cannot be accomplished by one bank alone—for this purpose we must have an international convention. The experts are quite aware of this, for they demand in Article IV that any member nation, purchasing currency from any other member nation may not deviate by more than a certain fraction from the established parity. I consider that demand as pure utopia. Even if the gold standard were restored, this demand could not be complied with. It has happened many times in the past that the low and high points of gold were exceeded in gold-standard countries, and it never occurred to any country to make sacrifices in order to preserve the gold parity of its neighboring country, when this parity was threatened in the above manner. Now these general sacrifices are to become the order of the day, without any clue as to the size of these sacrifices which every nation would have to take upon itself. Apparently there is no confidence in the adequacy of the gold reserve which every member country is to procure for itself with all speed.

Nevertheless it must be considered as a laudable admission that outside of this gold reserve, so called, one will set aside certain moneys, short-term obligations, and other holdings in other issuing banks (beyond the frontier), which by their liquidity are to supplement this problematic gold reserve.

Let us now define what might be meant by Stabilization of Credit. It appears to be a deep secret, closely guarded by the financial experts. They can hardly assume that it is possible to fix a maximum limit, because the potentialities of development cannot be foreseen for any country. Evidently this suggestion is based on a static and not on a dynamic point of view, and therefore the whole Stabilization of Credit program is ridiculous and impossible. The demand for credit will always change. It will always remain dependent upon the output and productive ability of a country, upon the role it plays or may play in world economy, upon the size of its domestic markets, and upon the speed of the domestic turnover of goods.

We need no new inventions, if we establish a Bank of Nations whose task it must be to limit its credits sensibly, in so far as these credits are based on bank note issues. In this respect the experience of national issuing banks during peace time will be of help to us.

Short-Term Credits of the Bank of Nations

Quite naturally in any economic territory there is a certain urgent demand for credit which can be limited and regulated according to the financial condition of the prospective debtor. First of all, we must consider the demand for raw materials and food which can be met if the Bank of Nations discounts short-term trade bills after investigating their soundness.

At present, however, confidence in the safety of credits granted to importers of weak-currency countries is shaken. Even the guarantee of bank drafts (Rembourskredite) is no longer considered adequate by the distrustful suppliers in gold-standard countries. That is why in the famous ter Meulen project there is a demand for the issue of fictitious gold values, by import countries, as security for their credits. For the interest and amortization of these they are to mortgage national capital objects and sources of income and private industrial or trade values. Besides that, they are to take over the solidary guarantee for any possible failure in the repayment of the credit; in this way they are to be given the right to supply any importer with gold bonds in the currency of the supplying country.

The latter payment appears especially droll to me. Instead of insisting on a uniform international paper money, every country is to receive the right to issue gold values in the currency of all other countries, and this under the control of a central commission, which would thereby become unchallenged ruler of the world economy. The commission is also to have the privilege of examining at any time all mortgaged objects and sources of income, and even to take them, over and administer them.

For what possible reason should the issuers of the gold bonds pay interest to themselves? Merely to prevent the exporters, in case of nonpayment of the credits, from getting rid of their bonds. But this would not happen, because the issuing countries would retain the right of sale and for the sake of decency would repurchase their bonds. The clumsy character of this system of credit security is really appalling. If the solidary guarantee of countries to which credits have been granted is introduced for all short- and long-term credits, in my opinion the mortgaging of objects would be superfluous.

What would happen if, in one of the weak currency countries, a financial crisis were to set in? In that case the mortgaged objects would have to be sold wholesale, and we would have the same experience as with the auctioning of French government estates as security for the assignates. Furthermore, we must not overlook the fact that, without serious treatment of national and international currency reform, the mutual guarantee for importers would often fail to function. Even with careful control of production for use, cases will arise in which bills will not be honored.

I therefore believe that we must first carefully test this idea of solidary guarantee on the part of the countries which were granted credits. According to present-day concepts, it contains unprecedented demands. If a national branch of the Bank of Nations were to make a mistake or miscalculation in its credit operations, all debtors in the nation concerned would have to meet the losses. This guarantee is not imaginable without some self-regulating mechanism of trade, industry, and agriculture. That such an organization is possible in Germany is demonstrated by the Hachenburg Draft for the Acceptance of a Foreign Loan.

With short-term credits the putting up of hypothecary securities is not impossible, as can be seen from the Dutch currency credit. But it makes the whole matter so much more complicated that it would be better to forego it if we are to make the most efficient practical use of credit. It would be preferable for the debtors to form a contingency reserve, which may take precedence over the repair of losses incurred.

The question may be asked whether the productive capital of countries weakened by sick currencies would suffice to pay the very high prices of raw materials, food, etc. (cf. the present [1922] situation of the Austrian industrialists). The whole situation would be changed as soon as these debtors could operate with the sound currency of the Bank of Nations. At the same time the distribution all over the world of newly produced products would be set in motion through the new credit system, if it were only possible to limit to the absolute minimum the inhibitions of trade, such as import and export restrictions, customs walls, etc. The fecundity of free trade would be immediately realized by the member nations of the Bank. Any country insisting on imprisoning itself behind unsurmountable trade barriers would soon enough discover the disadvantages.

If, at this critical time, there is a movement toward intensifying the outmoded high tariff system, such as is taking place in the U.S., it can be considered as nothing less than destruction of domestic productive facilities; it would be sad indeed if people continued to adhere to the illusion that they might continue to export in large volume without importing in the same volume. In what form can the United States, which, overnight, has changed from a debtor to a creditor nation, procure the interest on such a foreign investment? A gold payment to that extent would, in the long run, be quite impossible; the payment of war debts also must be accepted in the form of products. In the long run the destructive results of the high customs system will become evident to even the most reticent of states.

It is indeed a vain hope of American financiers that they may continue to grant dollar credits at the present high interest rate to the constantly weakening European countries, without driving them into bankruptcy. They are constantly creating new debit accounts, which are definitely unsound so long as this prohibitive system, ruinous for export countries, continues to exist. Unfortunately even in Germany there are politicians and financial tycoons who consider the enhancement of the German capital market through foreign loans as a cure-all, regardless of how high the interest is.

This is nothing better than a desperate *après nous le déluge* policy. Those who are deceived by high paper dividends might imagine that the productivity of this borrowed money would be higher than the excessive interest charged; however, this can continue only as long as the consumers of the products have an income sufficient to cover the consequent rise in prices. As is well known, even the shifting of interest has its limitations, and the paper profits of industry contain more of the substance of decaying capital than the adherents of such a credit policy would admit.

Long-Term Credit of the Bank of Nations

The appalling lack of capital which has gradually developed in all weak-currency countries cannot be healed, in the long run, by short-term credits. This is a basic fact which almost compels the Bank of Nations to establish a new system of long-term credits. To some extent this lack of capital is ameliorated by the fact that capitalists in strong-currency countries purchase property values and real capital in weak-currency countries. This procedure is profitable only as long as the returns from the acquired properties, converted into their gold values, suffice to pay the interest on such investments.

The increasingly diluted stream of paper money which thus flows into foreign countries would soon spoil the capitalists' enjoyment of these investments. The intermediate profits, also, derived from the resale of these objects, soon come to an end and represent nothing but the antisocial and anti-economic enrichment of some from the loss of others.

The only solution is to enable the financially weak entrepreneurs in weak-currency countries to renew outworn properties and to create new objects, by means of long-term credit. Upon this expansion of production the future purchasing power of financially unsound countries will depend. This is the only effective remedy against inflation.

Increased production means increased purchasing power, for only by creating products can other products be procured. It would be an unfounded fear if strong-currency countries, suffering from unsteady production, were to consider an extension of production in other countries as a threat to their own export ability. Generally speaking, this fear appears to have subsided, for there is a combined movement to develop the eastern European market by means of old-fashioned financial syndicates using capitalistic colonization policies, as practiced in China. Certainly, lip service is paid to the preservation of the complete economic equality of the country to be developed, but in practice this is not closely observed. Small wonder, therefore, that Russia and other nations have politely refused such economic guardianship.

Everyone must realize that only by means of huge long-term investments can we help backward and distressed countries to develop all their powers of production to the fullest extent. Countries such as France and Germany, which are greatly weakened by war and reparation payments, are in great need of such credits. They represent the only solution for them.

I should like to draw the reader's special attention toward events which may at present [1922] be observed in Germany.* Almost all new means of production and capital goods have risen in price so considerably that the customary method of writing off no longer suffices to take care of the renewal and reproduction of the depreciated capital. A new machine costs forty to sixty times as much as the old one which it is to replace, and no

* The reader is reminded that this was written before the breakdown of the German currency and its stabilization, November, 1923.

one knows what will happen when the prices of products manufactured by this machine can no longer be raised correspondingly, and even begin to fall.

In case of new purchases, great write-offs are permitted free of tax, but only well-endowed old enterprises with large reserves can afford such large write-offs. Thus the danger threatens, more and more, that the renewal of all productive capital is becoming impossible. Until now it has been possible for large corporations to combine in the form of trusts, thus considerably reducing their costs of production.

New establishment of industrial enterprises with newly built production goods (not simply transformation of existing private companies into share corporations) have become increasingly rare. The situation is even worse with new house construction, which, in spite of all subsidies, is still lagging far behind the demands of the increasing population. And this increasing need for more housing is evident not only in Germany but also in the majority of the other countries suffering from the aftereffects of the war. A lowering of rents is much feared, and the spending of the exceedingly high costs of materials and wages is avoided because of the uncertainty of being able to pay the interest and amortization on the required investment.

Many leaders of industry do not yet sufficiently realize the great significance this stoppage in the construction field has in connection with the economic development of their country. They are constantly aiming for large immediate profits from the turnover of their products, still lagging far behind the demand, and believe that they can exploit the monopolistic position secured for them by the protective wall of paper money.

It is erroneous to believe that we have at our disposal a strictly limited quantity of work (Arbeitsleistungen) which cannot by any means be increased, regardless of what system of capital expansion and capital creation may be applied. The need for a national economy to progress does not consist of maintaining only the profitableness of its existing large enterprises. It must lead to the formation of new productive capital in proportion to the constantly increasing population, and this means in the first place adequate housing facilities for the existing and growing laboring forces.

Until now it was deemed impossible to expand the basis of production in any economic field by any other method than the application of existing savings; these savings were formed by the reduction of individual consumption for the purpose of creating new capital. Certainly liquid capital of this kind is always available on the money market and is transformed into stable or circulating risk capital (either directly or by investment in securities). But

FUNDAMENTAL PROBLEMS

besides this there is another method of capital creation, which has been quite overlooked. This method is as follows:

In existing or newly established enterprises, certain additional productive capital is accumulated from the profits. I should like to call them productive savings, but let us not take this term too literally, because it includes all newly procured capital in trade, transportation, or insurance institutions. Frequently this creation of new capital is undertaken by means of long-term credits, bonds, debentures, mortgages or other obligations. So long as such securities could be issued in an amount corresponding to the demand, this process continued without trouble. It was then the entrepreneur's task to transform these outside funds into his own funds, by steady amortization from his net income.

In this way loan capital amounting to billions came to the aid of the German real estate market and the German corporate institutions. But the merciless suction pump of misapplied paper money has reduced to a minimum the creditors' interest earnings on these long-term investments. And yet, in this way the capital power of the debtors, i.e., of the actual owners of the properties, appears to have increased to a maximum. But the unmistakable danger remains that this whole credit system, already undermined by the war, may one day collapse completely, because it becomes unprofitable for the moneylenders.

Germany has been admired by many countries for its highly developed credit system. But at this time we need a supplement to this system if we wish to avoid the cessation of all mortgage issues. In order to attain this progress, we must carefully analyze the creation of new capital in the sphere of productive enterprise. In the acceptance of a long-term credit we may observe, during the life of such a capital fund, a double process of capital creation: on the one hand the steady repayment of the loaned funds, on the other the planned renewal of the existing productive properties up to the time of their complete depreciation.

The satisfaction of both these requirements has been possible only for very prosperous enterprises. The others have always remained in debt to the extent of a part of the accepted credits (bonds, etc.). Amortized mortgages have formed a conspicuous exception, for this system, better than any other, has been well equipped to perform the rational task of capital creation.

Much more detrimental than the retention of unamortized credits have been the numerous failures and interruptions of the regular systems of write-off and renewal, which frequently have occurred in less prosperous concerns. This usually has led to the economic ruin of the weakened enterprises, which

293

have consumed their capital proper, all the while trusting to a favorable business upswing to pull them out of their difficulties. Especially in times of great economic depression, as at present, the weaknesses and shortcomings of such an arbitrary, unscientific method become evident. The customary inadequate methods of writing off, handed down from generation to generation of entrepreneurs, have failed at the moment when revolutionary price changes have made the purchase of new means of production very difficult and have shaken the capital power of business men.

We must now take a new approach to this unavoidable economic situation. This is a task which can be completely solved only by the solidary cooperation of whole generations of entrepreneurs, and one which must be tackled without delay. All experience in the field of property renewal must be applied to this end. Only in this manner can the idea of a universal mechanism of capital renewal achieve practical significance.

It is today no longer considered utopian to propose the creation of institutions to enable us to organize the development of property values by means of voluntary cooperation toward a common end. This idea can be realized only through the medium of insurance. The discovery of this fact must be considered as one of the greatest progressive steps ever taken in the field of insurance.

After long years of preparation it has been possible by this method to bring to life a group of German property-life insurance companies, based on the principle of mutual preservation and renewal of capital.

I can but mention here that property-life insurance is built upon the concentration of renewal reserves. The insurance institution, in return for a risk premium, takes over the protection of the property against premature decay by indemnifying the vitally important repairs, and places at the disposal of the assured the means with which the property may be replaced at the end of its useful life. This is the development of a technically exact and universally acceptable maintenance method, enlarged and supplemented by our experience in the life duration and functions of objects (e.g., buildings, ships, or machines). It is the method by which all entrepreneurs may attain the continuation of their productive capital goods. It may also simplify their transformation into more productive capital goods (e.g., in the replacement of obsolete machinery by more modern equipment). This policy will form a new collateral, the value of which, together with the depreciated value of the property, will, in case of full insurance, correspond to at least the original value of the property.

It is, further, not without significance that, with the aid of property-life insurance, a secure protection is provided against any disturbing government encroachment upon the vital maintenance of capital. If this were merely a national matter, I would not emphasize the importance of this institution here. But there is not a single branch of world-wide economic enterprise which would not be benefited by the introduction of a solidary mechanism for the conservation of property values, and yet no one has even thought of such an institution.

It is a characteristic of objects that their technical conservation depends upon universal laws, quite independent of human arbitrariness. It follows, therefore, that the cost of gradual reconstruction, expressed in money, is equally dependent on definite laws, in spite of fluctuations in prices of materials and wages. If the insured amount were always adjusted to the rising and falling costs of renewal and reproduction, the participating property owners would reap the great benefits of securing the financial minimum of existence for their properties. Logically, in this field also, there develops first a national and then an international reinsurance, which will enable the coverage of all risks and finally lead to the greatly increased security of all enterprises covered, even in times of crisis.

In all countries of the globe there is a growing belief that a new system of credit guarantees must be introduced if the entrepreneurs of territories with shattered currencies are to be assured a systematic renewal of their outworn properties. As mentioned before, in years to come we can no longer count on the availability in adequate quantity of mortgages, bonds, etc. The financial losses before and after the war were much too large, the disposable savings are much too limited, the risks of investing in securities is much too great; for the interest and amortization on these securities depends entirely on the profitableness of the enterprises financed.

It is thus almost impossible for the average business executive to set aside in cash the amount necessary to replace his property. If, to do this, he lacks the necessary capital, or if all his savings are tied up, the only remaining solution is adherence to the principle that the enterprise itself must save the purchasing price of its properties from its future earnings. In other words, we need at present a most highly developed type of loan, one which will anticipate future earnings.

In order to provide an entrepreneur with the indispensable funds to cover his demand for capital, an international bank, I maintain and intend to prove, may grant long-term credits without the danger of abnormal losses, if, to support it, the bank attracts well-organized financing institutions.

Assuming that the Bank of Nations is given the privilege by all member nations to issue notes in a uniform currency according to previously agreed principles, in that case, undoubtedly, special safety measures will have to be taken if the credits are to be granted for long terms. It matters little whether these notes, in contrast to the short-term loans, are to be given special names, such as construction bank notes, or loan certificates, etc. What is important is that they be issued in series, based on definite groups of objects serving as a basis for the credit. If, for example, the construction of apartment buildings is to be financed, the buildings constructed in every year must be marked by the national construction bank responsible for the use of the funds as Series #1,2,3,4, . . . , etc. The period which has been fixed for amortization of each series from the rent receipts of the buildings concerned must also be set down. It will therefore be in the interest of simplicity to build the new houses according to certain standards, with a definite life duration. The amortization must be determined by a Bank of Nations statute.

In order to be carried out, these demands may be based upon the following safety measures, which I can no more than outline here: The amount, in terms of money, by which the building depreciates annually should be calculated in advance for the entire life of the building. The owner of the building, whether it be an individual or an association of landlords, would bind himself to the annual payment of these rates, by accepting a serial bill of exchange with detachable coupons which he would be legally compelled to redeem. Instead of serial bills, a set of single bills might be used, but I am inclined to believe that it would be quite in order to construct a new form of bills for this new form of credit. In any case the bank would require a sound security. Furthermore, it should be determined whether, during these times of economic insecurity, a solidary guarantee of the debtors within certain territorial limits and with certain series of objects should be required.

In the first place we must consider the liability of the national construction banks whose task it is to manage the work of financing. But this liability must be a subsidiary liability, because of the limited capital of the construction banks. The liability could take on a more definite aspect, if the construction banks would charge the debtors a certain addition to their amortization rate in order to build up a contingency reserve. In this way a relatively large fund might be accumulated with a minimum of individual effort.

The actual principal liability, however, would be accepted by the debtors, who could most readily be organized into associations. Any possible failure on amortization payments could, then, annually be corrected or be taken from the accumulated reserve. Against disturbances of a serious kind, the construction banks could safeguard themselves by means of indemnity systems, by forming certain reserves, or by reinsurance arrangements of all kinds.

The formation of separate reserves by the individual debtor might be desirable.

By the advance payment of rates in good years, the businessman could alleviate his position in less favorable times. Deferment might be permitted against adequate security, but only if the bank was in the possession of sufficient reserves. Compulsory management of mismanaged properties would be provided for; compulsory sale might be considered as a last resort. The sale of the financed properties would be based on the option of the construction bank. The purchaser would have to agree to take over the obligations of his predecessor in connection with the property.

Finally, there is a third type of credit security guarantee which should be required, for without it this whole loan system would be uncertain. As long as the credit obligation remains, the financed object must have its maintenance and preservation guaranteed. It is therefore imperative that the rational preservation of the capital (this does not include its replacement, which is optional) be safeguarded by means of property-life insurance. In this way cumbersome, bureaucratic control on the part of the construction bank can be avoided. By taking out a policy in the amount of the value of the property and by regularly paying the comparatively small risk premium for maintenance insurance, the debtor may cede the policy to the construction bank, so that the latter may handle the debtor's legal claims against the insurance company. The credits must be cancelable, in the event that the policy lapses for nonpayment of premium.

Until now the maintenance of financed properties has been left entirely in the hands of the individual entrepreneur. In the case of long-term amortized credits, however, control over the treatment of the capital, out of the earnings of which the amortization must be paid, has become a foremost principle. The amortization naturally proceeds in proportion to the depreciation of the financed productive property. When the property has totally depreciated, the amortization of the credit must be completed.

The experience of property-life insurance in Germany has made it possible to set up scientific tables and statistics for the predetermination of the length of life of buildings, ships, machinery, etc., so that the whole system of credit amortization can be placed on a scientific basis. The insurance company guarantees its policyholders the immediate payment of indemnities sufficient to cover the structurally important repairs as damages occur. The company must therefore have close contact with institutions which make these repairs thoroughly and inexpensively.

I believe that this measure, if carried out on a large scale, will be one of the most important financial steps in the advancement of projects designed to serve the rehabilitation of our disorganized world economy.

It is common knowledge, and has been confirmed by Russian experts on railways, that the condition of that country's railway equipment, with all its appurtenances, is in such a state of deterioration that reconstruction can take place only by means of credits with a system of amortization which requires only very low interest rates in the first years. Credits of all kinds requiring high interest rates right from the start are impractical and even impossible. So long as we delude ourselves on this point, we shall make no progress in this matter.

The situation is similar in the reconstruction of apartment buildings, factories, etc., in large Russian cities, such as Moscow and St. Petersburg. Millions, or even billions, are required here to enable the decayed properties to be rebuilt or replaced. Obviously the available savings are not large enough in Russia to pay for this. Here again, amortized credits may solve the problem, if issued in conjunction with a property-life insurance arrangement, to compel the owners and users of the properties to care for their maintenance in a scientific manner. Whether or not we would call this a form of economic education, the fact remains that it is a voluntary self-regulating mechanism which can never exclude or hamper the free pursuit of economic progress, but rather will invariably support and revitalize it.

Construction Banks

In all rational systems of annuity credit, the instruments of management which control the correct utilization of the loaned capital are indispensable. As an example I should like to mention the procedure of the Prussian High Commission in dividing large land holdings into small areas. The trust banks of the German electrical industry represent excellently administered institutions for the construction of power companies, railroads, etc., whose credit system would quite correspond to my suggestions for organization, if it were adjusted to present world economic conditions.

The specialization of the construction banks for classes or groups of properties to be created would correspond absolutely to the principle of division of labor. Without the help of such institutions, the necessary aid could not be available in the national territories to be supported. We must break ourselves of the habit of expecting all progress to come from private initiative or arbitrarily formed capitalist associations. Certainly we cannot get along without the initiative of captains of banking and industry, and I am the last to advocate that idea; but for the practical accomplishment of such gigantic tasks of reconstruction as those with which we are now faced, we must have a complex of financial and technical institutions which represent the systematic functions of capital. Even the leading large banks will readily appreciate the undeniable advantages of such trust institutions, when the task is approached in a practical manner. They have consistently and gladly participated in all existing arrangements of this kind, in solidary cooperation with large industries.

These self-evident facts should suffice to dispel the objection that the suggested construction banks might become a form of bureaucratic central agency under government control. There is absolutely no reason why these trust banks cannot be established in the form of stock companies. It would, however, be more advantageous if they were founded as semipublic institutions, i.e., with the participation of both private enterprise as well as public activity. The German settlement developments and the Rhenish Westphalian Power Company and associated companies may be cited as practical models.

Aside from the central construction banks, we must establish an adequate number of branch banks. Self-regulating mechanisms are to be added to the regularly employed officers as far as practicable. This whole apparatus will develop by itself under the influence of circumstances and will accustom itself to its natural functions, without being tied *a priori* to definite schedules. In the organization of mining ventures, for example, it will be possible to introduce miners' associations and settlements (and even participation of the organized workers in the profits). All these ideas will evolve with the passage of time and become practicable institutions, but it is imperative that the leaders of the work be imbued with the spirit of social progress.

By experience we know that it is in the nature of a trust bank to attract loan capital in great quantities in the form of bonds or debentures, for the support of its financial transactions. The optimists in our present capitalist system will perhaps blandly maintain that the subscribers to such securities will be available in sufficient numbers as soon as the invitations to subscribe are extended. However, in spite of my customary optimism, I doubt the immediate success of the usual issuing procedure. That is why, at least provisionally, I have proposed the use of amortized credits with the help of Bank of Nations notes.

I can almost see the horror on the faces of managers of issuing banks if, at their forthcoming conference in London, they should be approached with such an idea! Undeniably, bank note credits for the purchase of new capital have long existed in large quantities and especially in inflation countries, where they have been used in undesirable quantities (i.e., without sufficient security for the repayment of the credits). If we think of such practices as the constantly renewed acceptance credits of large enterprises, the uncovered current account credits of many Anglo-Saxon banks, the balances based on pure paper money credits and, worst of all, on national treasury bond credits, such as the excess price subsidies and settlement subsidies, then we can no longer maintain that it is impossible and unheard of to secure capital with the aid of bank note credits. I do not even hesitate to assert that not a single strong national issuing bank would run the risk of bad credits if it made use of my long-term amortized credit system in its own economic territory.

But how much easier it would be for the Bank of Nations, under the joint guarantee of all nations, to set in motion such a system of capital creation, after the frightful losses and disappointments of the war! Of course, there is still a great danger that practical economic solidarity might fall at the first attack of its narrow-minded nationalist and imperialist opponents. But fortunately it is impossible to wipe out completely ideas of enduring value by shortsighted individualistic opposition. Such an idea, once brought into the world, will assert itself and, with the help of leading progressive spirits, will create its institutions.

In the actual construction of this idea there is no limit to the number of variations possible. For instance, for those who consider the Bank of Nations as utopian, I might suggest the establishment of a system of uniform principles to be adopted by all European issuing banks. Then, I venture to say, the issue of an international medium of exchange would not meet with too many objections.

Compared to ter Meulen's bonds this proposal still seems much simpler and more practical. Vanderlip has thought of the formation of a European central bank whose central management and gold reserve would be located in the United States. If it were really possible to secure the financial coopera-tion of capitalists in the United States, then it would be in order, surely, to sacrifice for this purpose a part of our European independence; but, what-ever happens, we shall not be able to dispense with the development of a system of long-term credits, and in this respect all proposals of the Vanderlip type must be supplemented—this should be quite obvious.

As I have said before, with nothing more than the usual short-term trade credits, we shall never succeed in reviving our world trade. So far as that goes, I don't believe that Europe's condition is so desperate that it would be doomed to perish if American capital, selfishly shortsighted, refused to pledge its cooperation in the work of reconstruction.

FUNDAMENTAL PROBLEMS

If, in spite of all efforts, it should not be possible to form a uniform system of European finance, it may be necessary to create an eastern European banking system which would bring about financial reform for that group of countries and consolidate them into a uniform economic area. As a last resort we may have to be satisfied with the benefits of a purely national system of credit institutions and construction banks; such a system would still represent immense progress in comparison with the present shortsighted paper money economy which, like a vampire, saps the strength from all productive enterprise, investors, owners of treasury notes, and the unfortunate members of the middle class dependent upon a fixed income.

If the granting of long-term credits, such as I have suggested, were called "productive inflation" without further explanation, it would give the impression to the masses that any money loan in the form of paper money would, in conjunction with the excessive money volume, cause a terrible overflow. In view of this it should be noted that even the strongest opponents of every existing paper currency have admitted that there can be no financial objections to the issue of paper money for a definitely limited period, if it is made safe by loans and taxes; and in this form it can never be termed inflation.

It is mainly for this reason that I have suggested at the beginning of this book that the construction banks should, at the outset, issue bonds representing the full value of the paper money credits which they are to receive. Bonds are interest-bearing evidences of debt, sold to private purchasers by way of security issues. Even if, in the beginning, it were difficult to find a sufficient number of buyers for these construction bank bonds on the open market (this, as I have said, is strictly a matter of opinion), in that case the temporary retention of these bonds in the vaults of the construction banks would be in no way detrimental to their existence. In my opinion it is possible and practicable to dispense with the interest charge on these bonds for the duration of a certain free-of-interest period, which may last from three to ten years. Such an interest moratorium suggests itself, nay, is necessitated, by the present condition of the capital market. It is equally necessary to dispense with the interest charge on the amortized credits to be granted by the Bank of Nations to the construction banks. In times of great distress one may not shrink from lowering the rate of interest, even if he does not, as I do, consider this as permanently applicable.

Many a pioneer of relentless profit policies will probably strenuously object to my proposal of limiting the interest on the bonds which at the end of the free-of-interest period will have to be paid by the financed entrepreneurs to the construction banks. The interest should be limited to such an extent that it corresponds to no more than the customary interest rate for first-class securities, thus not containing any risk premium for the bondholders. Aside from this I suggested that the bonds be further provided with an adjustable share in the profits from the earnings of the capital goods constructed with the help of the banks' credits.

Desirable though a raise of the share in the profits may be, the unprejudiced observer will have to admit that in the first years of development the bondholders' variable share in the profits must be kept within modest limits. The entrepreneurs during the transitory period should be granted a rest period, so that they may look forward to a happier future. The happy prospect of mounting profits may make this method popular with the public; but during the first years the Bank of Nations or its branches will undoubtedly have to keep back a certain portion of the unsold bonds (instead of the cash money which would later return in Bank of Nations currency), until they become ripe for consumption.

On the other hand, it would be quite safe for the banks to accept deposits by their customers for the purchase of current accounts or balances and for the later acquisition of moneys and affidavits. In this way a new possibility of return is opened up for the international bank notes which may be seeking interest-bearing investments.

It will be hard to avoid a general rise in prices, as a result of the increased demand for building materials, raw materials, unfinished products, etc., because of the liberal granting of credits. But these boomlike symptoms can have a bad effect in weak-currency countries only if the construction banks give way to the temptation of excessive advances. In accordance with their structure they must observe a strict, well-planned production-for-use policy, in connection with their creation of new means of production and capital goods.

The Bank of Nations itself will be vitally interested in demanding documents concerning the limits of profitableness of the credit-financing institutions. The safety of the whole organization will be greatly enhanced by the cooperation of the entrepreneurs themselves, who are to give a solidary guarantee and construct numerous self-regulating mechanisms.

So far we have not touched upon the question of what proportion of the value of the property is to be given as credit; general standards can hardly be established for this, but I should like to mention the following points:

1. It is by all means desirable, if not necessary, to have down-payments paid by the debtors, in order that they may maintain their own interests.

2. The construction banks may consider the addition of small-risk premiums to the amortization rates, if circumstances permit.

3. In difficult cases the withholding of ownership may be agreed to.

4. For credits with small installments, the guarantee of associations, societies, and other bodies, including that of credit insurance companies, is not to be ignored.

5. In case of very-long-term credits the construction banks may provide themselves with new guarantees by means of life insurance on the debtors. In Belgium good results have been obtained in this way in connection with the cooperative housing construction (mortgage life insurance).

6. A voluntary abbreviation of the amortization period through part-repayment by the debtors will certainly be desirable for the construction banks, and will set capital free for new credits.

May I be permitted, in closing, to state once more that a good part of the institutions which should be used for the reconstruction work to be done have been in existence in Germany for many years and have proved very satisfactory. The basis of the whole concept of property-life insurance is well on the way to being established and is finding its counterparts in other countries. It will hold claim to its present monopolistic position only so long as no other institution of equal ability will compete with it. With increasing capital power the property-life insurance companies would be able to establish, with the means at their disposal, new credit institutions which would benefit, in the first place, those that participate in them. But too much time would pass before credits of this sort, which presuppose the complete renewal of capital by the businessman, were made possible by the self-earned savings of the assured.

Reparation Problem

Dangerous though it may seem to touch upon the subject of reparation in connection with the Bank of Nations, I should like to refer to the ideas expressed in my *World Credit and Finance Reform*.

The illusion is still being clung to that the debt burden will be lightened for Germany at least for a few years by means of loans by the billion, subscribed by foreign lenders, in spite of the fact that the interest and amortization obligations are enormous. Not even optimistic adherents of the giant credit or series of credits would dare hope that they might be small. Whatever the objections to such ideas, we must realize that the belief that these problematic billion-dollar loans will bring about the long-hoped-for stabilization of the German currency is nothing better than childish superstition.

It requires strong optimism indeed to hope for the complete abolishment of national inflation within a short time, if the German nation is not given a breathing spell. Without the most rigid and fundamental reforms of finance, there is no sense in conjuring up such lovely pictures of progress. Obviously, as a German, I am in complete agreement with all unprejudiced observers of the facts, namely, that only by means of a reduction of the reparation demands to a reasonable amount will their payment be made possible.

If we think of how small the actual gold stock of the whole world is, compared to the existing reparation demands of the victorious Allies, we shall realize, after adequate reflection, that a sum of about 30 billion goldmarks would be the absolute maximum amount of German reparation payments which could be paid with any degree of safety, within reasonable time. France especially could save herself many a sad and bitter experience if she would cooperate with organized German capital and labor in bringing about the restoration of its demolished territories with such a reduction of the German war debt. If only a final sum were determined upon, which would cover Germany's remaining debt and would not appear absolutely impossible or destroy her economic existence, I am sure that all the German people would gladly cooperate in order to pay this sum as quickly as possible. The amortization rates could safely be paid with the help of a credit association in the nature of the Hachenburg project, and an amortization tax could be imposed on the entire body of German real property (including all agricultural land holdings), if only, as I said, the total demand were reduced to a supportable sum.

Of one thing I am convinced: An economy as weakened as is the German will not be able to afford the interest on such an enormous sum to the extent required by the present condition of the capital market. It is already evident that the 5 per cent reparation bonds so far printed will not find a single voluntary buyer in the whole world. From the very beginning they were simply worthless speculation in the hands of their present owners. What Germany has paid so far would not even suffice to cover the ridiculous occupation charges. Any sensible Allied observer is well aware of the fact that this constitutes the worst obstacle to the reconstruction of the destroyed territories in France, in so far as Germany is liable for them.

I expect nothing better from the compulsory gratis delivery in products than the further destruction of the world market and equally serious financial ruin of the recipients.[2] Even if these deliveries took place over a period of time, without a complete depreciation of the German currency, the Allied businessmen would soon realize what havoc such enormous product deliveries would wreak with their own enterprise. Even if they succeeded in defending themselves against such wholesale competition of German "gifts" in their own markets, their world trade in other countries would still suffer immensely. Only to a very limited extent can carefully selected products be delivered, and only to that restricted extent can the system of payments be carried out without having disastrous effects on world trade.

These deliveries, however, would be immensely simplified by the banknote credits of the Bank of Nations. I do not hesitate to state here that the payment of all reparation deliveries with international currency would represent the least detrimental of all regulating systems for all countries concerned. The infallible logic of facts will sooner or later make this self-evident. If thereby the ever increasing interest on the huge reparations burden were dropped—in other words, if the German debts were restricted to the amortization quotas—then we might hope that they would be paid regularly (i.e., under the reduced conditions mentioned above).

The hope that from somewhere in the world there may come the credit billions of hidden benefactors who wish to sacrifice their fortunes for this good cause is an illusion. Even the fattest interest would hardly suffice to lure sufficient capital out of its hiding place. Even the wealthiest country in the world would keep its hands off this business and would utilize its disposable capital for its own productive purposes rather than for the amortization of the war debts of the Entente, and for the support of the armament programs of the enthusiastic French, Poles, etc. If we do not succeed in escaping the growing power politics of our impatient creditors, by substituting a sane consideration of economic facts and abilities, our "Europe without peace" may expect a further decline into the abyss of chaos.

[2] Cf. the excellent book of Prof. Dr. H. Mannstaedt of Bonn, *Finanzbedarf und Wirtschaftsleben* (Gustav Fischer: Jena, 1922).

CONCLUSION

La vérité est en marche,
rien ne peut l'arrêter.
—Emile Zola

GENERATIONS come and go; hatred, lies, envy and war alternate with love, truth, fraternity, and peace. We human beings sway from one side to the other, for our minds are not so constituted as to permit us to act rationally by instinct. That is why we require a mighty mechanism whose dynamic power and just order may relieve us of our economic cares and whose automatic functions, once set in motion, may demechanize our intricate lives.

The Bank of Nations is my conception of such a mechanism. Will it come true?

I have faith in the power of the idea, which will survive all conflict and opposition. Its accomplishment will require almost superhuman effort, far beyond the power of a few individuals. Thousands must strive assiduously, if the work is to succeed. And they will act as soon as the peoples of the world recognize the possibilities of this idea; for, no worldly or spiritual power will help those who do not help themselves in the struggle for existence.

A true Bank of Nations will come into existence, inaugurating a new era of human solidarity, and the sun of justice will shine upon a new planet.

306

EPILOGUE

To the "Atlantic Charter"

On August 14, 1941, President Roosevelt of the United States of America and Prime Minister Winston Churchill of England met in mid-ocean to discuss the war-aims of their respective nations. When the conference was over, they published the following mutual declaration of "certain common principles in the national policies of their respective countries on which they base their hopes for a better future for the world. The eight-fold joint statement is as follows:

"First—their countries seek no aggrandizement, territorial or other;

"Second—they desire to see no territorial changes that do not accord with the freely expressed wishes of the peoples concerned;

"Third—they respect the right of all peoples to choose the form of government under which they will live; and they wish to see sovereign rights restored to those who have been forcibly deprived of them;

"Fourth—they will endeavor, with due respect to their existing obligations, to further the enjoyment of all states, great or small, victor or vanquished, of access, on equal terms, to the trade and to the raw materials of the world which are needed for their economic prosperity;

"Fifth—they desire to bring about the fullest collaboration between all nations in the economic field with the object of securing, for all, improved labour standards, economic advancement, and social security;

"Sixth—after the final destruction of the Nazi tyranny, they hope to see established a peace which will afford to all nations the means of dwelling in safety within their own boundaries, and which will afford assurance that all men in all lands may live out their lives in freedom from fear and want;

"SEVENTH—such a peace should enable all men to traverse the high seas and oceans without hindrance;

"EIGHTH—they believe that all nations of the world, for realistic as well as spiritual reasons, must come to the abandonment of the use of force. Since no future peace can be maintained if land, sea and air armaments continue to be employed by nations which threaten, or may threaten, aggression outside of their frontiers, they believe, pending the establishment of a wider and permanent system of general security, that the disarmament of such nations is essential. They will likewise aid and encourage all other practicable measures which will lighten for peace-loving peoples the crushing burden of armaments.

* * *

The English no less than the Americans are great believers in the principles of free thought and free speech. In a democracy—even during war, in so far as strategical secrecies are not involved—important questions and events must be discussed and disputed freely. Nothing indeed should be hidden that can help in solving the superhuman and super-individual problem of peace and a new order of society.

Mr. Churchill as well as our President stand above criticism in matters of patriotism, social wisdom and statesmanship. Every word that might be said about their Atlantic Charter must be said with the distinct reservation that the layman cannot judge why at a given moment this or that point had to be formulated as it was.

English statesmen have a proud tradition in strategy and diplomacy in international affairs. Mr. Churchill knows better than any layman what may be revealed in a given situation, and he alone, as responsible British Premier, can know what is best for his Empire and for the now United Nations, and what are the ends of his policy.

On August 14th in mid-Atlantic he met President Roosevelt for the first time in person, and was seeking a manifestation of unity between the two responsible Western democracies . . . the two nations which will be largely responsible for the winning of the war and of the peace to follow.

No one can doubt that the two statesmen know how a real peace must be constructed and what are the ideals of a "just and lasting peace."

Perhaps they had good reason for not committing themselves at this early date to final peace aims. Perhaps their formulation of the eight points was the only means to their actual present goal, the formation of a strong unit, a phalanx among 26 nations, against the 14 of the Axis bloc.

This was no doubt the all-important aim of the hour (quite apart from many other political and psychological factors) before which the real issues of the future peace have to bow and give ground. First of all the two men want to crush Nazism, the most pernicious and devastating pestilence on earth, and in the second place to be the saviours of democracy and society. When they have done their job, they will listen to reason and be willing to pay the price in matters of brotherly love and mutual interest among nations.

The frank and, I hope, constructive criticism of the author, must be viewed in the light of these preliminary remarks. He believes he knows English leaders too well not to realize that they are interested in information about the reaction of contemporary American public opinion; in other words, that they can take it.

Mr. Churchill may be assured that the boundless admiration of the American people for his unique dynamism is genuinely compatible with certain suggestions which have occurred to them because of the Charter, because of current affairs and the state of events, and last but not least, in the hope of a better world to come.

First reactions to the Atlantic Charter found the American people divided between isolationism and interventionism. Both camps were aware of the unique opportunity for a social statement that would enlighten the world audience and that would bring about some change of heart inside Nazi Germany. They felt, however, that this chance was thrown away, and would not be come again so easily.

Public and press tried hard to underline the ethical highlights of the Eight Points, which were compared to the Magna Charta; an identification which resulted in naming them the Atlantic Charter.

Soon the realization grew that the "*laudanda voluntas*" of the statesmen and the "*principia ethica pro patria et pro mundo*" were fatally flavored with reactionary ingredients.

One thing is certain; the hoped for results regarding influence on our adversaries and particularly upon German public opinion, that might have led to a reclamation of the good or true Germans, were nil.

Goebbels pointed, and not without success to the "plutocrats," "the money-makers and money-changers"; in short, to the boogey-boogey capitalists who want to "enslave the world."

And Hitler could boast: "Blood fights the dollar," (he did not mention the Pound—the dollar works better on his herd), and the Nazi flock followed obediently their misleaders into icy Russia for mass destruction and glorious freezing to death.

If this was what the two statesmen wanted, they have certainly fiddled the right tune.

Let us not be cynical; the situation is too serious. It is not only the Nazi clique which calls us "money aristocrats" with amazing and growing results; the Japanese have followed their example. They want to "liberate" the peoples of Asia from the "exploitation" of the white man.

Let us, therefore, be strict and strong with ourselves and examine what might justify the Axis Napoleons in their use of such propaganda, with some effect on the conquered peoples.

What does the Atlantic Charter imply concerning Shylock-like exploitation; the imposing of economic or policital slavery, of the absolutist will, upon minorities?

When now the primary goal, the lining up of the Anti-Axis nations, has been accomplished successfully (except in the case of Argentina) the psychological moment may be near for committing ourselves to the perfecting and making practicable the ethical endeavours, the social reform ideology, equally at home and abroad.

There are first of all three main factors of debate which have caused much recent friction and adverse criticism.

(1) The beautiful ethical economic reform ideas of the Charter, such as the promise of free access to raw materials, economic advancement, social security and all the others, deteriorate into hollow phrases if all nations are not willing to create a super-ordinated economic mechanism to which the material application of these moral and ethical principles may be entrusted; an organism with sufficient sovereignty rights to enforce itself.

What are ideals such as free access to raw materials worth, if nations trade more unjustly than they did in the darkest mercantilist ages where the conflict between national need and foreign need was always decided in favour of national need. If embargoes, restrictionism, protectionism, and other prohibitive and provocative measures are not only given up but also outlawed and replaced by supra-national organisms like those described in this book, nobody will believe in the sincerity of the reformer's proclamation.

After the experiences of the inter-war period the peoples have rightfully become sceptical. Their scepticism is growing and will, revolution-like, destroy all good intentions and moral fibre of the statesmen and their nations, if they do not commit themselves to the supra-organization of the body economic.

(2) In order to satisfy the governments-in-exile of the poor enslaved nations (and other democratic nations as well) the Atlantic Charter promises them full restoration of their sovereignties and self-government. On the other hand territorial changes that do not accord with the freely expressed wishes of the peoples concerned and aggrandizements, territorial and other, are abolished in the charter. Excellent! But again the peoples of the world are becoming sceptical. Not only the economic but also the political organization of society was a complete failure and resulted in a sad catastrophe. Do these principles of the Charter imply that the old order is to be restored and revived? The author cannot believe that the statesmen have really intended this. From Mr. Attlee's statement (p. 239 *et seq.*) and others we know that not only Americans but also leading Englishmen are convinced that "Europe must federate or perish." Other major or minor groups may be formed; there may be a new partition of portions to the world, along geographically more energetic and economically more suitable lines. We need not ridicule the art of geopolitics; we must rather apply this youngest child of modern science universally, and not solely to the enhancement of one "master nation." It is possible for nations to expand and grow together without imperialist aspirations.

Much more decisive for the success of an enduring peace-order is the question of whether the nations or groups emerging from the present war and revolution are ready and willing to entrust sufficient sovereignty rights to a Federal World Authority, able to enforce its will upon the peoples and coordinated with the economic and social supra-organization.

This commonly considered "last best hope on earth" is also the key to the third question.

(3) Point Eight, which begins with a melodic statement of such aesthetic quality, develops toward an attitude that has done more harm psychologically and has aroused more active opposition than the other seven points taken together. It is the question of the aggressor and of one-sided disarmament.

Although a just and functional social and economic world organization must be considered paramount for the success of the peace to come in its political aspects, the matters of disarmament and policing are of no less importance and should be met with a plan of more universal practicability and appeal; with a more universal appreciation for the identical rights of all peoples, and their hunger and thirst for mutual confidence, security and justice. After the Nazi spirit has been crushed, and after a transition period when the threat of war—civil and international—has been removed, international security must not be entrusted to one group of nations as in past history, but to the community of all nations.

Knowing the attitude of a good cross-section of the American people, the author feels that point Eight would encounter the most violent opposition of the majority if put to the test in this country.

Let us take the Atlantic Charter as a step forward on our road to universal imagination. We must understand that in a situation of such grave danger to the very idea of democracy, the responsible statesman cannot yet produce the right proportions to the overwhelming requirements of a just and dynamic peace.

Now, with America in the war, a true and universal community of interest is established, and a world in ashes and ruins and new inspirations of a broken down society will force upon humanity the true and correct interpretation of its categorical obligations toward the ideals of permanent peace and change.

H. H.

INDEX

INDEX

314

INDEX

INDEX

INDEX

INDEX

318

INDEX

INDEX

INDEX